P R A I S E   F O R

UNSINKABLE
Princess

"*Unsinkable Princess* is a compelling international family saga of love, betrayal, heartache, and renewal; and of coming to terms with one's past so that the future can be bound by truth and courage. Faly Colaizzi writes with searing, unflinching honesty, taking the reader inside tragic and yet life-affirming chapters of a family's long journey to understanding."

— David W Berner, author of the award-winning novella, *The Islander*, Broadcast Journalist, CBS Radio and WBBM Radio Chicago

"*Unsinkable Princess* is an **emotional masterpiece** that takes the reader on a journey laden with terror. I felt as if I was...witnessing the tragic exchanges between a narcissistic monster and his helpless victims, how the pain never really subsides. This fuels a fire for Rachel and her daughters, Fallon and Soraya, to overcome the mountains before them. It is a wonderful read."

– Ron Onesti, President/CEO/Promoter, The Onesti Entertainment Corporation; Arcada Theater St. Charles, Illinois

"Faly Colaizzi's *Unsinkable Princess* is an honest chronicle of a family overcoming trauma, searching for hope and finding peace and understanding. Colaizzi describes how a family living with a tragic past can find strength with each other and triumph over their past adversities."

– Rick Gieser, public relations director for Zanies Comedy Clubs,
former producer at WGN Radio

"*Unsinkable Princess* is a scintillating tale of terror, heartache, survival, and strength. It casts a light on the dark topic of abuse and imbalance of power that often gets brushed beneath the surface and hidden from society, friends, and family. Rachel is a survivor; and she continues to thrive and helps her children succeed despite the crushing circumstances."

– Lauren Griffin Marica, Author and St. Charles Women's Club,
SCWC Book Club Chair

"*Unsinkable Princess* is the journey of an amazing woman, her life of luxury and love through years of explosive abuse to retribution and survival. It's gripping, raw, and unforgettable."

– Mitch Michaels, Legendary Chicagoland DJ
and Radio personality and author

UNSINKABLE
Princess

For events, photo gallery, and purchases of books, please visit:
www.UnsinkablePrincess.com

If you or someone you love is suffering from domestic abuse, help is available.
National Domestic Violence Hotline – 24/7 in English and Spanish: 800-799-7233

Design and Composition by: Tim Ogline / Ogline Design
www.oglinedesign.com

Editor: Joy E. Stocke

ISBN: 979-8-9897464-1-5

Publisher's Cataloging-In-Publication Data
Colaizzi, Faly
    Unsinkable Princess

Categories: Memoir, Family, Domestic Abuse

Tributaries Press
102 Sandy Ridge-Mt Airy Road
Stockton, NJ. 08559

UNSINKABLE
Princess

A MEMOIR

FALY COLAIZZI

Tributaries
Press

For My Mother, Rafaela Faly Hart

Table of Contents

what is happening. But you can't. All you can do is hope and pray that someday your mother will win and your father will pay with a slow demise full of every ounce of pain he's caused until all that's left is a useless pile of dust.

But life doesn't work that way.

As a child I felt like a ghost in the middle of the fury, walking through the fog of helplessness. I wanted to speak, yell, and shout, but no words would come. I wanted to cry, but the tears wouldn't come, either. I wanted to be strong, brave and have the power to destroy my father, have the capacity to pound him into the ground with my fist…but I was immobilized with fear.

That night in the kitchen, I saw Mama's bloodied arm, her shredded nightgown. Horrified and repulsed, I locked eyes with my father. But all I saw was a monster who would cut me down, too, if I made a move. For continuous years, we choked on my father's bitter poison.

I couldn't realize it then, but I would come to learn that in order to grow fierce and empowered I would need time, lots of it. I also knew that God is bigger and stronger than anything or anyone I could face. God needed to give us time, needed to give my mother, my sister, and me time to become strong…stronger than we were on that fateful night when everything broke apart.

power, but Abuelo knew better. He loved and wanted to be a part of the Buddhist religion, yet remained Catholic and was not fooled by his merciless relatives.

After Esther married Alfonso, he became an algebra professor before starting a successful fishing brokerage business. They settled into a fine house in La Coruña, and Abuelo's business grew. He hired drivers and bought small, refrigerated trucks to transport seafood to markets in small towns, cities like Madrid and Valencia, and many parts of Spain. Business was booming! By all accounts Esther and Alfonso had a camaraderie, a love affair, an intimacy that was difficult to find. Their emotional, mental, and spiritual togetherness was aligned to perfection. The doting couple and parents exuded old Hollywood glamor and treated their three girls like little princesses. Rachel dressed in the most luxurious clothing, traveled to many parts of Spain, Málaga, Portugal, France, and Switzerland, went to the best schools, and dined on the finest cuisine. She was in fact deliciously and lovingly spoiled rotten.

In the early 1940s Rachel and her family would spend long summers in the hot Spanish sun, swimming from May until late September at a popular country club. The country club had a sprawling park and veranda where she and her family feasted on paella with chicken, seafood, and chorizo sandwiches as they watched the flamingo dancers at sunset. The family would alternate days and head to the beautiful hilly beaches of La Coruña, where they would wash their cares away in the warm Atlantic Ocean. Rachel got the chance to indulge in one of her favorite activities: swimming in the sea. She loved the ocean so much that her family was sure she had once upon a time been a mermaid.

The family also belonged to a social and family dance club called *Fin-del-Mundo*, End of the World. Rachel was a natural and loved to dance. The steps and rhythm came easy to her, and the freedom was exhilarating. As she reached adolescence, boys started noticing her. There was no doubt that she was already a beauty. With the adulation, she, of course, had dreams of becoming a professional dancer.

A few days a week the family dressed to the nines and Rachel would remember how her elegant mother showed her how to slide long white gloves over her fingertips. She was grooming her three girls to become ladies and debutantes that fit perfectly into the fabric of the Spanish social scene. The training continued with outings to the theater and cinema to see the latest plays and films. In the fall, when Rachel turned twelve, she headed to a private boarding school, Saint Compostela de Santiago, along the famed pilgrimage route. The nuns were a harsh replacement for her loving mom, so she decided to run away and head for home. The consequence for her actions was laughter and a hug from her mother who could not believe that her daughter ran miles just to be back in her arms.

In 1951, Rachel turned thirteen and the family moved from La Coruña to the city of Madrid. Alfonso's fishing brokerage business was going strong, and he wanted to capture more of the market share that the larger towns could offer. He moved his family into an upscale penthouse apartment overlooking El Retiro Park near shops, salons, and cafés.

Life was good and the family had a personal seamstress who made gowns, dresses, and outfits to order for the girls and Esther. There were two live-in servants who looked after Rachel and her sisters. They cooked and cleaned and catered to Rachel who lovingly called each of them Nana. On days when the Nanas took Rachel and her sisters to the park and for walks, they commented that little Rachel would give her lunch away to an elderly widow or hungry child on the street. Always trying to help someone else have a better life, even if it was just bread and cheese to fill their bellies. Birds and animals got the same treatment. She would chase them in the park with her crackers. The Nanas would laugh, "Esta niña!" and told her that the lunch was for her. She would tell them, "But they have nothing and no one, no Nana or Mamma to care for them." The Nanas would tilt their heads sideways and smile.

That fall, Rachel and her sisters attended Saint Isabela, a private and exclusive school for girls where along with their studies, they learned to become proper ladies of the house. Along with math and history, they learned to cook, clean, and take care of their future husbands, the highest honor a young woman of means could dream of.

In 1955, destiny would take Rachel by the hand and tap her on the head with its sparkling magic wand. Her older sister Carmen had sent her picture to a local magazine setting a chain of events in motion that would lead Rachel to be crowned Miss Galicia. The different regions of Spain held beauty and popularity contests to find the perfect representatives that embodied the local culture and character of the ideal Spanish woman, and Rachel was tailor made for the role.

Magazines loved these events because they sold tens of thousands of copies all over the country. They looked for a well-mannered, educated, and classy socialite or debutante with the heart of an angel. They found one in Rachel Vasquez Borgia.

First, Rachel was crowned Miss Galicia. At another event on the southern coast of Spain, attended by celebrities and royalty, Rachel also took the title of Miss Benidorm in celebration of the beautiful seaside town. She loved the attention and at the costume party, she dressed as a French maid and stole the hearts of everyone in attendance. She pushed boundaries in her sleep without knowing it and without trying. She naturally created ripples of joy and laughter that left people cheerful in her wake. She made country folk and elite socialites feel bewitched. They took notice of every step she took as if magic rose pedals appeared under her feet and the sparkle of diamonds glowed in her eyes. Men wanted her, women wanted to be her, and the camera loved her!

Later that year, it rained day and night in Valencia. The region on the east coast of Spain was engulfed in severe flooding. Many homes and businesses and part of the orange crop were destroyed. When a year had passed and the area had been rebuilt, a group of local mayors got together at a summit meeting to organize a celebratory event to commemorate the flood and the region's recovery. They decided that the event should take place in March during the Fallas de Valencia, an annual celebration that signals the coming of spring.

Everyone from millionaires, world dignitaries, movie stars, European royalty, dukes and duchesses, locals, and people from all regions of Spain would attend the televised event, contributing money and funding for the reconstruction. The rich, chic, and elegant loved being "seen" flaunting their high-society glamor and opulence. The mayor of Valencia called Rachel's family three times to invite her to the event.

Finally, the mayor of La Coruña, Alfonso Molina, who was friends with Abuelo Alfonso, directly phoned Rachel, who was still Miss Galicia. He stated firmly that even though Rachel lived in Madrid and no longer lived in the province of Galicia, she was to attend and represent the region.

"Don't worry about anything," he told her. "You are the perfect representative for our beautiful Galicia."

The formal invitation came a week later from the mayor's office inviting Rachel to the celebration along with her mother and father as her chaperones. Immediately, the family's seamstress began working overtime to design a dress that represented the region. She spent days sewing an undergarment and blouse made of the purest white cotton, followed by a black velvet skirt with a matching bolero jacket. On her head, Rachel wore a lace mantilla, a red rose behind her ear accentuating her glossy black hair.

When Rachel and her parents' Iberian Airlines flight landed at Valencia airport, a group of dignitaries met them with flowers and escorted them to their Rolls Royce. From the moment she alighted from the plane for the six-day event, Mayor Molina, other dignitaries, and a local entourage in Valencia cheered for Rachel and greeted her like she was a hero. The crowd blew kisses and waved flowers. In return, she elegantly shouted well-wishes and expressions of hope for the region. She greeted the crowds with compassion and a momentary mission to spread bliss and laughter with her sharp wit. She knew how to rally her audience. Children sat on their parents' shoulders to get a glimpse of her as she passed by. Her heart was filled by the reception. "These were days I will never forget," she told my sister and me. "They were the best days of my life."

It was clear that Rachel had an exhilarating spark that the other women representatives did not have. Rachel triumphantly left the airport chauffeured by Mayor Molina's driver. Abuela drove off with family friends with whom she would spend the week, and who would join her and her daughter at the grand event hosting over 500 people.

The Fallas de Valencia began with elaborate cuisine for all the VIPs. They feasted on platters of tortilla de patatas, empanadas, and churros con chocolate for dessert. After lunch they would begin with the event of the day, a bullfight. The festival-filled days were spent with lavish and extravagant parades, social and theater events, and ceremonies honoring the Virgin Mary. Rachel was showered with gifts and flowers from many prominent attendees. She greeted crowds, shook hands, exchanged kisses, posed for pictures, and spoke with the newspaper and magazine reporters for hours. A natural at working a room, she met with all who wanted to say hello to the elegant and cheerful Miss Galicia. She broke out into dance with men, women, and children at the festival, laughing as if she was drunk on champagne without having one drop.

Rachel would crack a classy joke with the crowd who greeted her every day. A wave of laughter and cheers would arise when she delivered her punchline. She made everyone feel important, because to her they mattered, and she left people feeling better after she left. That was the true spirit of the representative Miss Galicia. With her electric star power, she was the people's liaison who crossed boundaries and limitations with laughter, making them swoon with her beauty and grace.

The evening's activities kicked off when Rachel was introduced to Sophia Lauren who, at 5' 9", radiated calm and glamor; Carmen Sevilla, the vivacious star of Spanish cinema; handsome bullfighters; and dukes and duchesses. Artists from all over Europe, commissioned to construct statues in the outside courtyard for the event, paid tribute to her as the patrons of the event placed flowers at her feet. Skies filled with fireworks exploding in the air created a dreamworld. It was as if Las Vegas and New Orleans combined events for New Year's Eve and Mardi Gras because everyone knew that the Spaniards were the best at throwing a party.

In the ballroom, hung with shimmering gold chandeliers and tables set as if to honor a queen, the master of ceremonies introduced each of the mayors of the different regions of Spain, along with the women representing those regions. The mayor and the representative from Alicante were announced, the crowd applauded. The mayor and representative from Seville were announced, the crowd applauded. Mayor Molina and Galicia Representative Rachel Vasquez were announced, and the crowd stood on their feet to give her a standing ovation. It was clear that Rachel was their favorite, and she was now the face of Galicia.

The Fallas de Valencia festivities were winding down after the six days, and the local chairmen and mayors hosted meetings to figure out how to commemorate the extravaganza. They chose to put together a book with all the pictures of the events, guests, quotes, and stories that took place during those glorious six days. The event and a national magazine put out a copy of the book sold countrywide. Rachel Vasquez made the front cover. To this day, each year on its anniversary, television stations across Spain play clips of the Fallas and my tia Carmen sees Rachel plastered across TV.

4

A Flurry of Suitors

By the time Rachel's sisters were eighteen, they had already married. But Rachel, who was nineteen, wasn't yet ready for marriage. She was out to have fun and still benefit from the shelter of her parents. This made for a difficult compromise, or one would say it created a ping-pong match in Rachel's mind. Her parents chaperoned and guarded her from the occasional predator like a precious jewel, but she craved her freedom.

She had the lion's share of men knocking at her door, mostly due to her incredible looks, celebrity, and her family's social status. She also had star power. A line of suitors came from far and wide. Professional soccer players from Barcelona and Madrid, lawyers, doctors, actors, bullfighters, and sons of dignitaries all pursued her. One famous bullfighter, Victor Valencia, and many of Rachel's chaperoned dates, made the society papers.

On a summer trip to Málaga in the south of Spain, Rachel and her mother stayed on the coast near Puerto Banús, a playground for the rich. There were social gatherings on the beach, pool parties, and day trips on yachts out to sea. Rachel and her family would constantly run into people they knew from Madrid and around Spain. The society papers captured pictures of Rachel and Italian movie star Raf Baldassarre hanging by the pool. Raf knew that it was a great career move to get in the magazines and papers next to a pretty lady with a bit of her own star quality.

American actor Ty Hardin, star of the TV series *Bronco*, was at the same pool party that day with Rachel and Raf. Ty loved Spain and had lived there for a while. He knew Rachel's family, too. Soon, the society papers put together a full page spread of Ty, Raf, and Rachel. It was classy and tasteful and gave Rachel more intrigue with everyone wondering, "Who is this beautiful woman popping up in society?"

Funny thing was she didn't care one way or another for the fame. She loved her privacy and her innocence as much as the attention she received from charming men. Still, everyone wanted to get a picture with Rachel. Little did they know that one of her passions was photography. She loved getting behind the camera to see what it revealed about the person standing in front of her.

Along with over twelve marriage proposals, Rachel also had numerous movie, modeling, and television commercial proposals. Rachel and family were friends with the Mexican movie star Cantinflas. Some of his films were *Around the World in Eighty Days*, *El barrendero*, and *El bolero de Raquel*. Cantinflas loved Rachel's style and knew that the camera would love her, too. He asked her on many occasions to star in a few movies with him and he would jump start her career. He told her that they could make a lot of money together. Rachel was flattered by the offer, but politely declined.

She knew that a lifestyle and career in film would possibly leave her exploited and exposed. She was too cultured and refined. In other words, she had been raised to be a lady. She was made aware of this lifestyle by Abuelo and friends of hers that were in the movie business. She heard horror stories of movie directors always wanting payback for that leading role. Rachel loved dipping her toes into the waters of her fifteen minutes of fame but wanted no part of that sleazy regime. She would not allow her life to be manipulated by a career that she simply did not want, even if offered by her good friend Cantinflas. She did what she wanted, even if the result did not have dollar signs attached. She loved fashion, dance, hair, and makeup.

She received a diploma in Spanish and French cosmetology, taught by a world-famous cosmetologist.

Back in Madrid, Rachel was invited to a high school class reunion. Many of her classmates were the children of dignitaries and nobility. One of their honored guests was the son of the King of Morocco of the Royal Palace of Tétouan, Prince Ismail Hassan. His father worked with a few of Rachel's friends' fathers on business and real estate deals in many of the surrounding countries.

At a party, chaperoned by Rachel's mother, Prince Ismail took one look at Rachel and had to know more. He began writing letters, and after a period of correspondence, he called to invite her to the palace. She agreed. Arrangements were made for her and her mother to make a month-long journey. Prince Ismail sent plane tickets and arranged for a private charter to pick them up for the one-hour flight from Tarifa, Spain to Tangiers.

An elegant stand of palm trees guarded the entrance to the palace. Along with her mother, Rachel alighted from the car, passed between the palms and through the gated entrance where graceful, intricately carved arches made of marble and stone from Greece greeted her. Inside, a fountain bubbled in a stone courtyard inlaid with beautiful mosaic tiles. Forty bedrooms, seventeen bathrooms, ballrooms, and banquet rooms surrounded the courtyard. The hallways were carpeted with fanciful Moroccan and Persian rugs. Lanterns glowed in jewel tones. Low tables were inlaid with mother-of-pearl. It was as if she had entered a tale from the Arabian Nights.

When she joined the prince and his family in the dining room, she was surprised to see them sitting in a circle on pillows on the floor and eating with their hands. She had been raised to sit at a table and dine like a cultured proper European lady. But the prince and his family were welcoming and warm, offering her every luxury she could wish for.

The days passed in a hot, languid haze. To get relief from the heat, Prince Ismail arranged for his staff and entourage to prepare his yacht for a day's outing. During a magical afternoon, Rachel, her mother, and the prince laughed and dined on the sixty-foot ocean cruiser gazing at the coast of Tangiers and the sea's wildlife. They spent three separate days on the yacht swimming, feasting on fresh lobster, then heading back to the palace in the evening.

The prince was falling hard for Rachel and would take her and the family on shopping sprees in the Casbah. Rachel loved the colorful locals, sights, music in the streets, and the smell of spices and meat grilling on spits. The prince had beautiful gowns and dresses shipped in from Andalucía from which Rachel and her mother could pick and choose anything they wished. By the time Rachel returned to Madrid, Prince Ismail's head was spinning with thoughts of marriage to his Spanish beauty. There would be many trips back and forth over a six-month period.

Rachel and her parents were back in Tangiers under the care of Ismail's ladies-in-waiting when he came up with the idea to dress her in a full burka that showed nothing more than her striking eyes. Rachel playfully complied with his wish and the ladies transformed her into a Moroccan princess. They left the Palace of Tétouan for the streets of Tangiers. With a full entourage they walked through the stalls as the locals wondered, "Who is this mysterious woman with the captivating eyes on the arm of Prince Ismail?"

When the royal posse returned to the palace there was a brand-new white Mercedes with a giant silk ribbon wrapped around it waiting at the gate. Rachel then knew that there was more than whimsy involved in dressing her in a burka. This would be her future. Rachel was momentarily excited about the gifts, yachts, endless dresses, the palace and the new Mercedes staring right at her. Rachel looked at her father as he politely declined the extravagant gift.

He wisely spoke to Rachel in a whisper. "Please, cariña, never take a gift that invites compromises."

Rachel nodded her head in agreement, never meaning to insult the prince for his elaborate gift.

After she returned to Spain, the prince came to visit. He knew that time apart could mean losing her. Not wanting to risk the loss of the woman he loved, the prince proposed with the most exquisite royal diamond that she had ever seen. In a bit of shock, she caught her breath and let the prince down easy.

She was a young woman exploring the world around her, she told him. And although he was kind and worthy of abiding love, she wasn't ready to settle down.

The truth was simpler. She certainly didn't want life in a palace with all the compromises that would come with it. She certainly didn't want the responsibilities or complications that came with the title of princess. She didn't want to become one of four wives, or part of a harem. She was a leader, not a follower. She knew she would become a prisoner of the burka, a prisoner without the rights she valued as an accomplished woman.

She had a way out and she used it. She told Ismail that her Catholic upbringing and strong faith would not allow her to become a Muslim. She had no way of knowing that she was leaving one prison guarded by a man who truly loved her but had to honor his duty, for a maze of prisons to come. She took Prince Ismail's hands in hers, they tenderly said their goodbyes, and she never saw him again.

5

Switzerland and the Road to Saint Sebastian

It was December, 1958, just a few days before New Year's Eve. Rachel was looking forward to a few days of freedom away from her parents. Gloria, an old school friend, had called and said that her family was flying to Gstaad, Switzerland for the holiday and wanted to know if she wanted to join them. Gloria explained that there would be a few parties and some fun activities in the snow, plus sightseeing around town. The trip, hotel, transportation, and food were all paid for by Gloria's wealthy father.

The plans were set, and Rachel, Gloria and family were off in first class splendor to Gstaad. It took some muscle from Gloria's father to convince Rachel's parents to let their daughter go unescorted, but the family had been good friends for many years, and her parents relented.

The group arrived at the intoxicating and opulent Gstaad Palace Hotel. It was like a castle in the alps and the surrounding town was a fairytale fantasy. Rachel twirled around in the snowy mountain landscape under a canopy of towering pine trees. A glow of luminous lights filled the village, bejeweled with exquisite illuminations. Everyone from industrialists and capitalists, to royalty, dignitaries, and movie stars had been seduced by Gstaad's magnetic field of guilty pleasures.

Rachel and Gloria, exhausted from their trip, browsed the shops and cafés, and grabbed a hot cocoa before jumping into their snuggly king-size beds. The next morning, the clock tower gonged, the silverware and glasses clinked in the hotel's banquet rooms, and the scent of brewing coffee filled the daybreak as the sight of champagne-colored snow glistened off the mountain tops. Rachel, Gloria, and her family met up for coffee then headed over to the horse and carriage in front of the hotel for a half-day excursion up the mountain's gondola.

The group trekked a bit through the snow into the majestic and lofty mountain range, and then to a lodge for an elaborate brunch, punctuated by bouts of laughter and storytelling.

The next day was New Year's Eve, and the evening festivities would soon be underway. A gala to rival all other galas. Everything was carefully orchestrated from the champagne fountains to the entertainment, food, and extravagant fireworks display. Jetsetters got naughty, sloppy, and drunk, reveling into the night as Rachel barely sipped her champagne. Yet she was always the life of the party. Five minutes after midnight the crowd pressed their noses to the windows, hung out of doors and ran out into the snow to watch the rockets explode, illuminate, and glisten in the night sky.

On New Year's Day, Rachel and Gloria slept in till noon. After they awoke Gloria's father had a fleet of Mercedes sedans awaiting the group and another party of family friends for an overnight excursion to another nearby ski town. They spent another carefree day sightseeing and dining into the night.

When the group decided to stay longer, Rachel asked if it was possible to go back to the Palace Hotel in Gstaad for some fresh clothes. One of the friends asked their son Arlo to take Rachel back to the hotel. All her life Rachel was trusting, untroubled, and relaxed with people and her surroundings. She believed in the protection of God, her faith, and her devoted parents. Now she was alone for the first time with a strange older boy on an open road between the mountain range. She was naturally friendly and could give the wrong signals. She started to feel uncomfortable when he pulled the car over.

Suddenly, he began touching her and leaned over to kiss her. "Rachel, are you thinking of what I'm thinking?" Revolted, she looked out the car window, horrible thoughts running through her mind. She thought he could kill her and throw her on the side of the road, and no one would ever find her. Desperate and afraid, she came up with a plan.

"Arlo, I have a great idea," she said softly. "Why don't we go back to the hotel where we can be alone? Doesn't that sound like a better idea?"

Arlo fell for it, agreed, and drove fast. Rachel tried to make small talk while, in her mind, she prayed to God that her plan would work. When they arrived at the hotel, he rushed her to his room. Nervous and full of adrenaline, she allowed him to enter the room first.

"Don't you dare touch me, you disgusting pig!" she screamed and kicked the back of his legs, causing them to buckle as he fell forward. He got up and turned around to grab her, ripping her blouse, and the two became entangled in a struggle as she screamed again, hoping a staff member would come to her rescue.

Screaming louder and not believing the words coming out of her mouth, she spat in his face. "Don't you touch me. Don't even think about it!"

She turned and ran as fast as she could down to the front desk to get help, but to her dismay most of the staff spoke a Swiss-German dialect. In a dark foreshadowing glimpse into her future, Rachel ran to her room breathing heavily, locked her door, and awaited Gloria's return.

When the family returned, everyone acted as if nothing had happened. Rachel never spoke of the incident, never even mentioned a thing to her parents. She was a lady and did not want guilt by association, and she certainly didn't want to cause trouble for Gloria's family. If she got the authorities involved, the society papers would have had a field day with the teenage socialite.

Months passed and Rachel put the confrontation with Arlo behind her. Her friend Suzie from school called and asked if she would like to go to St. Sebastian in France for the weekend. Rachel said that her mother would have a difficult time saying yes to the trip but asked anyway. To her surprise, her mother, thinking that she had done so well on her trip to Gstaad, granted Rachel permission to spread her wings again.

More cautious this time, Rachel agreed to the weekend trip. This was no ordinary trip. Rachel's friend Suzie was lovers with Juan Antonio, a multi-millionaire and the former vice president to Juan and Eva Peron of Argentina. Juan Antonio was married but, in that era, there was no reason to divorce and create a mess. The rich and famous simply added a secret partner to the mix.

Juan Antonio arranged for a private plane to take the three to St. Sebastian and to the swanky Chateau Le Mas Hotel and Casino. At that time gambling was prohibited, yet certain pockets of France indulged the rich and their vices. Rachel looked around the casino floor of gamblers, smokers, and drinkers. She knew what she was, and she knew what she wasn't. She watched the wealthy clientele indulging their pleasures and knew even then that this lifestyle with its endless cocktails, flirtations, and affairs was not for her.

Suzie coaxed Rachel a bit to try the roulette table.

"Sure, but I don't know the rules, Suzie," Rachel said.

"Take some of my chips, pick a number, then place the chip on that number."

Rachel placed her chips on number 13 and yelled it out to the dealer. The wheel spun and landed on 13. Stunned, Suzie and Rachel jumped in elated disbelief. Rachel played again, picking lucky 13. She won again! The cheers coming from the roulette table caused a small crowd to gather.

Rachel placed all her chips on 13 and yelled the number out to the dealer. The roulette wheel spun, landing on number 13. The crowd cheered.

Now, Juan Antonio and a larger crowd joined them. They were now ten-deep around the roulette table. Rachel placed a stack of chips on number 13. Won, then won again! The number 13 had never won five in a row at this casino, because no one ever played unlucky-lucky number 13.

"Stop, while you're ahead," Suzie whispered. "Let's collect your winnings."

Rachel grabbed her chips while men played tug-of-war with her, begging for her to stand by their table for luck. Juan Antonio's entourage protected and guarded her as she turned in her chips. She had won thousands. "Beginner's luck," she said, and never gambled again. Yet, to this day, her favorite number is lucky 13.

6

Alejandro Levine

In 1962, the British Invasion began and Rachel felt change stirring all around her. She loved shopping at the boulevards of Madrid and getting the latest hair style at multiple upscale hair salons, one of them called Carita's. She loved hair, makeup, and the swank fashions of the sixties. It was at Carita's that Rachel met the handsome celebrity hairstylist Alejandro Levine, who was of Sephardic Jewish heritage. Like Warren Beatty in the movie *Shampoo*, Levine was renowned for catering his services to the rich and famous.

Things moved fast and a love affair between Rachel and Alex blossomed. Alex showed up at Rachel's front door with a gorgeous diamond ring. He talked with the abuelos and asked for Rachel's hand in marriage. The abuelos were not convinced that even though he made a good living, he was good enough for Rachel. They wanted a man that had her etiquette and education. Alex was an orphan baby and was adopted by a woman that ended up with a drinking problem and a father who died young. Alex felt forced to live with his drunk mother in order to take care of her. Alex let Rachel know that he wanted to leave the home of his troubled mother and getting married would be the perfect excuse. Within months Rachel's parents had bought a hair salon for the two of them. They couldn't believe that after dating a prince, bullfighters, and professional soccer players, their daughter would find true love with a hairstylist. Still, they wanted to ensure Alex's success and make sure their princess was well cared for.

A few months later, the couple married in front of two hundred guests with little Esther, her niece, as her flower girl. Dukes, duchesses, contessas, sultans, lawyers, dignitaries, family, and friends were all invited. In truth Rachel would have preferred a simple wedding without all the pageantry and hoopla. But her honeymoon, a month in the sun on the island of Palma de Mallorca off the coast of Spain, made up for it.

Life was good. The couple returned and moved into an apartment in the heart of Madrid. Business was booming at the double-decker full-service salon named Alex, after Rachel's husband. It had massage rooms and hair, nail, and makeup stations. They hired a part-time chef to prepare elaborate appetizers and cocktails to serve to their elite guests.

Six months later, Alex shocked Rachel when he told her that he had made plans to fly to New York City to meet with a possible business partner, a friend named Liam Katzman. Alex would travel first to Manhattan to set everything up before sending for Rachel.

Liam owned a salon on Fifth Avenue that had become a central meeting point for American movie stars. The clientele was right up Alex's alley. While he was in New York, he worked as a stylist at Liam's salon for clients such as Elizabeth Taylor, Zsa Zsa Gabor, Sophia Loren, and Shirley MacLaine.

Alex was infatuated with New York and told Rachel that he wanted to move permanently to America. Rachel couldn't fathom why he wanted to leave their beautiful Spain and the salon that her parents had bought for them as a wedding gift. She hated leaving her family, friends, and devoted parents, she told her husband.

But she was raised to be a proper lady and wife, so with her parents' anguished blessing, she took a train from Madrid to Cádiz and a ship from Cádiz to Manhattan, arriving twelve days later. The ship carried all her cargo and belongings ready to move into her new apartment on Second Avenue, three blocks away from the salon. Liam, who was openly gay, looked at Rachel and told Alex, "You have a million-dollar wife." Rachel and Liam were instant friends.

A year went by, and New York proved to be as exciting as Madrid. Rachel took a pregnancy test and excitedly told Alex the news. He asked her to give him time to let it sink in. The next morning, jittery and disturbed, he said, "Let's go back to Spain."

"Why?" asked Rachel. "You're so happy here."

"Listen," he said, "I know of a private place where we can get an abortion."

Abortion was illegal in most places, but he explained that through contacts at the salon in Madrid, he knew of a safe place to get it done.

"Are you out of your mind?" said Rachel. "I'm not getting an abortion."

She noticed something else. He had begun to show signs of volatile behavior. He had a habit of calling her seven times a day. She hadn't thought it was strange until she started putting things together after he demanded that she have an abortion.

She remembered the morning she left the apartment to go to the market for strawberries, he had asked her what time she had returned. Later, he brought her back to the market to ask the staff. "Was my wife here to buy these strawberries and who was she with?"

When the shopkeepers verified her story, he acted as though it was nothing. She had dismissed it too, making an excuse that he was her husband and truly cared for her. But he was showing strange patterns.

Yet she agreed to go back to Spain with him anyway. She knew that once she was home, with the muscle of her family behind her, she could convince him that there was no reason to have an abortion.

On the flight back she asked again, "Why are we doing this? Why are you forcing me against my will to have an abortion?"

"I see you with your nephews and nieces," he said. "You are so good with them. You will love this baby more than me."

"You're insane, Alex," she replied. "I'll only love you more."

When they returned to Spain they moved in with Rachel's sister, Esther. Rachel begged her mom for help in talking Alex into changing his mind.

Rachel's strong and loving mother sat with her, held her as she cried, and prayed for a resolution, but explained that her hands were tied. For women of Rachel's generation, when a woman married, her husband held all the power. It was up to Rachel to listen to her husband.

Rachel was now putting all the puzzle pieces together. Alex was jealous and deeply insecure. She guessed that he had moved her to New York to keep her away from her friends and male admirers. Her acclaim and vibrant personality had given her power in Spain. She could see now that he was happy to cut those roots. Her mother and father took up the cause, agonizing with Alex to stop this horrible abortion from happening. Didn't he understand that he would not be replaced by a child?

There was nothing to be done. With tears in her eyes, her mother told Rachel that she would have to go through with the illegal procedure. Rachel was already three months along so there was no time to wait.

In the doctor's office, she could see her mother's shadow behind a partition. "Lie down," said the doctor. And when Rachel lay on the surgical table, he carefully tied down her arms and legs.

"May I have pain medication?" she asked.

"There is none," the doctor said matter-of-factly.

She felt the cold speculum prepare her womb and the procedure began, slow and agonizing as if they were cutting her body apart piece by piece.

"It's a boy," the nurse quietly told her when the procedure was done.

In shock, Rachel went back to her sister's apartment and wept. Weeks passed and still the nightmares came, and she woke, crying out for the soul of her lost child.

She had barely healed and already Alex was demanding his conjugal right. Two months passed and to her horror, she was pregnant again. Again, she went to the doctor with her mother. Again, she learned that she had lost another boy.

The nightmares and fitful sleep plagued her, a demon reminding her of her sins. Finally, she kicked Alex out of the apartment and moved home with her parents where she filed for a separation.

A month after the separation, Alex's housekeeper called her. "Alex cut his wrists and tried to commit suicide," she said. "You need to come immediately."

She agreed and returned to care for him for a month. After Alex was healed enough to take care of himself, Rachel sat him down. "We are finished," she told him, and went home to her parents. They sold the beauty salon to Jean d'Estrées, a world-famous hairdresser and cosmetologist from France, turning a solid profit.

It was 1964. The Beatles were gaining global popularity. Rachel was trying to get on with her life, enjoying the fact that she was young and living in beautiful Madrid. Soon Alex followed her to shops, salons, and cafés. If he couldn't find her, he would wait in her parking garage with flowers.

"Please come back to me! We can try to have children again," he said.

But she had had enough. "Do you have any idea what you put me through? My family thinks you're crazy. Please, leave me alone…let me go."

Alex refused. He sent packages, love letters, flowers, and candies to her apartment. He would show up when she was at her favorite salon and beg for her to come back. Rachel got a restraining order. It did absolutely nothing.

One evening Rachel was out with friends at a restaurant. As they were ordering wine and tapas, Alex showed up and sucker punched the man sitting next to Rachel, knocking him to the floor, yelling, "Who is he? Who is he?" The maître d' and staff saw the uproar and rushed to wrestle Alex to the ground while a waiter called an ambulance.

"You're mine," Alex shouted, and pushed his way out of the restaurant.

He grew more aggressive and dangerous. Weeks went by and she was afraid to go out, but some friends convinced her it would be safe. She went to a tapas restaurant and halfway through dinner the maître d' stopped by her table to tell her that her husband was outside, and he would like to talk to her.

Rachel told the maître d' to please tell him to go to hell and that the restaurant would be calling the police. Rachel and her friends immediately paid the bill and left out of the back of the restaurant. Rachel's family had no choice but to get involved. Her brother-in-law Pepe, sisters Carmen and Esther, and her parents went to the authorities to work out a game plan.

But seven months of stalking was taking its toll.

"Querida," said her mother, "Your father and I think you should leave Spain for a while." The abuelos knew that Rachel could no longer hide from Alex anywhere near Madrid.

"Where would I go?" she asked.

Abuela Esther had been talking to her cousin Carlos. Rachel could fly to Houston, Texas and travel from there to Mexico to file for a divorce. If not, it would take ten years to get a divorce in Spain.

Rachel thought, cried, and prayed. She didn't want to leave Spain, her parents, or her sisters. But what could she do? If she got the divorce, at least she would be free of Alex.

Her parents flew with her and stayed until she got settled, and then she waited. Carlos knew lawyers who could help her. The process would take a few months, but it could and would be done.

When all was ready, Carlos set Rachel up in a small hotel in Laredo, Texas on the Mexican border. She would ultimately have to cross the border and sign the papers in Mexico.

The hotel was a nice reprieve with a swimming pool and air-conditioned rooms. She was feeling good about herself again. She put on her pink bikini with its border of feathers at the waistband and sat by the pool, enjoying the sunshine.

One afternoon, a handsome man approached. She laughed because with white zinc oxide on his lips it looked like he was wearing the latest trend in lipstick.

"I heard you were from Spain, nice to meet you. My name is Henrik, Henrik Baumann," he said. His Spanish wasn't perfect, but it was good. He was charming and soon they were having a conversation. They talked for a while by the pool and Rachel finally asked what he was doing in Laredo.

"I'm here with some friends enjoying the sun. We come out on weekends from Chicago from time to time."

Henrik then started asking Rachel for information about her life. They talked about each other's marriages and Rachel was polite but not trying to start anything new with this strange man. Henrik told Rachel that he was divorced and by the end of the weekend, he asked for Rachel's contact information in Houston and even went as far to ask for her phone number in Spain. Rachel reluctantly gave him the numbers. She figured he would never follow up.

She was wrong.

7

Dark Days of Demons Made

Let's take a moment and travel back in time to New York City, 1929. Wall Street, to be exact. The roaring twenties are ending in a free fall along with the crash of the stock market. The crash caused the well-heeled to lose their fortunes, but it was the worker who lived on Main Street who truly suffered as the Great Depression began to suffocate the world. The year of 1930 began with high unemployment, poverty, deflation, plunging farm incomes, and lost opportunities for economic growth. Soup kitchens, bread lines, and homelessness grew as the unemployment rate rose to 24 percent.

In the dead of winter, January 28, 1930, my father Henrik J. Baumann was born. If you paralleled my parents' lives, you would find very few similarities. Henrik was born to poor German immigrant parents who moved to Chicago in 1924. Henrik Sr. and Ethel Baumann came to the United States by ship from Germany. Later, they took a train across the country to Milwaukee before settling down in Chicago.

Henrik was a cranky, moody child, always whining if he did not get his way. Later, his father said that if his son saw another child with a bottle and if he didn't have one in his hand, he would grab that child's bottle and throw it on the floor. His mother sobered Henrik up with cracks across the face, berating every rebuttal her son threw her way. Like Superman bending steel in half, Ethel twisted everything into an argument, throwing in some violence for good measure, a slap across the face, a crack on the bottom, or a jar smashed against the wall. Ethel even went as far as hitting her husband over the head with a frying pan.

Ethel's nickname was "the Little General." And what she loved most was degrading people with her words and vicious tone. I believe it filled up her insecurities as she must have been self-conscious about her horrible disposition and unattractive looks. She had grown up in poverty in Germany and couldn't seem to get past her own degradations of her early years. She was trash. In those days, you didn't get divorced, so my kind and handsome grandfather remained stoically married to my unhappy grandmother and enabled her bad behavior.

By the time little Henrik turned three, Franklin Delano Roosevelt was president and rallying the economy. Henrik was already equally fluent in German and English and would become multilingual. By the time he turned twenty, he would have fluency in Spanish and an ability to converse in Italian. You could see from a young age that Henrik had a rational brain with very little interest in others. He took no interest in his baby sister Chloe or baby brother Ted. Henrik always felt superior to both of them.

When Henrik was seven, he started selling candy bars to his friends and neighbors. He would sell his wares to strangers and tell people that a larger shipment of candy was coming in a week or so. If they could pay him up front, he would deliver the candy to their door. The candy never showed up…neither did Henrik. By the time his customers realized they'd been *had,* Henrik had already slithered away, down the streets on the far west side of Chicago. Early warning signs of his genius and lunacy were right there before your eyes.

His duped clients surely chalked his antics up to kids' stuff because Henrik never sold to the same people twice. Getting away with this prank gave him a sick satisfaction that he didn't have to play by the rules. He was a well sculpted *Schiesser*, or operator, as the neighbors called him. If you understood Henrik's mindset at this point in his life, you could see the unfolding of a master predator and manipulator.

As the dark days moved forward, Henrik Sr. and Ethel struggled to have enough food to feed their family. They used the *Daily News* for toilet paper, hoarded rubber bands, disposable cups, and reused wrapping paper from gifts. Many souls, including Henrik Sr. and Ethel, despaired that the American dream was out of reach. But Henrik made a different decision. He vowed that poverty would never define him. No, he would have success and power. He would never stop building his empire. Not only that, he would make sure that people knew who he was.

With no financial means, Henrik's impeccable grades earned him a scholarship to the University of Illinois where at 5'11", with dark hair, long sideburns, and thick glasses that he wore even in the swimming pool, he cut the classic figure of a nerdy intellectual.

He graduated with a double engineering degree and left quickly after graduation for the armed forces. Rapidly, he worked his way up to become a second lieutenant. He moved up the ranks again to become an intelligence officer stationed in Berlin behind the Iron Curtain. He was assigned to the intelligence unit posing as a double agent, where he held an alias as a German civilian. He would later use his military training as a tactic to psychologically and emotionally break innocent people. It was a strategy he relied on for the rest of his life to paralyze and manipulate his unsuspecting victims.

After he returned home, he worked at International Harvester and married a woman from Germany named Elsa, who mysteriously stole thousands of dollars from his first business, a local hardware store. With that money, she picked up her things and took off back to her home country, never to be seen again. It all seemed odd at the time but this peculiar reaction from Elsa foreshadowed a dark undertone in Henrik's character.

But Henrik was determined to move on. He worked day and night at the hardware store, Alloy's True Value, which was walking distance from his home. Slowly, he built a small financial empire buying buildings, houses, 20-flats, 10-flats, and land. Henrik was quick in turning bullshit into cash. He acted as a slumlord, renting out his properties. Next came the stock market. It was on the upswing and with the money he made, he bought all the buildings surrounding his hardware store and collected rent from them.

Henrik's brother Ted was a different story. He was more interested in beer. As he slouched on his bar stool and stared out the window of the local tavern, he could watch Henrik zip by, out to collect his rents. By the time Ted raised his latest glass to his lips, Henrik would surely have bought another slum-like building.

Henrik wasted no time in finding a new wife, Carol, who turned a blind eye to Henrik's antics and the fact that he flirted openly with other women in front of her, never mind what he did behind her back.

By the time he met Rachel, he was on the hunt for something better. In fact, he told Rachel that he had been long separated from Carol. The marriage had been short and lonely, he told her, the divorce was a done deal.

He was so charming and persuasive, Rachel had no reason to doubt him.

Back in Chicago, Henrik sent letter after letter and postcard after postcard to the hotel in Laredo. He phoned Rachel nearly every day stating that he had fallen in love with her and that he would take care of her if she moved to Chicago.

Still reeling from Alex, lonely on her own in Texas, Rachel felt herself succumbing to Henrik's charms.

"Querida," he said, "you should see the house I'm building in Chicago. It will be finished in a few months. Come and see for yourself. I'll take good care of you, I promise."

Rachel's divorce from Alex was now final and she moved out of the hotel in Laredo and back with Cousin Carlos and family in Houston. She had every intention of going back to Spain, but she was rightly worried about the revenge that Alex would take against her, so she stayed in Houston for a few more months. She would not become another headline in the Spanish press: "Beauty Queen Murdered by Jealous Husband in a Fit of Rage."

She also felt burdened with guilt for what she put her family through and the shame she brought on the family name. Crying on the phone from Texas, she called her mother and tried to apologize for the failed marriage. In those days in Spain, you did not file for divorce. And the fact that Alex had forced her to have two abortions was too much. Her mother completely understood the reason for the separation and supported the divorce.

Months passed and Henrik's letters and postcards kept coming along with visits from Chicago. Rachel was exuberantly enticed and persuaded by Henrik's invitation to his home. She longed for her old life in Spain and missed her family dearly, yet the thought of starting over in a new country with a man she was equally falling for could be an exciting change. Henrik was so unbelievably charismatic, charming, and doting toward her. He promised her the world. He shared his heart with her, letting her know that, like her, he was very conservative and moralistic, that he loved children as much as she did and couldn't wait to start a family with her.

Rachel felt completely desired by Henrik in a way she never knew was possible. She truly believed that they loved each other and could have a great future. Henrik reminded Rachel that she could not get remarried in Spain because of the strict divorce laws. This immediately cut out the option of living happily ever after back in Spain.

On October 10, 1966, Rachel moved to Chicago into a luxurious condo on the Gold Coast with sweeping views of Lake Michigan. Henrik was still in the process of building their dream home in the suburbs, but soon it would be finished.

Rachel, enthralled with America, settled into her new life. She met her neighbors, Alice Tricocci, who managed the building, and her husband Jimmy. She and Alice quickly became best friends, going to lunch and sharing all their secrets.

Henrik was busy running his hardware store and taking care of his rentals, yet he found time to show Rachel the highlights of vibrant Chicago. He introduced her to his parents and brother within the first few weeks. He also took her to meet close family friends, Tante Annie, Onkel Paul, their niece Karin Kaffie, her husband, and their two sons, Marc and Ralph. The Kaffies lived in a duplex a few blocks from Henrik's hardware store.

Eager to show Rachel how successful he was, Henrik took her to shop at fancy department stores, Marshall Field's and Saks on Michigan Avenue, for fur coats, the latest fashion, and whatever she wanted. He went out of his way to spoil her.

But the novelty soon wore off and Rachel found herself desperately missing her parents and the country she loved. She spent a lot of time on the phone with her parents planning her next trip home and when she could see them again.

She was also pregnant again and faced off with Henrik's mother, Ethel. "Send Rachel and her unborn child back to Spain," Ethel commanded. She looked at Rachel, beautiful and happy, and her jealousy blossomed. Ethel wanted to be the powerful matriarch without the stunning Spanish princess to make her look and feel more invisible. The Spanish princess had to go.

Henrik ignored his mother's advice. Instead, he brought Rachel to Arizona to meet his sister Chloe. From there, he and Rachel drove to Las Vegas. Henrik also started looking at farmland to buy in and around Ontario, Wisconsin, northwest of Madison, the state capital. Per usual, he had many irons in the fire.

In March 1967, Henrik took off for Mexico. He told Rachel that he was going to open a new bank account near Acapulco. He traveled there so often he told her it would be a great idea to have extra cash on hand when he needed it. At one of Rachel's monthly pregnancy checkups, Doctor Lopez, her beloved Spanish-speaking doctor, told her that it might be safer if she did not travel with Henrik. If she caught a bug, flu, or dysentery, she could put her pregnancy at risk. That was the last thing Rachel wanted.

A month had passed, and Rachel checked in with Doctor Lopez letting him know that she had some discomfort and irritation and was worried about the baby. He told her not to worry, that due to changing hormone levels some women suffer from some discomfort. Still, he ran some tests and called Rachel and Henrik back into the office. "Rachel," he told her, "Henrik has an infection on his hands and that infection is causing your discomfort." After the strange behavior she had experienced at the hands of Alex, Rachel squashed her suspicions and said nothing to Henrik. Slowly, her suspicions boomeranged into denial.

Dr. Lopez was concerned that the infection could harm the baby but wouldn't know until the child was born. He took Henrik into the next room. "You have a venereal disease," he said. "One you did not get from Rachel."

Keeping matters completely private from Rachel, Dr. Lopez spoke sternly to Henrik about the dangers he had exposed to his unborn child. For Rachel's sake and the sake of the relationship, he would keep his mouth shut. Disgusted, he left the private meeting with Henrik and came back to Rachel to discuss a treatment plan without divulging the truth. Instead, he told her that she would have to come in for regular appointments. They would have to coat her insides with topical antifungals, antimicrobials, and suppositories, not knowing if anything would work.

The incident was somewhat forgotten, and in May, Rachel and Henrik were married in Saint Joseph, Michigan. Things changed quickly after their marriage. Henrik had become another person. On their honeymoon, he asked Rachel if she wanted to have another couple over to watch pornography and he always invited sex toys into the bedroom. This disgusted her but most of the time she would laugh it off as if he were trying to pull off a college boy prank, but the frequency of his extreme sexual queries had her alarmed.

It was the Summer of Love, and the newlyweds flew to Spain so that Henrik could meet Rachel's parents and Rachel could get the visa and the passport she needed to travel freely between countries. With his worldly ways and fluent Spanish, Henrik put on a show and charmed the entire family. They were smitten with him.

Henrik said he needed to return home early to close on the farmland he had bought in Wisconsin, so Rachel stayed behind. Basking in the joy of her family and her pregnancy, Rachel swam in the ocean, spent time with her adoring parents, and shopped and dined with friends. When Rachel came home in time for her checkup, she noticed that Henrik had a robust tan, the kind of tan you couldn't get in Midwestern sunshine.

"Where on earth did you get that color?" she asked. "It looks as though you were in Mexico. I thought you were closing at the farm?"

"I was in Wisconsin all this time," he said. "It was really hot there. And I needed to explore our new four-hundred-acre farm. Congratulations! I can't wait for you to see it."

He leaned forward to kiss her, but Rachel turned away. She couldn't understand why he chose a getaway five hours from Chicago in the middle of nowhere. She would have preferred a house in Lake Geneva, Wisconsin, only an hour away. She loved the quaint coastline, marinas, and boats, which made her feel like she was back in La Coruña. But in the end, it was Henrik's money, and he was going to do whatever he wanted with it. Besides, her new home was almost finished, ready for them and the new baby who was due in a few months.

When they finally moved in, the house seemed like a dream. It had everything she could have needed. It was a brand-new bi-level home and the nicest place on the block with large windows that would let in light even in the dead of winter. It had a custom leather-wrapped bar with a zinc top, a heated dance floor with strobe lights in the ceiling controlled by a dimmer switch, and en suite bathrooms, a newer concept in the late sixties. The fireplace had a custom rock wall whose stones were handpicked by Henrik. Henrik liked to hunt, and he collected and sold guns. In fact, he loved them so much he built an elaborate gun cabinet with a wrought iron design and glass doors.

As for Rachel, she now had a beautiful dream home, a husband who had traveled to Spain to meet and charm her parents, and the greatest gift of all, a new baby on the way.

Rachel's late October due date was approaching, and Henrik wanted to throw a party before the baby came.

Feeling the exhaustion that pregnancy in its later stages can bring, Rachel asked that they wait until after the baby was born. But Henrik refused to listen, and the party would go on as scheduled.

On the day of the party, Rachel woke up feeling unwell. "I'm not sure what is wrong but I'm really tired," she said, catching her breath.

"You'll be fine," said Henrik. "We have to have this party. My family will be here tonight! I need you to start getting things ready now. I've already picked up stuff at the grocery store!"

His voice had grown angry and urgent. She shot him a look, got up, and began cooking and cleaning. That night, as the guests were making their final toasts and taking their last bites, Rachel began to feel pain. She stayed quiet because Henrik was in his glory, and she didn't want to ruin the night.

The next morning, she noticed that she was bleeding, and asked Henrik to call Dr. Lopez before taking her to the hospital.

After he examined her, Dr. Lopez paused. "I just checked you five days ago," he said. "What have you been doing? This baby's head was down and ready to enter the birth canal, now its head is turned around. This baby is breech and you're in labor. What happened?"

Rachel was doubled over in pain. "Oh my God," she said. "Henrik wanted to have a party with his family and friends, and I cooked and cleaned for over ten hours yesterday!"

Furious, Dr. Lopez turned to Henrik, "Do you realize how dangerous this could be for your wife? I can't turn the baby!"

"She'll be fine," scoffed Henrik. "She's strong like a bull."

On October 15, 1967, at 6:14 p.m. after more than twenty-four hours of labor, and an episiotomy that required over forty stitches, Rachel bore her first child, Rachel Fallon Baumann, a healthy, strong baby with no sign of the ravage of venereal disease. The abuelos flew over from Spain and hired a housekeeper to take care of Rachel and the baby.

The holidays came and went, and everyone was in the glow of baby Fallon. In the middle of winter, 1968, Henrik and Rachel flew to Spain to introduce Fallon to the family. Henrik hung around for a while, but as would become his pattern, he took off for the States, making up an excuse that he needed to order products for the new season at the hardware store. Rachel and the baby stayed for two months basking in the love of the abuelos and the beautiful life Rachel and Henrik were building in America.

In May, Henrik and Rachel were about to celebrate their first anniversary. Henrik had planned the entire evening. They would drop the baby off with his parents and spend the night at a hotel downtown. He told Rachel that he had a surprise for her and to pack an overnight bag. Rachel was excited. Surely, he had booked a room at the Palmer House or the Drake Hotel. After, they would have a romantic dinner and then possibly attend Lyric Opera House for a performance. Rachel loved the elegant Michigan Avenue area. She dressed in a glamorous Chanel suit of cream chambray silk and packed her favorite lingerie. As they drove into the city Rachel grew giddy with anticipation of a romantic night with her husband. They had so much to celebrate.

On the outskirts of Chicago in a run-down neighborhood, Henrik pulled the car over.

"Where are we?" asked Rachel.

"You'll see, it's part of the surprise," he said. "C'mon." He motioned for her to get out of the car.

They walked for two blocks and Rachel asked again, "Where are we going? Is the car going to be okay here? What on earth is this place?"

In all of Rachel's circles she had never seen much poverty. As they got closer, they approached a small cinema with posters of naked women posing in sexually suggestive positions. Rachel noticed strange sexual pictures of acts that she had never seen before. She was confused. There were only men in the theater, and she could feel them staring at her when they sat down in matted red velvet seats. The film began and within minutes three men and three women were doing things on screen that she never imagined was possible.

Rachel jumped out of her seat.

"What *ees* this dirty thing you take me to?" Rachel's strong accent grew worse when she got upset. She had never learned to use the word porno or pornographic, so she called what Henrik took her to see "the dirty thing."

Rachel's voice grew louder as she got up from her seat and headed toward the exit. "You take me to this sex movie on our anniversary?"

"Calm down, calm down, you're causing a scene," Henrik chimed in, but Rachel wasn't listening.

"I don't care! This is disgusting. We either leave or I call a taxi. This evening is over, take me home."

Shocked that Rachel had spoken up for herself, Henrik followed her out and drove her home.

In the bedroom, disappointed and upset, Rachel unpacked her pink silk nightgown and matching robe, the pretty underthings. Moments later, Henrik rushed upstairs to say that he had just received a phone call and the hardware store's alarm had gone off. "I need to deal with the police," he said. "I'll be home when I can. Don't wait up."

Before Rachel could even say that she didn't hear the phone ring, he was out the door and into the night. Fitfully, Rachel fell asleep waiting for Henrik who stumbled in near dawn.

When Fallon was a little girl, she loved listening to the small white radio that sat on a shelf in the kitchen. It was set to WLS, and in later years, 97.9 FM, the Loop, home of classic rock. Rachel learned English from radio and television programs, and as Fallon grew, so did her love of rock and roll.

They had wonderful neighbors. There was Edwardo and Janette, who lived next door. And there was Sheldon, who was gay and lived a few doors south of their house. His name was Sheldon, but he liked the more feminine version, Shelly. He and Rachel became best friends and loved singing along to the radio.

One morning, as she unpacked boxes and brought trash to the curb, Rachel noticed a strange woman driving past the house. At first, she thought maybe this woman lived in the neighborhood. But as days went by, she noticed the woman circling the block and slowing down when she passed the house. It gave Rachel an uneasy feeling. She pointed it out to Henrik one day when she saw the woman drive by. Henrik recognized the car. "Don't worry," he said. "That's my ex-wife Carol. I'm sure she'll go away in a few days."

Rachel thought it was odd that he said the name Carol because she thought Henrik's ex-wife was named Elsa. But he reminded her that Carol had been his second wife. Carol soon called the house and hung up. "We've got to do something," said Rachel.

"I know," said Henrik. "I'll take care of it." Within days, Carol was never heard from or seen again.

Rachel had a sinking feeling that something horrible had happened to Carol but she had no physical proof of any kind. Life was good for her and Henrik and their new baby. There were trips home to see her family, the new house, car, and four hundred acres of farmland. She didn't want the thought of an ex-wife destroying her happiness.

Months later, in the winter of 1969, Rachel and Henrik left Fallon with her godparents, Tante Annie and Onkel Paul, for a week-long trip to Acapulco where the weather was perfect and the water was inviting. On the third day, Henrik befriended a wealthy couple whom he met on the beach.

Bruce Wilcox was an executive for a television station and his lovely blonde wife Sherry reminded Henrik of the actress Sharon Tate. What was even better was the fact that the couple lived in downtown Chicago. He invited them out for an afternoon on a private chartered boat to scuba dive and snorkel. When the foursome returned to the beach, Rachel noticed Henrik making eyes at Sherry, rubbing the sand off her feet, and giving her a massage while she giggled.

Embarrassed, Rachel, brought up to be dutiful and loyal to her husband, wondered what was wrong with Sherry.

Henrik knew he could do whatever he wanted, and his wife wouldn't say a thing. She was raised to be a proper Spanish lady. Besides, with her beauty, all she had to do was walk down the beach and men would turn their heads. When their vacation ended, Henrik made sure to get Bruce and Sherry's phone number.

That summer, Henrik often brought the family to the farm. Some of the farmers had herds of extra milking cows in the barn as well as goats and chickens. Always looking to make a buck, Henrik had found a way to make the farm cash positive. Miles away at another farm in Bethel, New York, the Woodstock Music Festival was in full swing. Over four hundred thousand peace-seeking teenagers and folks that wanted refuge from the Vietnam War attended. Rachel loved music and on their little radio in the kitchen she would listen to Joe Cocker, "I get by *weeth* a little help from my friends…" Many of the bands that headlined at the festival would become her daughter Fallon's favorites in years to come.

The fall had come and gone, and Rachel befriended a new neighbor, Kelly, a travel agent who could help her book flights to Spain. Cultivating new friends felt good to her soul because she missed her family.

After dinner one night, Rachel was at the kitchen sink washing dishes and talking to Henrik. "I met a new friend a few days ago," she said. "A travel agent who works just down the street from Dominick's Groceries. I told her we travel a lot and…"

Henrik violently slapped the mail off the kitchen counter. "I know what you're going to ask me," he suddenly raised his voice. "How dare you embarrass me. You don't call the shots around here. Who the hell do you think you are? I've been using my travel agent for twenty years and I'm not gonna change now. You will use *my* people. *My* contacts!"

Startled, Rachel dropped the plate and sponge in the sink. "I'm trying to make new friends."

"New friends? You'll be friends with my friends, only. I don't give a damn what you want. I make the money around here. I pay the bills. And another thing, I'm leaving a sheet of paper taped to the wall! From now on, you will record the time you spend talking to your parents in Spain!"

He was looming over her, spit flying in her face. And then he walked out, leaving her to stare through the window and wonder what she was going to do. *How did I get into this terrible situation*, she wondered. *I only want happiness for all of us. Maybe he's oversensitive and feels threatened? He knows how much I need my parents. He can't control everything.* She wondered what caused this outburst that seemed to come out of nowhere. His personality had changed in a matter of seconds. She had never witnessed anyone flying off the handle like that. It didn't seem normal.

Worse, she was pregnant with her second child and didn't want to rock the boat. The travel agent friend was never mentioned again. And when she flew home for two months that summer and Henrik called to say he couldn't come, she let it go, even though her suspicions about what he was doing with his time were growing.

Fall and the holidays came and went. January 1970 was brutally cold with days hovering below zero. Rachel had flown to Spain just after the holidays and was now home and settling in when she got a phone call from neighbor Shelly.

"Can you come over?" he said. "I have something to tell you." Rachel grabbed her coat and Fallon's snowsuit, bundled Fallon up, and off they went.

"Rachel!" said Shelly, opening the door against the bitter wind. "You look beautiful. How was your trip to Spain? And Fallon, you're such a big girl. You're going to have a baby brother or sister soon!"

They settled in over coffee and leftover Christmas cookies. Soon, Shelly's face grew somber. "Rachel, I wanted to tell you this. It's been eating away at me since you've been gone. I really don't know how to tell you and it's made me a bit sick. When you were away, your husband came over and was making small talk with me. I didn't think anything of it at first. I figured Henrik was lonely and maybe wanted supper."

"Yes?" Rachel tilted her head to the side.

"Then as he was leaving, he asked me to call him one night and he would come over. He said it in a way that sounded like he was propositioning me. I was in shock. I'm a gay man and I know when I'm being approached…if you know what I mean."

Rachel sat in stillness.

"Of course, nothing happened, Rachel. I never called him. I would never do anything like that to you."

Rachel sat for another minute hugging her belly and not saying much, she was trying to process it all. When she finally got up to go, Shelly hugged her, "Remember, I'm always here for you," he said.

She walked back to the house numb and wondered who and what she was married to. The couple on the beach in Acapulco had been bad enough, but this was too much to think about. She had Fallon to worry about, and another baby on the way, but she couldn't put this out of her mind as she had with the other indiscretions.

February was just around the corner and Henrik told Rachel that he was heading back out to Mexico alone. They had talked about wallpapering the front hall. "Listen," he said, "when the wallpaper samples come in, just leave them on the dining room table."

"What samples?" she said. "I have some ideas for colors and…"

"JUST LEAVE THE GODDAMN WALLPAPER ALONE! I'll take care of it when I get back!" He flung his arm over the coffee table, sending an ashtray crashing to the floor.

Rachel's head jolted in Henrik's direction. "Don't you dare talk to me like that and don't you dare touch me when you get back from Mexico. God knows what you'll bring back!"

"You don't know what you're talking about. I pick out the wallpaper and paint for this house! I pay for everything around here and I'll do whatever the hell I want!"

Rachel walked out of the kitchen and went upstairs, slamming the bedroom door behind her.

"Don't you dare turn your back on me and slam the door!" he shouted, but she ignored him.

The changes had come over him gradually, but now they were in full force, volatile, argumentative, secretive, controlling, tyrannical…the list went on. She would no longer blame his intensity on the new baby on the way. This was more, much more.

The weeks that Henrik was gone were peaceful and within days of his return on March 5, 1970, Soraya Yvonne Baumann was born. The first time Rachel settled her into Fallon's lap, Fallon told Rachel and Henrik, "She's so big! I can't wait to play with her!"

Everything seemed perfect from the outside looking in.

Trails of Betrayal

Early summer, 1970, and the trees were in full bloom. Baby Soraya was getting bigger and fun to watch as she slept in her bassinet. Fallon loved taking her hand in hers and feeling how warm and soft it was.

Whenever Henrik picked Soraya up, she began to cry and fuss. Rachel thought it odd that she fussed around him. Was her child feeling a vibe about her father?

Henrik noticed that his baby was uncomfortable with him, and he also noticed that Rachel knew too. Out of nowhere, he turned his rage on Rachel.

"Is this how you make a Goddamn bed? This room looks like a piece of shit since the baby was born!"

In a rage, he threw the pillows on the floor and ripped the blanket off the bed. Like a wild animal backed into a corner, he berated Rachel and sent Soraya screaming at the top of her lungs.

Rachel sternly spoke back. "What is wrong with you! What the hell is wrong with you!"

He was now shredding the king-size bed, his glasses flying off his face and landing on the sheets strewn across the floor.

Fallon hid in her room. Rachel, with Soraya in her arms, stormed downstairs. There was nothing wrong with the bed, of course. The comforter was folded up on one side because Rachel was storing some of her

Hola magazines from Spain. They sat next to a huge stack of Henrik's *Playboy* magazines. Rachel always kept an impeccable house, clean and neat.

Later that evening Henrik got a call that one of his dear friends Harold Krause had passed away. They were good friends from the hardware store and Harold was a good customer.

The wake was the next evening and he insisted Rachel join him. They dropped Fallon and Soraya off at their grandparents' house. Child-free for the night, Henrik mingled at the wake like it was his own private cocktail party, working the room with Rachel quietly by his side, laughing and joking. She saw a very tacky, inappropriate, obnoxious side of him that had no clue how to behave around grief. She also noticed that he would never let anyone get a word in edgewise, had no filter and the conversations were always centered around him and his accomplishments, boasting about his travels, conquests, money, and how brilliantly smart he was.

As the wake drew to a close, he narrowed in on Mrs. Krause. From the corner of her eye, Rachel watched him kiss and hug Mrs. Krause, rubbing her back as if Rachel wasn't there. Then she heard him say, "I will come over tonight."

Rachel spoke softly, disappointment in her voice. "Henrik…what are you doing?"

"Be quiet… These are my customers!" Henrik spoke swiftly and sternly. *Oh my God*, she thought, *what is this, what is happening?*

On many levels Rachel knew that this behavior was not because of her but that there was something deeply wrong with him. But she could never put her finger on it. When they returned home, sure enough Henrik came in long enough to change and put his coat back on.

"Where are you going?" said Rachel.

"Mrs. Krause is a good friend of the family and a good customer of the hardware store. She sounds really upset. I need to be there for her."

Disgusted, she went to bed only to awaken at 2:30 a.m. when the front door opened. The parasite slithered back in thinking his indiscretions were undetected.

The weeks of summer progressed, and Henrik flew Rachel's parents in from Spain. It made Rachel happy but Henrik's ultimate plan was for Rachel to be preoccupied with family so he could do more of what he wanted. The abuelos loved the summer months in Chicago, and they loved to play with Soraya and Fallon in their little baby pool in the backyard.

As the abuelos settled in, Henrik suggested that they watch the girls and that he and Rachel go downtown to visit, "Our friend Sherry…do you remember her?"

"Sherry from Acapulco…and her husband?"

"Yes…that Sherry."

Rachel had wondered if all this time Henrik had been keeping up the friendship with Bruce and Sherry and she wondered why today of all days they would head downtown for a visit. As Henrik drove, Rachel noticed that he used no written directions on how to get to their high-rise apartment in the city. He seemed to drive on autopilot. When they got to the building Rachel and Henrik took the elevator up to the twenty-seventh floor. Henrik knocked and Sherry answered, tall and blonde and self-confident. Overdoing it a bit, she threw her arms around Rachel.

"My dear, so lovely to see you! Henrik, great to see you too!"

Henrik and Sherry were walking quickly to the stairs in the building. They looked like they were on a mission and Rachel asked, "Where are we going?"

"Down a flight to the twenty-sixth floor," said Sherry. "I've got these very cool friends who own a store on Michigan Avenue. They have tons of samples of their clothing at a fraction of the price!"

"Rachel, wait until you see some of the stuff," said Henrik. "Have fun and buy whatever you'd like."

Before Rachel could say anything, a door opened, and she was inside

Margaret and Amy's apartment. More fast talking. Henrik, Sherry, Margaret, and Amy seemed to speak in a frenzy. There was no possible way for Rachel to understand the rapid-fire English.

Warm and friendly, Margaret and Amy ushered Rachel toward the clothes, showing her hot pants and tops.

Somehow, Sherry and Henrik graciously made their way to the door. "We'll be right back," said Henrik. Rachel, whose politeness had been ingrained from birth, watched them go.

Soon she was distracted. Margaret waited hand and foot on her while Amy brought fresh lemonade. Soon, they were engulfed in laughter as Rachel tried on outfit after outfit, the latest miniskirts along with matching purses and shoes. Soon there was a pile of outfits that Rachel put aside to show Henrik. She was getting worried. An hour had passed, and he was nowhere to be found.

"Can you show me where Sherry's place is?" she said. "I think I'm done shopping now."

"Don't worry," said Margaret. "I'm sure they'll be down soon enough. I'll call Sherry on the phone."

As Margaret dialed Sherry's number, Rachel was sure she saw an anxious look across her face.

Within five minutes Henrik and Sherry were back in Margaret's apartment. Rachel saw the pink in Sherry's cheeks. She saw the look in Henrik's eyes and heard a giggle from Sherry's lips. She looked at both of their faces as her heart sank. This shopping spree was just a hoax, and she knew what her husband was doing while she was being polite and shopping with the ladies. Rachel knew that Henrik had banged that nasty Sherry, and there was nothing she could do about it.

Summer turned to fall. For weeks Henrik would be loving and fun, then out of nowhere he became an inhuman beast. She didn't know what she was going to do. She had been educated to take care of her husband, cooking and cleaning for him, but she had no marketable skills, none of her own money, no family in America, and only Henrik's friends. She was terrified of talking to her parents about another divorce. And she had Soraya and Fallon. Unsure of her future, she told herself to make the best of it and that maybe things would get better.

In late September, the family piled into the car and drove to The Peacock for breakfast, a local family place where Henrik knew the owner. They sat in a booth, and since Fallon could never sit still, Henrik began yelling at her. Always yelling and screaming, always chaos until his friends came around. Then he turned his personality on and off like a switch. Almost like he was a different person. Nick, the owner, came over and shook Henrik's hand and the waitress took the order.

Rachel gave her order and ordered toast for Fallon to nibble on. Henrik started asking the young waitress where she lived and was making small talk with her like they were friends. Rachel shot him a look of disgust. Then Henrik whispered to the waitress as she walked away.

"If you come back to the table with your top unbuttoned, you'll get a bigger tip."

The waitress's face turned flush and she pretended she didn't hear him.

"What's wrong with you?" Rachel pleaded as Henrik's eyes followed the waitress. "The girls and I are sitting right here, and you talk to the waitress like she's a prostitute!"

"Never mind. It keeps the staff on their toes."

Rachel knew that Henrik flirted with every waitress who crossed his path and threw his money around thinking that service people were hard up and that if he waved around his cash, he would get what he wanted. He threw out the offer to the masses knowing that when an agreeable person came along, his offer would be accepted.

On the way home, they drove to the grocery store to pick up a few things. Henrik said, "I want to invite my family over for a dinner party tonight."

"I'm sorry," said Rachel, "Can we do it another night? Soraya hasn't been sleeping and I'm up with her at all hours, I'm exhausted."

"I don't care what you want!!" he shouted, pressing his foot on the gas. The car jolted forward. He was now swerving in and out of traffic. "This is my god damn family and you will do what I say! I don't want to hear another word out of your Goddamn mouth! You *puta!*"

Cars were beeping in both directions. "Stop!" shouted Rachel. "Stop the car! The children!" She held Soraya tight, grabbed my hand in the back seat and braced herself.

"Shut up…shut the hell up…*shut the hell up!* You Goddamn bitch!" You will do what I say! It's my car, my house, my rules!"

The car was now going double the speed limit. Rachel wept in the front seat. "Henrik, you need help…! Dios mío!"

"What did you say to me? You need help! Not me, you Goddamn ungrateful bitch!"

Alex had caused her deep and lasting pain, but Rachel had never even observed this kind of violence. The car hit the curb. They drove past the sidewalk and ripped up the grass. Fallon's head hit the front seat and she began to cry. Soraya was screaming in the front seat as the car jolted with a sudden stop near the tree line. Henrik got out of the car and began screaming again as he pointed to the grass.

"LOOK WHAT YOU MADE ME DO! You make me go crazy! Look at the girls, they're crying because of what you made me do!"

Rachel spoke softly. "Please Henrik…take us home."

Calming down slightly Henrik said, "You're so Goddamn lazy. You don't work and you don't have the energy to put together a last-minute party. I'll show you what real work is. All you do is take care of the girls."

Rachel looked down at the car's front seat and did not utter another word. She waited until Henrik was done checking for any damage to the car. She knew trying to reason with him would be fruitless as anything could set him off.

His anger spent, Henrik got back in the car, drove home long enough to drop Rachel, Soraya, and Fallon off before heading to the grocery store to get supplies for the dinner party.

Rachel had no idea that the worst was still to come. She got herself together, wiped off the smeared makeup and started vacuuming and cleaning for the party.

The weeks turned into months of unprovoked verbal assaults. Rachel tried to analyze what triggered his chronic explosive and violent outbursts. She played things over and over in her mind trying to make sense of it all. She couldn't. The puzzle pieces of Henrik's psyche were a mystery to her, and his unpredictable behavior seemed out of proportion for the situation. She started to snoop around trying to discover anything that could solve the ambiguity of the man she married.

She called the hardware store at different times a day. He was never there to answer her call, he was always out at one of his buildings or out on an errand. She kept notes on what the hardware store staff was telling her and would compare his answers when he came home. She began to visit the hardware store unannounced. Henrik was nowhere to be found.

At home she started looking through his paperwork. She didn't know what she was looking for, but she kept searching. She discovered a few exorbitant checks that Henrik made out to some of the priests at their church. She thought it odd and kept a mental note of it. Rachel was good friends with neighbors Frank, who was a cop, and Laurie, his wife. She had asked him to take a look at some of Henrik's paperwork to see if anything stood out to him. Sometimes she had trouble understanding everything that she read. Frank became a second pair of eyes for her, and he and Laurie came over periodically when Henrik wasn't home.

On one occasion, Frank showed Rachel a hardware store tax return. "Look at this," he said, pointing to the bottom line. "It shows that Henrik makes $12,000 a year in profit at the hardware store. He's lying, Rachel. There is no way that store only makes 12K a year. This is tax evasion! Be careful if you sign off on these papers. If the IRS comes after him, they can also come after you."

"What do I do?" she asked. "He's always getting me to sign this paper and that."

"I just wanted you to be aware. They will probably go after him and keep you out of it, but you can never be sure."

Rachel had a sinking premonition that this would cause a terrible amount of concern in the near future. Frank also found paperwork that stated that Henrik sold his hardware store for a dollar to what looked like to be a relative. Frank also found Henrik's ex-wife Carol's signature on the paperwork, a signature that looked identical to Henrik's handwriting.

"Rachel… It looks like he forged Carol's name to take the hardware store away from her before their divorce. I'd be careful not to sign anything with this asshole."

Rachel stared off into space, quietly nodding her head in agreement.

Henrik knew that Rachel had grown indifferent to him and was more on her guard. Still, he did whatever he wanted thinking that her English was not good enough and that she was too naïve to know the truth. But she was working every day to improve her English, getting better with her reading until she was no longer duped by his indiscretions.

A year had gone by, and Rachel brought Soraya and Fallon to Spain. It was nearing the Thanksgiving holidays. Once again, Henrik made the excuse that he had things to take care of when really Rachel knew he had planned to go to Mexico in search of prostitutes or take his latest girlfriend up to the farm. Plus, he had the house to himself. He promised he would fly to Spain in a few weeks, but in truth, Rachel couldn't have cared less.

Rachel not only loved spending time with her family, but she was also relieved to have time to herself. Her parents, the girls' abuelos, smothered them with love while she took time for lunch with her old friends, never letting on that her second marriage to her handsome American husband had turned out to be a disaster.

She returned after the new year. It was now 1972. She found herself regularly digging through Henrik's paperwork looking for something… anything she could find. She stumbled across something with Henrik's signature on it and noticed that Carol, his ex-wife, also signed the paperwork. She looked closer at the signatures side by side and noticed that both signatures were signed by Henrik. She knew his handwriting anywhere. At this point all she had as proof was that he was capable of forgery. She knew that his calculating and manipulative mind was adept at so much more. Her heart sank and she had no idea what to do.

That summer Henrik invited five families from the neighborhood to join their family at the farm. Some of the neighbors rented mobile homes and campers so that all had enough space to sleep. The four-hundred-acre farm sat on a ridge overlooking a valley of lush green forest. The white farmhouse, barn, horse corral, machine shed, and water pump house were spaced out perfectly almost as if in a dream. The air smelled of freshly mowed grass, oak and maple trees, and chamomile.

They rode horses in the fourth of July parade, swam in the pool, and everyone helped with the cooking, cleaning, and food prep. One particular clear night, everyone gathered outside. Some played guitars and others sat by the bonfire. Henrik put a five-gallon bucket of water near the fire in case of an emergency. The kids were all playing Ghost in the Graveyard, and Fallon was learning the game for the very first time. They ran, jumped, and played for what seemed like hours.

After some time, Fallon heard Henrik calling her name. It seems he had been calling and calling her name for a minute or so but none of the kids could hear anything amongst the chaos and laughter.

Fallon looked up, and playfully ran past him, a happy ghost in their pretend graveyard. Suddenly, she felt the shock of cold water, the thud of the bucket on her head, the handle catching her lip. She looked up at him, the water had caught in her throat, and she was finding it hard to breathe. He seemed to be yelling in slow motion, silencing the guitar, the singing, the laughter.

The neighbors were now quietly staring at Henrik and Fallon in disbelief. Rachel ran toward her daughter. "Henrik, what is wrong with you! She is a four-year-old child!" she shouted, scooping Fallon up in her arms. Fallon couldn't stop shivering.

"That's what happens when you don't listen," said Henrik, his voice cold. "I was calling her, and she didn't listen to me."

Rachel glared at him. "What kind of sick torture did your mother put you through. Your mother must have mistreated you for you to act like this. God knows this couldn't have come from your sweet father. I can't believe he stays with her."

"Keep my mother out of this!"

The metallic taste of blood leaked from Fallon's lip. She was trembling, humiliated, and didn't understand what she did wrong.

Henrik walked in the house as Rachel was putting some Vaseline on Fallon's bloodied lip. He walked in the bathroom, and Fallon looked at the floor to make as little eye contact as possible with her father, the devil in the graveyard.

"Henrik get out of here. Who do you think you are? You don't treat a child like that. She's not a dog. She's our child! You treat me like shit, you're not going to do it to her. Understand?"

"She wasn't listening to me."

"I told you to get out of here. I'll march right outside and embarrass you in front of all your friends!"

Henrik left with a scowl on his face. Rachel knew that it would vanish the moment he returned to his friends by the bonfire, toasting them with a freshly opened beer.

Back in Chicago, Rachel grew more tired and suspicious, but Henrik was always one step ahead of her. He was now aware that Rachel was onto him and had begun drafting fake and blank documents for her to sign. Little by little he was taking her name off all the properties they owned together by forging her name.

One afternoon, Rachel was sitting in the kitchen rewriting one of her recipes when Henrik approached her.

"I need you to sign this piece of paper," he said, waving it in front of her.

She grabbed the sheet, turned it over and handed it back.

"That's an empty sheet of paper…I'm not going to sign that. I know you think I'm stupid, but you better think again. I'm not signing it."

"Sign the papers, Rachel!"

"No!"

Henrik's face got red. "Sign this Goddamn piece of paper!"

"No…I'm not signing a blank sheet of paper, and why do you need me to do that! Besides…keep your voice down, the girls will hear you."

"The girls…the girls…they have no idea what's going on!"

"The girls know more than you think. They hear you screaming and yelling every day. They will carry what they hear for the rest of their lives."

Henrik's thumb was now poised over the detonation button. The cockroach grabbed her hand and forced the pen between her fingers. Froth gushed from his mouth. "Sign this fucking paper…sign this Goddamn motherfucking paper. You will do as I say, sign this paper, YOU GODDAMN…!"

They were wrestling with the paper that now ripped in half. Henrik crushed the pen in her hands, then threw it against the wall in the kitchen.

Rachel felt her own fingers bruising purple. She had begun a new tactic. When Henrik became violent, she would run outside to get away. This way he would stop because he worked hard to show the neighbors what a good guy he was. One by one, she talked to the neighbors. Her escape plan: run to their homes for safety.

Now, Henrik stood in the doorway, laughing and taunting her. "Where do you think you're going, bitch?" he said.

Tears and black mascara ran down her face. She was gently grasping her bruised fingers as she glanced and saw the shadows of neighbors peering out their windows. She didn't know when or how to get out, but she knew a divorce was long overdue. She walked to the backyard and waited for him to calm down. She heard his car door slam then screeching around the corner. Her brow was sweaty, her heart pounded as she felt overwhelmingly alone and in complete despair. She looked up into the sky and wished she could have vaporized into the clouds.

9

A Private War

By the spring of 1973, Rachel was hanging on by a thread. Fallon was five and working on Saturdays at the hardware store, not because she wanted to but because Henrik told her she had to. He believed that you were never too young to start working and Fallon made the best of it. She wheeled lawn mowers in and out of the store in the spring, and snowblowers in winter. She put together nuts and bolts, walked paint cans to the paint mixers, and watched the timer for the customers. When things got slow, she would make the most of her day by playing on the tall stacks of cement bags in the back storage room. Even as a young child, she felt that every minute was accounted for. She was always at her post, her nose to the grindstone. Fallon had to earn her keep; she never learned the art of doing nothing. As she got older, she felt that working long hours and keeping busy would stave off the emptiness she felt inside.

Summer came and the family took off to the farm. Henrik surprised Soraya and Fallon with three new ponies that he bought from a horse breeder near Elroy, Wisconsin. They named them Orange, Nancy, and Pat, and when the family left, Henrik rented barn space for them at Neven's farm a mile up the road.

When they got back from the farm, they flew to Spain. Henrik came with them and they spent a few days on the Costa del Sol in Marbella before he flew back to the States. They had the time of their lives swimming in the hotel's pool and in the ocean. The abuelos flew down to the coast with them and played with them in the sand, where they rented paddle boats and ate fresh calamari on the beach until the sun went down. Life was momentarily perfect, and it was good to see Rachel at peace.

Fallon was practicing her Spanish, eating ice cream every night after dinner as the family took long walks by the marinas of Puerto Banús. Even as a young girl, Fallon loved looking at the beautiful boats and yachts in their slips bobbing up and down in the gentle waves. She loved watching Rachel so happy and how much her abuelos loved her. She had such an amazing relationship with them, especially her father, Alfonso. Fallon also knew that you couldn't take the bad away with trips to Spain.

Their six-week holiday was winding down. Rachel had been talking to her mother, telling her the horror stories she was living back in the States, explaining in detail about Henrik's sexual issues and how he was with other women in public. She worried that if his violent tendencies increased, he might start beating her. He was sick, she said. He had explosive behavior patterns. When she asked him to get help, he threw it back in her face that she was the one with the problem.

Her mother vowed to come and stay with them if things got bad. Rachel confirmed that she was going to look for an attorney and ask Henrik for a divorce. She had no choice.

Before they boarded their flight home, the abuelos hugged them tight and wouldn't stop kissing them. Tears fell from Abuelo Alfonso's eyes. He told Rachel to please call if "that animal puts a finger on you."

Rachel sadly knew she couldn't trouble her aging father with all her marital problems and would have to deal with them on her own. It made the abuelos sick to think that another divorce was looming.

By September, Rachel was leaning on her friends and neighbors for help looking for and interviewing divorce attorneys. Mary Jenkins, a good-hearted resourceful friend and neighbor, lived around the block from them. Fallon befriended Jenny Jenkins, Mary's oldest daughter, and stayed at their house. Fallon split her time there and at Tante Annie's while Rachel organized meetings with lawyers and counsel.

Mary sat down with Rachel, talked to attorney friends, and called others from the phone book. Rachel had made appointments with lawyers in Chicago before she picked one that she liked. She was nervous and sick to her stomach even thinking of confronting Henrik, but she knew that she could no longer take the abuse and cheating.

It was time to absorb and swallow what she was about to do. She feared that retaliation could be worse than what she had already been through, but she would walk through the darkness to get to the other side.

The next few days Rachel was quiet and melancholy, trying to stay out of Henrik's way. She pretended to be preoccupied writing letters to her mother, father, and family in Spain.

One morning, she got up as Henrik was getting ready to leave for the hardware store.

"I don't know how to tell you this," she said quietly, "I've thought about things for a long time, so I'm just going to come right out and say it."

Henrik looked up at her as he set his toothbrush down.

"I want a divorce."

"WHAT!"

"I want a divorce."

"Are you crazy, Rachel… Don't I give you everything you want?"

"I don't care about things. I care about a normal happy life."

"You have this house and trips to Spain anytime you want, your GTO, fur coats, land…more land than you know what to do with!"

"All those things don't mean anything if you don't have a peaceful life," said Rachel. "Look…you cheated on me."

Henrik glared at her. "Don't give me that bullshit!"

"I know about you and Sherry. Stop lying to me! I know there are many whores in your bed!"

"That's ridiculous. I never touched Sherry!"

"I don't want to hear any more of your garbage. You leave here to go mail a letter, then you come back three hours later. You say you're going to the farm, then you come back with a tan like you sat on the equator. Don't even think about getting out of the lie that you went to Mexico and came back with an infection on your hand. I'm not stupid! You gave me a venereal disease when I was pregnant with Fallon. You treat me like garbage. Look at what you did to me when I wouldn't sign your blank piece of paper. Do I need to go on?"

"You're making a huge mistake."

"I don't care. I found an attorney."

"Oh, did you, now? You had better watch it because we'll see to that!"

Henrik stormed downstairs into the basement then out the front door, slamming it as he left. The one thing Rachel could count on was that when Henrik was furious about something, it would get worse before it got better. He would stew on it and she would pay later. He never let anything go. He held grudges for months, years…even a lifetime!

That night Henrik never came home. Rachel knew he must have been plotting his retaliation or having a sleepover with one of his whores. The next morning Henrik came in through the front door. Fallon was eating a bowl of cereal, but when she saw him, she began laughing, giggling, and bouncing in her kitchen chair calling out to him.

"Daddy… Daddy!"

He slapped the cereal spoon out of her mouth. The spoon hit the wall as he knocked the bowl over, spilling the rest of the cereal on the table, floor, and Fallon's pants. For a moment Rachel froze. Fallon sat in the spilled milk and cereal mess as the tears ran down her face, looking up into the face of her father, blaming herself for what she did wrong.

Rachel broke her trance. "What is wrong with you? Do you see? This is why everyone in this house hates you!"

She cleaned up the mess and took Fallon upstairs to change. As we walked upstairs, Henrik said, "Rachel, I want to talk with you in the basement." His voice was frighteningly calm.

Soraya was still upstairs sleeping. Once Fallon had changed into fresh clothes, Rachel told her to stay in her room, and went downstairs.

"You are really sick Henrik," she said. "That's not how you treat a child. You touch her again and I'm calling the police."

"I don't give a damn what you do anymore Rachel. I've got a bunch of papers for you to sign."

"Henrik, you really don't get it. There is a child upstairs who will have psychological damage because of you. Did your parents lock you in a dog's cage when you were young?"

"Keep my Goddamn parents out of this and sign these papers."

"What kind of papers?"

Henrik's voice levitated and shook every molecule of air in the room. "Tax papers…and never mind…you can't read English anyways!"

"I don't read perfect English, but I'm no fool, I can read! What am I signing other than tax papers?"

A bomb went off in Henrik's head. "Just sign the Goddamn papers, sign the Goddamn papers! SIGN THESE GODDAMN PAPERS YOU STUPID BITCH!" The windows were now shaking.

"I'm not signing anything without my lawyer!" She knew what was coming and braced herself.

He grabbed his overnight bag and slammed it into Rachel's head, then kicked her in the shin with his heavy work boots. She went down to the ground, hitting her shoulder on the floor. He kicked her again and again. Blood spattered the tiles hitting the wallpaper. Papers scattered everywhere. Rachel grabbed her leg. It was now bleeding heavily. Still, she picked herself up and ran up the stairs. Henrik screamed in a fury, knocking down three of the basement chairs while Rachel locked herself in the bedroom.

"Don't you run away from me. Just wait til I get home later tonight. If you think that little kick in the leg was bad, just wait!"

Rachel heard his tires screeching down the street and phoned Karin Kaffie and Tante Annie. She begged them to take Soraya and Fallon, then packed a bag for all three of them. In the car, Fallon had a sick feeling in her stomach and a throbbing sensation on her lip where Henrik had knocked the spoon from her mouth. Soraya was crying, not understanding what was going on.

Karin and Tante could not believe it when they saw Rachel's leg and they wondered if she should get some stitches.

"No Karin, I can't go to the hospital. Henrik, as well-off as he is, does not have health insurance. He would come after me again, if he got the bill. Second, if the hospital reported who did this to me, I might have to stay in the hospital for the rest of my life after Henrik was through with me."

Karin and Tante Annie made eye contact with each other. They were trying to process the violence against their beloved Rachel. Rachel didn't know it then, but she would have the scars on her leg over fifty years later. Tante Annie and Karin gave her some aspirin and checked the bump on her head. They asked Rachel what had happened, and she told them she asked Henrik for a divorce a day or so ago and he went crazy when she wouldn't sign some of his papers earlier that day.

Tante got some bandages and taped up Rachel's leg, then made beds. Rachel told the family what Henrik had to say as she was escaping to the bedroom from him. Karin and Tante's entire family were astonished by Henrik's behavior, and they said that they had tried to talk to him about his disturbing conduct on other occasions. Onkel Paul told Rachel that before she walked back in that house that he would have a talk with him.

"If Henrik touches you or the girls again, we will call the police and make lots of trouble for him. This man should be incarcerated for his unbelievable behavior. We will tell his parents. Henrik won't like that at all... but I don't care!"

Rachel cried herself to sleep but felt safe at Tante Annie's family home, even if it was just for one night. Later that night Rudy, Karin's husband, took a bag outside to the garbage and he saw Henrik's car driving around the alley in the back of their house. Henrik did not see Rachel's car because the Kaffie family hid it in their garage. Rudy kept this information from Rachel until morning.

Later the next day Onkel Paul and Tante Annie called Henrik at the hardware store and told him to meet them at the house on Pittsburg. Henrik agreed.

"So, you and Tante Annie had my wife and my girls over at your house last night! What gives you the right to do that!"

The elderly Onkel Paul got in Henrik's face as his own turned red from the tension in the room. Onkel Paul was wearing his usual white short-sleeve, button-down shirt. His dark-rimmed glasses slightly moved up and down on his face as he spoke. His silver hair was always cut short and perfect.

"It gives me every right when you beat Rachel up! Did you look at her leg for God's sake? You have terrorized all three of them."

Henrik smirked. "A little kick in the leg never hurt anyone. Who do you think you are telling me what to do with my wife? That's my wife! You two have been my friends for years and," his voice was rising, "THIS IS HOW YOU TREAT ME? YOU TAKE HER SIDE?"

Henrik was now in a full-blown rage, ransacking the kitchen, knocking papers, cups, and glasses on the floor, and breaking everything in sight.

"Onkel Paul, you need to stay out of my business. I'll do exactly as I please with my family! Goddamn it, get out of my way!"

"Oh, no you don't. That's why we're here. If you don't calm down, we're not leaving. Rachel will *not* come back. Do you understand me? I will call the police. I will call a psychiatrist."

"A psychiatrist…for what, old man! *She's* the one that wants a divorce!"

"For *you*, Henrik…you get crazy out of control. Something is very wrong with you! Henrik, you need help, we have told you this before! Your behavior is not normal! You go from nothing into a rage in seconds!"

Onkel Paul sat in the living room chair next to the kitchen, trying to catch his breath. He was upset and sobbing a bit trying to get the words out. The accusations and the spit flew. "Little Fallon…you knocked a spoon out of her mouth while that poor baby was just calling for her daddy? What kind of an animal are you? She's just a little girl and she's already afraid of you. She's my godchild, I don't have my own children. I've vowed to protect her, even from you. You show no remorse for things you do. You are scaring all of us! *Please!*"

Henrik walked up to Onkel Paul. Tante Annie grabbed his arm trying to pull him back. He knocked her hand away. Tante, with her short wavy gray hair and sturdy build, stood there in a state of shock.

"Shut up…shut up you old stupid man, you have no idea what you are talking about! Fallon *is not* afraid of me!"

Onkel Paul stood. "You don't touch my wife! I just saw you throw her hand! You better watch your step, Henrik. I've known you since you were a boy. What happened to you?"

They argued with him for over an hour before he calmed down. They begged him to get some sort of help. They told him something was deeply wrong inside his brain. Henrik wouldn't listen. But he promised that he would not touch Rachel or the girls. He promised to behave himself. He just wanted the confrontation to be over.

Tante Annie and Onkel Paul should have never taken on arguing with such a dangerous man, especially at their age, but they believed that Henrik would respect them as he would his parents.

They were wrong, but the confrontation shed light on who Henrik really was. This was Henrik's destructive creation, he loved chaos all around him for it was all he knew as a child. Tante Annie and Onkel Paul did not believe Henrik would change his behavior, but nodded their heads in agreement as he falsely reassured them. He could fool, trick, and deceive anyone when his personality switched over to his phony charm.

Rachel and the girls carefully moved back home, grateful that Henrik was no longer around all that much. But when he was, he was always cranky, and explosive, throwing things and pointing out that he was in the right. Rachel was torn up inside. She didn't know what to do or where to turn. She couldn't ask her parents to come every time there was an incident with him.

The abuelos only knew small fragments of what went on in Rachel and Henrik's marriage. Rachel was afraid that if they knew all the details and confronted Henrik, it could mean World War III once they returned to Spain. She would pay a heavy price for involving them and pointing the finger at Henrik. Also, the abuelos were getting older and living off of their investments and the government. She didn't want to impose on her parents for financial support. Plus, she was embarrassed to ask them for money since they knew she had married a wealthy man. At times she had no choice when things got desperate, but she always made up an excuse (Henrik was buying a new building and needed cash, or she wanted to do a few extra things for the girls).

Thanksgiving had arrived, and Rachel had finished her shopping the day before. They would have a normal dinner and the families would come over around three in the afternoon. Rachel had a full day of cooking to attend to. Henrik came and went whenever he wanted. Sometimes he slept at the house, at times he stayed out all night, where she never knew when he was coming home. Rachel knew he was with a different whore every week.

Soraya and Fallon were unaware of all of this since Rachel tried to protect them as much as she could. Excited for the big feast, the girls set up their dolls in the basement while Rachel bustled about in the kitchen mixing the ingredients for the homemade stuffing. She learned to make this from one of the neighborhood ladies.

Suddenly, they heard the door burst open.

"Hello, girls!" shouted Henrik. "Stay downstairs, I'll be there in a minute."

Without saying another word, Henrik grabbed the pound cake on the dining room table and smashed it against the curtains. As the cake imploded, it landed in a thousand tiny crumbs all over the floor with a few big chunks landing on the dining room seats.

He raced over to Rachel as if a time-bomb had detonated inside his head, grabbing her hair and pushing her to the floor. He was now dragging and wiping her face back and forth across the kitchen tiles as if he was punishing a dog that pooped on the ground. Rachel was screaming and grabbing at his boots.

"Fallon…Fallon…help me, get this animal away from me!"

The television was loud downstairs, and the girls couldn't hear much of what was going on. Henrik bellowed above it all, screaming so loud the air molecules vibrated, levitated, and split in half.

"You fucking bitch… I got the letter from your attorney and some of your demands for the divorce! When I'm through with you…you should be begging for your life!"

"Henrik no…no…stop!"

"You'll never get your hands on my stuff…my land!"

Rachel yelled for Fallon again and tried to get away from him. She grabbed his legs to pull herself up. He grabbed the collar of her blouse and one of her arms, and dragged all 110 pounds of her up the flight of stairs. When they reached the bedroom, he let go of her collar and arm. Rachel sat on the floor, gasping for air and trying desperately to catch her breath. Blinded by a fit of rage, his spit flew in Rachel's face.

"If you think for one minute, I will give you *anything* you asked for, you're fucking crazy! I own *everything* you touch; you hear me?"

Rachel dragged herself to the door. She pulled herself up and ran down the stairs to the kitchen.

"Don't you run away from me!" he yelled. "I WILL KILL YOU!"

By now Fallon had crept into the kitchen to find Rachel desperately making a phone call.

"This is 911…what is your emergency?"

"Please, it's my husband. He's beating me up and my two small children are here. I don't know what to do!" Rachel was breathing heavily.

"Ma'am, I'll send an officer right away!"

Fallon saw her father enter the kitchen and walk past her as if in a trance. It was almost as if Henrik didn't see her standing there. He began yelling again. "You ungrateful *bitch*!"

He took the phone receiver and pounded it into the drywall then tore the phone off the wall and smashed it on the floor. Chunks of drywall and wallpaper came loose.

"Now try calling the cops again!"

Fallon was crying and screaming as she looked at her mom's scraped up face. Her collar was torn, and her neck had dark red marks. Soraya was crying in the basement.

Fallon yelled, "Daddy stop! Stop it! STOP HURTING MOMMY!"

He pushed Fallon aside and told her to get out of his way. Rachel grabbed Fallon's hand and ran downstairs; she grabbed Soraya and a blanket off the couch. She wrapped Soraya in the blanket. They left through the basement door and headed to their neighbor Edwardo and his wife.

Rachel rang the doorbell and waited. Edwardo answered the door. Fallon only wore stockings and her feet tingled from the cold cement.

"Rachel…is everything okay?"

"No! It's Henrik again. He has gone crazy; I called the police! Can we wait here?"

"Of course! Come! Oh, these poor little girls are in tears on Thanksgiving. What on earth has that asshole done now? Look at your face Rachel, you have scrape marks all over!"

"I know. My shoulder is killing me. I'm going to have to ice it later."

"Rachel, this is horseshit! I'll help you any way I can! What happened?"

"You know I asked for a divorce a few months back. He's gone crazy after reading the letters from my attorney. I'm not sure anymore, he screams at everything. I'll tell you more later. I'm sick to my stomach right now."

Rachel, Soraya, and Fallon waited in Edwardo's living room. Fallon's heart was pounding fast. The minutes seemed like hours.

"Rachel, the cops are here."

"Will you come outside with me?"

"Of course. Girls, stay here with Aunt Jeanette. Let me get my coat for you."

Rachel noticed some of the other neighbors looking out of their windows seeing the police car in front of her house. She felt a measure of relief. *At least they're witnesses to the hell I'm going through*, she thought. She walked up to the officer and began telling her story, pointing at her house and explaining that her husband was still inside. As the officer went to her door, she found herself wondering how long her turkey had been in the oven.

Within a few minutes the officer returned. He seemed a bit different when he came back outside almost as if he turned this beating into a joke.

"Now…Mrs. Baumann, you don't want to have your husband arrested on Thanksgiving, do you? Do you know what that will do to your children not having their father around the holidays? He will be locked up in jail."

"Yes, I know. My children would be happier without their father. He's an abusive and controlling bastard!"

"Come on Mrs. Baumann, I talked with your husband and he's sorry for everything. I'm sure you can find it in your heart to call off an arrest in front of his neighbors and your kids on Thanksgiving."

Edwardo chimed in. "But officer, look at the cuts and scrapes on her face! He's done this before!"

"Sir…who are you?" the officer stated.

"I'm Rachel's next-door neighbor, Edwardo, and little Soraya is my son's godchild."

"Why don't you stay out of this."

"I most certainly will not!"

The officer, who seemed to be siding with Henrik, put up his hand as if to motion to Edwardo to stop and shut up. Rachel's heart sank and she guessed that Henrik paid the officer to make all this go away. Rachel turned to Edwardo.

"Henrik also tore the phone off the wall…if I have an emergency, can I use your phone?"

"Of course, Rachel."

Rachel turned to the officer and asked if Henrik could at least get out of the house until he calmed down or she would press charges.

Rachel hugged Edwardo and told him that she wanted to cancel Thanksgiving but couldn't call anyone to do so. She woefully turned back toward her house to finish cooking and did not speak to Henrik for the rest of the evening. The charming man who had courted her so gallantly was nothing more than a monster.

Weeks went by and Christmas was approaching. Rachel had meetings with her attorneys as Soraya and Fallon jumped back and forth from

Tante Annie's and the Jenkins's home. Rachel was trying to keep the peace around the holidays because she knew that Henrik could explode at any time. She wanted to have a normal Christmas if possible. She told Douglas Marshall, her attorney, that Henrik broke and yanked the phone off the wall. She couldn't call her family and was worried that if there was an emergency she would have to go to the neighbors. Her attorney began to advise her.

"I can make a polite phone call to Henrik to fix the phone situation," he said. "But if he doesn't listen, we're going to have to try something different."

"What can we do? I have to call my family in Spain. They're worried about me."

"Well let's try the phone call first…then I can file what's called an injunction against him. Henrik won't like it and it will cost him, so he better listen to the phone call."

"What's an eenjunction?" Rachel messed up the word with her accent.

"Basically, you file an injunction to have someone stop doing something or to make them do something."

"Can we do this to stop Henrik from hitting me? Can we get him to move out of our house? Or at least get him out of my bedroom? I've kicked him out many times; all the arguing and fighting is affecting my girls. I've asked him to leave, and he refuses. I've called the police, and he paid the cops off. My girls are witnessing nothing but traumatic events. This is going to be devastating for their future."

"We'll try a restraining order, and I can talk to the judge and see if we can get an order to kick Henrik out of the house. If he flies off the handle like you say he does, he's gonna take all this out on you. This is gonna cost him and with the courts, this stuff takes time and money. From what you say, that looks to be Henrik's favorite thing, *money*!"

"Oh, yes! It's his creation, his life! So what's the alternative? He kills me first? Then what would happen to my girls?"

"I understand. Let's try and take the simple route first then take action with court orders."

A few days went by, and Henrik fixed the phone on the kitchen wall blaming Rachel for the incident. "Your Goddamn phone is fixed. Just so you know, this is how crazy upset you get me, and this is what happens!"

"You're trying to blame me for the phone?"

"You're damn right I am! I should have your fat-ass mom come and fix this. You call her enough!"

"Everyone is fat, stupid, or the wrong color with you. Everyone around you are idiots with the exception of you!"

"Shut the hell up, Rachel!"

"Stop yelling. You will never make anyone happy!"

"Your damn attorney called me the other day. I got his name and law firm. We'll just see about that, now, won't we?"

Christmas Eve was in full swing and despite the looming divorce, Henrik's family was over for all the festivities. Henrik expected perfection. If one crumb was out of place, Rachel would be hearing about it.

On Christmas morning, Soraya and Fallon woke up early to see what Santa brought them. It was just the four of them, Rachel, Henrik, Soraya, and Fallon. The rest of the family wouldn't be over until dinner. Excited, Fallon pranced around the Christmas tree picking up presents, giggling and giddy.

"Just settle down, Fallon! You will open presents when I'm good and ready and the adults have had their breakfast," Henrik snapped.

Immediately, Fallon settled down. She knew that if she talked back, she could expect a spanking…and a bad one.

The cloudy Christmas morning rolled on, and the tree was packed with presents. Henrik seemed agitated with the high level of energy in the house. Rachel was pretending to be happy for the girls. Soraya always fed off Fallon's energy, and if Fallon was a bit rowdy, she would try to follow. Fallon began running, skipping, and parading around the living room and it started making Henrik nervous. He couldn't handle an unwanted scene of exuberance. Rachel had put on a Bing Crosby Christmas album, and Fallon scurried around with joy and excitement.

"Fallon...stop it...stop it! Sit down, stop running around!" Henrik hollered from across the room. He was up in a flash, grabbing Fallon's arm and dropping her to the floor.

Rachel got up to see if Fallon was okay. "Just calm down, Henrik," she whispered. "It's Christmas and the girls are excited. Please let them enjoy it."

"Oh yeah. Don't tell me to calm down! When the girls are out of line, they're out of line and I'm gonna say so!"

"I understand, but it's Christmas and they're overexcited. Just let them be kids."

They started opening gifts one after another. There were so many, it was almost a sea of Christmas presents and wrapping paper everywhere. The noise in the room got higher and unbeknownst to Soraya and Fallon, so did the level of tension. Even as a child, Fallon would sing loud, laugh, and make up songs and phrases in her head. She was simply happy and joyful just like her mom in her childhood. Fallon didn't want to be the center of attention, but this unintentionally put her there, taking the spotlight off Henrik Baumann.

"Knock it off, Fallon," he shouted. "Settle down!"

"But Daddy, watch me! It's so fun to cover Soraya in the wrapping paper."

"Oh, I'm getting tired of opening so many presents." Rachel softly spoke.

Fallon began singing Christmas songs.

"Tell Santa, I wanted the dolly with the yellow dress," little Soraya cooed.

This simmered Henrik's cerebral capacity, now brewing a storm in his brain. His sensory malfunction went into overload. Just like that, the tinderbox was lit, the detonator went off and the nuclear bomb launched itself into the stratosphere. There was no argument or fight, Henrik just blew up out of nowhere for no reason other than everything seemed to aggravate him. He abruptly grabbed as many unopened presents as he could carry.

"You Goddamn ungrateful bitches. Nothing is ever good enough for you! Now you're gonna see what happens! I'm gonna show you what happens to the Goddamn ungrateful!"

Soraya screamed louder than they ever heard her scream. She ran behind Rachel who stood up to see Henrik running out the basement door and into the backyard.

"What are you doing?" Rachel's mouth dropped open with bewilderment. She looked around the room, confused. They had just been opening presents on Christmas morning and now this madman was taking a stack of them outside. Her brain could not wrap around the situation as she held Soraya.

Fallon stood up, not knowing what to do. Her father was dropping the Christmas presents in the snow, grabbing the outdoor fire pit stoker. They heard his violent rant through the glass but had a hard time making out the words as he bashed the presents into extinction. Fallon began to cry, "Mommy, why? Why? Our presents. Why?"

They saw the boxes shred into chunks and pieces and the wrapping paper scattered about the yard as if a wild dog was attacking their gifts in the snow. Seconds seemed like hours. Rachel grabbed Fallon's hand and held Soraya. They went upstairs and hid in her bedroom.

She needed some time to think. She didn't want to bother the neighbors and was embarrassed to call the police again on Christmas after what happened on Thanksgiving.

She looked out of the bedroom window, hoping the neighbors had witnessed some of the happenings, but no one was there besides them. This was the way Henrik did things. He tormented his victims in private. This was to keep them isolated and under his control. Sometimes things spilled over, and other family members would witness his domination but for the most part no one saw anything but a charming charismatic face. Rachel, the girls' warrior and protector, vowed to do her best to let the world know what Henrik was perpetrating behind closed doors.

As they hid behind Rachel's locked bedroom door, she put frightened Soraya on the king-size bed and began to pray. She prayed as the tears streamed down her face. She prayed as Fallon looked into her sad and tired eyes and took hold of her hand. She cried as she cradled Soraya in her arms until Soraya closed her eyes and fell asleep.

All of a sudden, they heard a loud series of bangs that sounded like garbage cans tumbling down the street. They heard a car screech out of their driveway. Terrified, Fallon ran to the windows in the front room. She looked outside in disbelief with a tear that ran down her face. Henrik had kicked their plastic Santa and reindeer staged on the front lawn. Santa and sleigh were mutilated, chunks of red plastic were strewn about laying in the snow. The smashed-up reindeer covered the sidewalk, some missing their antlers.

Fallon turned from the window to report her sad findings to her mom, when she heard the kitchen radio playing quietly. She wouldn't realize it for years, but the song was "River," and the voice was Joni Mitchell. The lyrics rang out, "I wish I had a river I could skate away on; I wish I had a river so long; I would teach my feet to fly." Fallon walked upstairs slowly, listening to the haunting music. She wanted so badly to take her mother and sister and fly, fly away…but didn't know how. As she reached the bedroom Rachel asked her to look out in the backyard again, and Fallon told her that all the packages were destroyed and thrown everywhere. Fallon also told her that the front yard almost looked worse.

What Henrik didn't realize was that he not only destroyed this Christmas, but memories of Christmases to come. Nothing would take away the horror they experienced on that day, forever cemented in their minds. They fell back to sleep in the king-size bed that morning, their eyes puffy and swollen with tears. They were safe together. They were a team of protection for each other. Still, Rachel knew she needed to make another desperate call to her attorney after the holidays.

10

An Heir in Despair

Somehow, they made it through the holidays. January 1974 rolled in, and Rachel was hoping for some good news from Doug Marshall and his team, any news. Things moved slowly, if at all. Phone calls did not get returned and questions went unanswered. Rachel called Doug and left a message. She wanted Henrik out of the house. Her girls had suffered another violent holiday at the hands of a sadistic, inhuman, greedy, sick man.

The phone call to Doug never got returned. But supposedly Henrik had talked to his attorney. The judge in their case made the ruling that Henrik was to get out of Rachel's bedroom and move into the basement bedroom. Henrik was a powerful businessman and threw his weight around to get his way. Appalled at the judgment Rachel called Doug again and got his secretary.

"I'm calling again looking for Doug, my attorney...Douglas Marshall. Is he in?"

"No ma'am...I can leave him a message. Mr. Marshall is in court."

"Look...I've been leaving messages. Many of them. My husband is violent, and I heard the judge made a ruling that my husband is to move downstairs in the basement? My husband is dangerous and crazy, I'm worried for not only my safety but the safety of my two girls. He needs to move out of my house."

"I'm sorry ma'am...I'll leave Mr. Marshall a message."

Rachel felt discouraged and frustrated. Henrik was controlling, manipulating, and pulling the puppet strings of her life. She was in control of nothing.

The Moody Blues was playing on the small kitchen radio. The lyrics rang out, "Listen to the tide slowly turning, wash all our heartaches away. We're part of the fire that is burning and from the ashes we can build another day." Rachel let the lyrics sink in and called the abuelos.

"Mama, please come and stay with me," she said. "I feel safe when you're with me."

"Querida, I'm so sorry," said Abuela Esther. "Your papa's having surgery and we'll have to wait until it's safe for him to travel."

February brought one snowstorm after another, and Henrik left for Mexico. The house became peaceful bathed in the soft glow of falling snow. On Saturday mornings, Rachel rolled dough and fried it, dusting the doughnuts with powdered sugar that looked just like snowflakes. They tasted like heaven.

When Henrik returned, Rachel and the girls had to watch everything they did or said, for he was constantly correcting them and cracking his whip to keep them in line. He tried to control their every thought and movement.

They were grateful that he was gone most of the time, and exhausted when he was home. They were a different species, and Henrik was an alien. The girls weren't perfect, but they were peaceful and kind, and couldn't understand why he constantly conspired against their mother.

One morning in March, a few days after Soraya's fourth birthday, Rachel was drawing a bath for herself when Henrik came upstairs in a rage with a stack of papers.

"Where are you, you miserable thing?"

Rachel turned around and gave Henrik a blank stare.

"If you think for one minute, I'm gonna let you and your attorney chisel away at my wealth, you've got another thing coming."

Rachel had a puzzled look on her face. "I haven't talked to my attorney in weeks, maybe longer."

"Your attorney is trying to divide up my estate and give you half!"

"Well, we *are* married. Doesn't that make it our estate? I don't want anything. I just need money to live and take care of the girls and the house. We just want peace. The girls deserve peace!"

Henrik pushed his way further into the bathroom. "I don't care what you or the girls want."

"They're your daughters, Henrik!"

"The house, the land, the buildings are fucking mine you bitch. You need to sign these papers, or I'll kill you. You just wait to see what happens to that Goddamn attorney of yours."

"I'm not signing anything."

Henrik kicked the bedroom door shut; the papers went flying over the bathroom floor. He grabbed the hair on the back of Rachel's head and shook her. Rachel tried to scream and get away, but Henrik dragged her to the bathtub. He tightened his grip on her hair and neck and slammed her head underwater. The water churned under the wake and Rachel choked on gulps. Something caused Henrik to come to his senses and let her go.

Fallon heard the commotion going on down the hallway and walked slowly toward it, not knowing or understanding what she was about to see. Rachel sat on the floor of the bathroom gasping for air as she tried to scream at this thing that was the girls' father. Her voice was hoarse from choking. Her wet hair dripped down her face.

Dealing with Henrik was like waiting for a nuclear bomb to go off in front of you. All you could do is watch it happen. Rachel sat for a moment trying to get her bearings. Henrik breathed heavily above her. She was having an out of body experience. She knew if she cowered under his gaze, Henrik could make another attempt. She made a decision. Very slowly and deliberately, she stood up and walked away. "You, sick bastard," she said as calmly as she could and pointed toward the front door. "Get out of this house and away from my children. Now." Her voice rattled.

Henrik stormed past Fallon in the hallway.

Fallon walked over to her mother and wished that she were fifteen or so years older to protect her. She wished she could have sentenced her father to an extra hundred years in hell for what he had done. The seeds were already planted and had sprouted. Thoughts of pummeling him to the ground started to engulf her mind.

Fallon wished so much that she could stop him, but she was a scared, frightened little girl whose brain felt as if it were flying away into the clouds, taking her with it. Why couldn't she speak up? Why wasn't she brave enough to choke her father in his sleep, or poison his food, or set him on fire for all the brutality she heard and witnessed? Why? Because she loved and forgave, and forgave and loved. He was the only father she knew.

Rachel cleaned herself up, put on dry clothes, and walked downstairs lost, confused, and in a daze. She called the police again and her heart sank when she saw the same police officer arrive at our front door. She told him what had happened and this time she wanted a restraining order. The officer chuckled a bit and told her that he thought she was making this all up.

"How could you have drowned in the bathtub when you're standing next to me?"

"No, officer," she said. "This beast tried to drown me in the bathtub. How do you not understand this? This isn't funny. Did he pay you again?"

The officer walked away saying, "I will see what I can do," but did nothing. The incident was never discussed until, years later, it would get dismissed in court. Injustice was growing around Rachel and her daughters like a prison.

Rachel sat on the steps that led to the basement. Fallon sat with her, and she showed Fallon her arm. It was red and looked sore as if the blood vessels under the skin were broken. Fallon also noticed what looked like red fingerprints and scratches on her neck, not understanding at the time that those markings were also caused by her father. Rachel's tears rolled down her face.

"Mommy don't cry. You will make me cry."

They sat together, Fallon put her head on Rachel's shoulder, and Rachel began to pray.

"I'll pray too."

Rachel was quiet and Fallon felt her nod her head yes in recognition.

"What's going to happen to us, Mommy?"

Rachel's eyes looked empty and out of answers.

A day went by and Rachel called her mother to tell her what Henrik had done. Her mother paused and wept. "Please move back to Spain," she begged.

"The judge won't allow it and Henrik has threatened many times to kill me if I talk about bringing the girls back to Spain with me," Rachel said quietly. When she got off the phone, she called her attorney and made another attempt at leaving a message.

She thought it was so strange that he was blowing her off, but she also knew that some negotiations were still going on between the judge, Mr. Marshall, and Henrik's attorney. Next, she called Mary Jenkins to see if she would help her brainstorm and find a new attorney. She told Mary that Douglas Marshall was doing nothing for her and that she needed a new game plan as Henrik became more violent.

March became April and Henrik moved a bed into the basement refusing to leave the house. He told the judge that he wanted to be around Soraya and Fallon. But, in truth, Henrik was trying to save enough money to build a new house and pay cash for it without selling any of his rental properties. Meanwhile, Mary Jenkins had referred three new attorneys to Rachel, and she was in the process of interviewing them.

One Saturday night, Soraya and Fallon were supposed to be asleep upstairs, but Fallon could hear Rachel and Henrik arguing downstairs. Henrik had installed a gun rack on the basement rec room wall. Rachel was now worried that Soraya and Fallon would get hurt or worse. She was also terrified of bringing up anything about the removal of the guns, Henrik would go crazy if she did.

Rachel was so nervous about the guns that she wasn't sleeping much, and when she slept, the nightmares came. She would see her girls taking guns from the shelf, pointing them at each other, pulling the triggers. Night after night, she dreamt that Henrik was pointing a gun at her. She was desperate to move on with her life. But how would she survive on no sleep, no court case, no money? Where could she turn when she didn't know what would happen next?

"Please Henrik, you can do anything you want, go anywhere. Have your freedom. I need to move on with my life. You could get an apartment and you could see the girls on your scheduled days."

"How dare you? By the time I'm finished with you, you and the girls will be in a dumpy apartment, not me. This is *my* house! I built it."

"How would you like it if I told the IRS that you cheat and lie about what you make at the hardware store and on your tax returns."

The minute the words rolled out of her mouth, Rachel knew she had made a mistake. She had gone too far.

"You fucking call them and I will kill you! You understand me? I will kill you and no one will ever find your body!" He flipped over the coffee table in the center of the room. "You are not going to run the show! I CALL ALL THE SHOTS HERE!"

The maniac jumped behind the bar and opened the cabinet. His face had become deep red as if it could explode. Instead, vodka, bourbon, and cognac flew across the room, thudding against walls, shattering on the floor. Heavy cut glasses for old-fashioneds and Manhattans, a cocktail shaker, a bottle of Galliano liqueur, one by one he whipped them at Rachel, glass shattering against the stone fireplace.

As she dodged the flailing bottles and glasses, the truth flashed through her mind. He was right. He could easily dump her body in the forests of his farmland, and no one would be able to find her. In desperation she thought, *But he wouldn't hurt our children, would he?*

Liquor had saturated the carpet. The stink of whisky and vodka filled the air. Rachel braced herself and ran out of the strike zone. The only way out was through the basement door. She ran through the yard and around to the front of the house, knowing that Fallon's bedroom window was right above the front door, which was locked. She pounded on the heavy wood, rang the doorbell, and screamed, "Fallon! Fallon! Please answer the door! Fallon!"

Our new next-door neighbors came out. Lorraine scurried up behind Rachel. "What's going on?" she asked.

"It's Henrik! He's gone crazy again!"

"I'm calling the police. This is ridiculous!"

"You can try to call the police, but it does no good!"

"I'm calling the police now!"

Awakened from a deep sleep from all the chaos, Fallon rubbed her eyes and got out of bed. She felt like she was in a bad dream, walking out of her room, down the hall, and down the stairs. Henrik ran upstairs away from the stench and broken bottles around the fireplace. Fallon sat on the bottom step that led into the living room and pleaded with her father to open the door for her mother.

He pounded his fist on the drywall next to the door. "Be quiet! Be quiet out there. If you want to come back into the house, you'll have to come through the door you left."

Fallon was dazed and not completely awake, and Rachel was still screaming outside for her. She was trying to wake up. She was in tears now and feeling the terror begin to build.

"Daddy, please let Mommy in the house. Why are you leaving her outside? Why, Daddy, why?"

He stared at Fallon. His face held no remorse. Not an ounce of empathy. "Be quiet. Go back to bed, Fallon. This doesn't concern you. Nothing is wrong with your mother!"

Fallon looked at the floor. Her father's tone was mounting and soared in her direction. "LOOK AT ME FALLON WHEN I'M TALKING TO YOU!"

Fallon looked up, crying uncontrollably, but she did not leave her mother's side. She wet her pants a bit. She had to change her underwear and PJ bottoms, but she knew in her gut that she needed to stay put on that step and hold her ground. A moment or so passed until Henrik left her there crying on the steps as Rachel looked at her through the front door window, her eyes widening in fear. In the kitchen, he started breaking and knocking things around. Tears welled up again as Fallon softly mumbled under her breath, "Don't break my radio, Daddy."

Moments later, Fallon heard him head down the stairs to the basement. She quickly looked back at her mother. Rachel had a terrified look on her face and a haze of exhaustion. Fallon got up slowly and walked to the door. She kept her eyes on Rachel as she told her which way to turn the knob to unlock the door. Fallon let her in and fell into her arms.

By now they heard Soraya crying in bed upstairs. "My tummy hurts, my tummy hurts, Mommy!" she called.

"Wait here," said Rachel, as she ran up the stairs to get Soraya. She was back in a moment when the doorbell rang. Through the window, they saw a policeman.

"We were told of a disturbance at this address?" he said, his voice ending in almost a question.

"Why don't you go see the wild animal who lives in the basement," said Rachel.

Down the stairs the officer went. Rachel could hear them talking. "Listen, it won't happen again," she heard Henrik say. "Where can I send a donation? I'll write a check right now." He was working his manipulation magic again, and after the officer left, Rachel was sure there would be no consequences.

Fallon walked past the stairs that led to the basement and saw her disgraceful father cleaning up the smashed liquor bottles with a broom and dustpan. She didn't understand the smell back then, but she caught the scent of booze in the air, a scent she immediately hated. She could sense trouble and tension around her. Moments later, Rachel came for her. She had picked up her pillows and blanket and now locked the girls and herself in her room for the night. She put Soraya in bed and then she gathered Fallon, sobbing and shaking, into her arms.

"Fallon…I'm so sorry for all this." Her voice cracked as she wiped her tears.

"I know, Mommy. I don't like to see you sad. It makes me sad." Fallon was still shaking uncontrollably.

"I know, my baby."

Rachel's head spun with anxiety. Soon she would make an appointment to see her doctor about sleeping pills and would find a professional counselor to talk to about the unmanageable, overbearing, and mounting stress in her life. She also contemplated suicide a few times, but the thought evaporated with the larger fear of leaving the girls alone with a man whom she knew was capable of murder.

The next morning was Sunday, and on Sundays Rachel, Soraya, and Fallon went to Mass. The familiar ritual of a service Rachel had attended since her birth added a sense of normalcy to her life and the children's. Even though Rachel reached out to a few of the priests, as she told them some of the stories about Henrik, they seemed to take Henrik's side and offered her no help. She couldn't believe it. But she had attended Mass since her childhood. She had always loved the Virgin Mary, mother of Jesus, and protector of all mothers. And so she went to Mass, ignoring the priest and focusing on the statue of Mary gazing at her from an alcove, her eyes full of love.

Later she found checks Henrik had written to the church, large sums of money. She didn't know where to turn. But she believed that her faith was bigger than any church she could belong to. She went every Sunday and saw a bigger picture for her life.

Henrik was not Roman Catholic and did not attend Mass, but one morning, he showed up in the parking lot.

"How dare you go to church without me? We are a family. Don't you dare humiliate me." Henrik was in complete denial of the looming divorce.

Rachel grabbed the girls' hands as they walked away from Henrik toward their car.

"GET BACK HERE!"

"Humiliate you? We're going through a divorce! Leave the girls and me alone."

He lowered his voice. "Get back here. I'm talking to you. Don't walk away from me!"

Rachel knew he was surrounded by many witnesses, and that she was respected.

Quietly, so that only he could hear, she said, "Go find one of your whores and leave us alone! And stop talking to me like I'm three years old. The only child here is you!"

Tired of his bullshit, she was now tentatively fighting back. She knew it made matters worse, but she felt good whenever she could do it. Fallon looked at her father's face as they left and knew that he was planning revenge.

On Monday, Rachel contacted Michael Ward, an attorney recommended by Mary Jenkins's brother.

"You won't recognize your husband after we are through with him, Mrs. Baumann," he said. "Don't you worry."

"Michael, what if I left my house? You know, I could move in with friends or my family back in Spain. I would be safe. My girls and I would be safe from the violence!"

"Rachel, whatever you do, don't leave your house! Stand your ground. If you leave you could lose everything, the house and all. Stay put!"

Optimistic, Rachel shook her head in agreement and told Ward to bill Henrik who would be paying for the divorce. Ward asked for Henrik's social security number and told Rachel he would conduct a full discovery of properties and businesses. This made Rachel a bit nervous, but Ward said that it was standard procedure.

A few days passed and Henrik refused to leave the house. In between his explosive brutal tirades and menacing silence, Fallon moved in a mind-numbing fog. She was six years old and had seen and heard things that her little brain couldn't comprehend. She knew her mother was always there for her, but her father was a monster. And Fallon was too young to realize that she needed not only her mother's help, she needed professional counseling, too, but no one saw her. No one saw her suffering, lost and invisible. She witnessed more shocking distress than most adults could bear. But how could her mother understand what Fallon desperately needed when she was fighting for her life?

Later that week Fallon went out to play in the beautiful spring air in her backyard. She walked over to the sandbox where she planned to build her own small city with roads and sandcastles.

Henrik had bought Soraya and Fallon a bunny rabbit. Fallon named him Cocoa.

"Come here, baby," Fallon said, hugging Cocoa's soft body as she took him out of his cage. She watched him roam around the sandbox as she built the city. He was so tiny. She started to fill up her buckets with sand to build a row of castles and then used a soda can to roll out the mini roads.

But Cocoa had hopped away a few inches. Fallon got up and brought him back to his spot. She continued working and saw him hop even further away. She picked up her pink shovel and placed it in front of him to stop him from leaving the sandbox. The movement seemed to scare him a bit and he quickly darted away from the shovel.

Fallon didn't know what came over her, but time seemed to stand still. All she wanted was for Cocoa to stay in place. It felt as if someone grabbed the pink plastic shovel and took it out of her hands. She began to beat the helpless Cocoa into surrender. He quickly darted, and before he could leave, Fallon cornered him and pummeled him into the sand. Not understanding what she was doing, she kept beating him. "I TOLD YOU TO STAY, COCOA," Fallon shouted. She couldn't stop. She wished Cocoa was her father. "STAY!"

Fallon wanted to protect her mother. She wanted to stop, but she couldn't. It was as if she had become her father, who beat her mother senseless. But she always got up. Always! But Cocoa. Cocoa wasn't moving. Could Fallon have been wrong about herself? Was she really a monster like him?

Fallon was her mother's protector. Like the angels in church, she sailed on the wind, a joyful seed. Now Fallon stood ashamed. She understood that she betrayed her own spirit, that her father's brutality had brought her into darkness.

Cocoa, so tiny, so beautiful, looked up at Fallon with lifeless eyes. "Look at what you've done to me," they seemed to say.

Lost and alone in tears, Fallon tried to hide her despicable act. She picked up Cocoa and threw him in the garbage. Remorse filled her veins and nightmares filled her subconscious. She made herself a promise that she would never hurt another animal as long as she lived. She would take responsibility for her own actions and be a voice of peace, not malice. Fallon did not understand the catastrophic consequences of her father's actions and was too young to comprehend the meaning of displaced anger. Yet, that day was a turning point. Even though she was still so young, she knew, going forward, she would only direct her anger at the hands of the man who caused the insurmountable turmoil in their lives.

Fallon closed her eyes and imagined Cocoa running through the yard into the summer grass and freedom. She would follow the light, too. Because her mother had shown her that there was light. Rachel's love for her daughters would make Fallon stronger. She and that light would show Fallon the way.

Summer came and the agonizing days moved forward. Rachel decided that the attorneys should send the divorce papers to Henrik while he was at the hardware store. She figured if he read them there, it would give him some time to cool off before he got home. On the morning they arrived, it took only minutes for Henrik to scan them before he was out the door in a flash.

Fallon was at the kitchen table when Henrik's car came screeching into the driveway. She heard him pounding on the door, which Rachel kept locked at all times, and ringing the bell like his life depended on it.

Fallon went into the living room. Time stood still. Her mind could not keep up with what was happening. Henrik pounded on the door with the force of a freight train hitting a building at top speed. She heard the wooden door frame make a twisting and bending sound, saw the inside of the door frame crack, and watched the frame shatter.

She went to her knees, then buried her head in the carpet. Henrik barreled through the front door with his own brute force. Twisted and warped like a pretzel, the door fell to the ground with a jolt, breaking the tiles on the floor below. The foundation shook. The sound of the crashing door reverberated through the hall. Fallon's mind shut down and she felt as if she was suspended, hovering just outside her body. It seemed to mute her senses. Fallon said to herself, "Our front door just came down as if my lunatic father had a stick of dynamite in his hands."

Rachel came downstairs thinking the front foyer had collapsed. "What on earth was that?"

Henrik exploded. "Get upstairs, you Goddamn *puta*! I got your papers from your new attorney. You are so stupid. You will never get anywhere with him!"

"You better fix this door, you crazy animal!" Rachel sobbed as she hurried upstairs to get Soraya. "I can't believe this nightmare you've put us in!"

"Don't tell me what to do! You have no idea what you are in for!"

"Think of your daughters. What kind of insanity are you showing them?"

"Your attorney is doing another discovery of my properties! You told him that you will go to the IRS."

"They're our properties! Our marital properties!"

"You just wait to see what I do with that. I TOLD YOU RACHEL, I WILL SEE YOU DEAD FIRST!"

Henrik lunged forward and grabbed Soraya from Rachel's arms. Soraya started to scream.

Rachel reached for Soraya. "What are you doing with her?"

"She's my daughter, too. I'm taking her to the store," he said, and stormed out the broken front door.

"Mommy, Mommy!" Soraya cried.

"Stop!" Rachel screamed and ran after him. Henrik did irrational things that didn't make sense. Rachel never knew if one of his manic acts could result in injury or death for the three of them.

He opened the driver's side of the car, threw Soraya in the front seat, got in next to her, and started the car.

"Stop! Please!" shouted Rachel.

Tires shrieked as he backed his car down the driveway. Then, he stopped, gunned the motor and flew forward, ramming into Rachel's car.

Soraya hit the dashboard. He pulled out of the driveway and took off.

Their neighbor Frank passed by with his dog. "Rachel, I saw the entire thing! Do you want me to call the police?"

Rachel ran down the driveway. "Oh my God, Henrik took Soraya," she sobbed.

"I'm pretty sure Soraya will be okay. I don't think he'll hurt her." He was staring at Rachel's car, then he turned toward the front door. "Rachel, what on earth happened to your front door?"

"This *animal*, who else would do this? I don't care about the front door or my car…my daughter!"

"Listen, I can call the police chief if you want me to. Excuse my language, but what kind of an asshole does this?"

"If he doesn't bring Soraya back soon, I'll call them. He's always taking the girls somewhere, but not in a rage. I don't know how much longer I can take this. I'm trying to get my parents here to stay for a few months and hopefully he won't touch me."

"Call me in thirty-five minutes or so, or if there's any more trouble. I'm here for you Rachel. I'm gonna call some of my connections and see what I can do. I worry if I tell this asshole off, he could become violent with you, when I'm gone."

Rachel stood in the driveway trembling. Fallon hid behind the front window curtains.

They saw Henrik's car turn the corner.

He screeched to a halt and Rachel flung open the door, gathering Soraya in her arms.

Once Soraya was back, Rachel decided not to press charges. Instead, she bandaged up Soraya's forehead and documented what had gone on, saving her painful notes for the courts.

In the following days, Henrik brought her car to the garage to have it fixed. He also boarded up and ordered a new front door.

Everyone held their breath until the end of summer, when the abuelos came for a three-month visit and peace returned to their home.

11

No Handle...
On this Scandal

The year 1975 seemed to appear out of nowhere. Queen's "Bohemian Rhapsody" hit the airwaves and took it by storm. Henrik joined a scuba club that held local meetings and dive trips that took him around the world. Rachel stayed at home with the girls, worrying and waiting for a resolution to her unbearable marriage. After her parents left, Rachel held on, missing them and dreaming of returning to Spain.

When Henrik was around, Rachel was distracted by more fights and arguments with him, and time flew by. Other times, between court dates and meetings with her attorneys, time seemed to stand still. After a year and a half and two different attorneys, a court date was set. Rachel got a call from her new attorney.

"Rachel... How are things, this is Michael Ward."

"Hi Michael... I'm sure you know how things are. You've heard my story and I've given you lots of information on this."

"Don't you worry about a thing; you sound like you have lots of letters and testimony against Henrik. Everything will be fine."

"I hope so... I can't go on much more like this."

"Well...I wanted to call you and let you know that our court date will be more of a mediation with both attorneys present. We will do a discovery of all the properties that you both own and try, in a civil manner, to divide everything up. That is also called filing an interrogatory, but discovery seems to be an easier word."

"Michael... What's a mediation again?"

"That's when both attorneys, plaintiffs, and defendants get together and discuss terms. We will be going over all the properties in the estate this time around."

"Well, we did the discovery thing the last time."

"That was with a different attorney."

"I understand."

"I'll see you next week."

Rachel got off the phone. It seemed that things were moving nowhere. The next week arrived, and she had a sick feeling in her stomach. She drove downtown a few minutes early to calm her nerves before the mediation and waited for Mr. Ward. They walked into a conference room with eight leather chairs, an oval table, a tall dragon tree plant in the corner, and a wall of bookshelves.

Both attorneys were present, but Henrik never made an appearance. The three waited for fifteen minutes or so and proceeded.

Ward began to speak. "This is a discovery...Baumann versus Baumann. As we can see, it appears that Mr. Baumann has failed to appear for this meeting. Mr. Sherman, are you aware of Mr. Baumann's whereabouts?"

"Yes...Mr. Ward...Mrs. Baumann. It seems that Mr. Baumann called me saying that something was wrong with his mother, and he had to go to the hospital."

"And you believed him? He's lying...my husband is lying. He lies about everything. What do they call that? He's a compulsive liar."

"Mr. Ward, it seems you already have to take control of your client." Sherman snickered loudly.

"Mr. Sherman, everything is fine. Let's move on to the discovery." Ward motioned to Rachel to calm down and keep things moving forward. He slid a small stack of papers across the table to Mr. Sherman who read over the papers quickly and discussed them between the three attorneys.

"Mr. Ward...Mrs. Baumann, I will now read the list of properties that are owned by Mr. and Mrs. Baumann and any tax discoveries that we may need. Let's make sure we're not missing anything."

Sherman cleared his throat. "The list includes 20-flat and 10-flat apartment buildings, hardware store, farmland, homes, other properties, six to seven different bank accounts, stocks, life insurance, and other assets that were in joint tenancy in the Baumann trust."

"Mrs. Baumann," Ward said. "Does that seem to be the entire list of properties?"

"Yes, that's the list, or at least the properties I know of. What about my alimony and child support?"

"We'll file a motion for support and another restraining order to get him out of that house," said Ward.

"Okay Michael."

"Mr. Sherman...that is the list for now, we will do our due diligence in finding out property values and a settlement amount the closer we get to some court dates." Ward stated firmly.

"What about custody for my children?" Rachel whispered to Ward. "I also want to get rid of the guns that Henrik keeps in the house."

"Rachel...we will get to that after all of the property is divided."

"But...Mr. Ward...my husband threw it in my face that I would get nothing!"

"Let me take care of the details," Ward said, quietly. And turning to Sherman, he said, "Thank you for your time. We'll be in touch."

"Good day to both of you." Sherman got out of his chair.

Rachel was cautiously optimistic about the meeting, but she knew that Henrik always had something evil up his sleeve. Her head spun with the details she had to keep straight and remember. Her saving grace was that she was methodical in keeping notes and tabs of Henrik's whereabouts.

Spring arrived and Rachel had a wedding to attend. She asked her girlfriend Alice to go with her since they were both friends of the mother of the bride. Rachel never went anywhere, she always stayed home with Soraya and Fallon, but knew that she didn't want to miss the wedding of a good friend.

How Henrik found out, she didn't know, but as she was getting the babysitter she had hired settled, she saw his car drive up and park in front of the house. Her stomach dropped; panic overtook her. In he walked, full of power and confidence. He glared at Rachel and turned to the babysitter. "How much do I owe you?" he asked.

Rachel knew better than to complain. If she said a word, he would remind her of who was boss. "You don't trust me," he would shout, and beat her until she was too bruised to go anywhere.

"You didn't need to do that," she said quietly, gathering her purse.

Fallon sat with Soraya on the step, willing her mother not to go, but she knew the pattern.

"Girls," Rachel said, kissing their heads. "I won't be late."

And with that, she walked past Henrik and out the door, her head held high and her dress swishing elegantly against her legs.

They watched her GTO slide out of the driveway and what seemed like moments later, the doorbell rang. A woman they had never met stood on the porch, smiling.

"Girls...I want you to meet Millie from the scuba club." Henrik spoke in an uncharacteristically joyful tone.

"Hi girls...I have a daughter in between your ages."

"Hi," Fallon said cautiously, not knowing why this woman was in their house when her mom was gone.

Henrik began to make dinner for the four of them, which was a shock because Fallon had never seen him cook anything before. They sat at the table in the kitchen and the strange lady asked questions about the farm and school. It was awkward and Fallon gave yes or no answers.

After dinner, Soraya and Fallon were sent to bed and Millie and Henrik went downstairs. Rachel came home at about 10:00 p.m. When she turned the handle to the front door, she found that it was locked and began knocking. It took a few minutes, but Henrik opened it. Immediately, she knew something was wrong; the delay and a look in his eyes tipped her off. She ran to the window. "Did you have a woman here while I was at the wedding?" she asked, turning toward him.

Rachel quickly ran down the stairs to the basement.

"No…are you crazy?" Henrik replied.

"Really? I smell candles and incense! Everything is dimly lit. You don't use candles…ever! Can you explain that?"

"We had candles in the basement, and I thought I would light some."

"Nice try Henrik, but I saw your latest conquest running down the street and getting into a red car. Was that your plan? To have her run out the basement door on the opposite side of the house?"

"I don't know what you're talking about."

"I saw her, Henrik! With the girls upstairs sleeping?"

"That could have been anyone running down the street."

"I'm checking on the girls and then I'm going to bed. You're a liar and a pig! You disgust me."

Rachel couldn't believe the web of deception that she was in and had never met a more loathsome human being in her life. Henrik was nothing more than a cockroach, cheating, beating, and manipulating his way through life. She knew her decision to divorce him was the best decision she ever made. She missed Spain but she knew she would have to stay and fight for her home and for her girls. She waited with anticipation for

Monday morning when she would call her attorney to see how things were progressing.

Elton John was singing "Someone Saved My Life Tonight" on the little kitchen radio when she called. The lyrics made Fallon sad: "You're a butterfly and butterflies are free to fly, high away, bye bye," sang Elton John. Rachel always told her that when she passed one day, she would come back to Fallon as a butterfly.

"Don't leave me, Mama," Fallon prayed.

Now, she left a message for her attorney. He called her back quickly.

"Michael how are you...or should I call you Mr. Ward?"

"Call me Michael if you wish, I got your message. I'm just calling you back."

"Yes Michael, how is the progress going? Do we have a court date or anything yet?"

"I'm looking at the paperwork right now. I was going to mail this out to you later today. The court date is three weeks from tomorrow. The address to the courtroom will be on the summons."

Rachel sighed with relief.

"I knew this would make you happy. I have your petition for divorce ready and we'll be all set."

"What do I need to do?"

"Don't worry. I'll call you the week before and we will go over everything. Okay?"

"Yes. Okay!"

Rachel was hopeful with the news from her attorney. Her divorce was already one and a half years in the making. She had called her friend Mary Jenkins about the news, the court date, and they talked about a game plan. Mary asked Rachel if she had all her paperwork ready. Rachel told her that she had letters and documentation from Karin Kaffie, Tante Annie, and her friend Alice Tricocci. They were letters describing Henrik's physical and mental abuse, including letters from neighbors documenting the women who came to the house when Rachel, Soraya, and Fallon were in Spain. Rachel was embarrassed that the neighbors saw such dreadful things but most of them were aware that Henrik was, in their words, a "complete sociopath," and were happy to prepare some testimony for her.

Three weeks later, Rachel drove to Karin Kaffie's house. Alice Tricocci would meet her in court because she already lived downtown. Tante Annie would pick up Soraya and Fallon after school if she wasn't back in time.

"You're gonna win this, and when you're through we'll be here to help you start your new life," Karin promised.

They waited in the hallway outside the courtroom. Alice arrived minutes before Michael Ward, who came bustling down the hall. "Are you ready, Rachel?" he said, his smile friendly. He seemed relaxed, which unnerved Rachel.

"Yes, I am." She nodded.

Ward spoke first to Karin Kaffie. "From what I understand," he said. "Your family was friends with the Baumann family for years and you're now taking sides with Rachel?"

"Yes Mr. Ward, the brutality and temper tantrums brought on by Henrik are completely unforgivable, not to mention the way he ignores his own children. It's disgraceful. My Aunt, whom we call Tante Annie, is Fallon's godmother and both of us have written letters to the judge testifying against Henrik Baumann for his cruelty and abuse."

He turned to Rachel. "Do you understand what is going to happen today with the judge?"

"I think so Michael."

"We have your petition for divorce and all the properties that we will try to divide up. Be forewarned that these things take time and none of us knows what the judge will say."

"Okay," Rachel said softly.

"Ladies," he smiled. "Let's head into the courtroom and wait our turn."

Rachel, Michael, Karin, and Alice walked into the courtroom and searched the room for Henrik. Rachel's stomach was tied in knots. "Henrik's not here," she whispered.

"Don't worry," Ward assured her. "We still have twenty-five minutes before our case is called." He nodded toward Henrik's attorney, Mr. Sherman.

Twenty minutes passed, then thirty. "Baumann versus Baumann case number 714556," the judge bellowed.

Rachel and Michael Ward approached the podium. Sherman followed.

The judge flipped through some paperwork. "Counsel, are both plaintiff and defendant present?" the judge said sternly.

Sherman spoke first. "Your Honor, Mr. Baumann has called me this morning about an emergency with his farm properties in Wisconsin. Mr. Baumann will not be present this morning."

Rachel tugged on Ward's sleeve and whispered, "He's lying! There's no emergency!"

Ward motioned respectfully and inconspicuously, bouncing his hand up and down signaling Rachel to settle down.

Alice leaned over to Rachel and whispered as Ward addressed the judge, "This is bullshit Rachel. I come from Texas, and I speak my mind. This is pure bullshit!"

"Your Honor, my client has come here in good faith with a petition for divorce, testimony from solid witnesses, and documentation."

"Counsel be informed that I will make a motion for a continuance. Next case please!"

Rachel was on the brink of tears. "What is going on?"

"Don't worry we will get another court date; I'll file for a notice immediately. Sorry for this, but it happens."

"I'm telling you. Henrik is doing this on purpose!"

On the drive home, Karin tried to be gentle with Rachel who stared out the car window. "Henrik gets away with everything," Rachel finally said. "He manipulates everyone to get what he wants and then when he gets it, it encourages him to keep controlling people. Crazy thing, he honestly believes his own lies."

"It sure looks like that!" Karin said.

"Did you know that Henrik sells guns illegally at his hardware store and in Mexico?" said Rachel.

"I believe it."

"He sells them on the black market. His buddies look for customers to buy his guns. He flies the guns to Mexico and sells them on the beach."

Rachel and the girls didn't see Henrik for days after he missed the court date. Soraya and Fallon didn't ask where he was because everyone felt better when he was gone.

But one morning, after Soraya and Fallon had left for school, the phone rang in the kitchen.

"Hello," Rachel said, picking up the phone.

"You better watch yourself, pretty lady," came a muffled voice. "That gorgeous little head of yours is going to end up in the garbage can one day."

The man laughed and Rachel recognized him as one of Henrik's friends. She felt the blood rush from her head to her feet. She dropped the phone and sat on the steps next to the kitchen. "Nights in White Satin" by the Moody Blues was playing softly in the background. Rachel pondered the haunting and melancholy lyrics: "Breathe deep the gathering gloom, watch lights fade from every room."

She had terrible premonitions of her life in danger. She had not been eating much or sleeping. Now, she felt faint. She was losing her hair, and the thought of suicide was never far from her mind, except for the fact that her precious girls needed her.

She gathered her thoughts and called Alice who told her that she was going to think about what to do and call her later. Still terrified, she called Mary Jenkins to see if she could come over with the girls. She needed support now that this nightmare was closing in on her.

She told Fallon about the call, too, because she wanted as many witnesses as possible to know what was happening to her. Fallon was glad that she told her, but at the same time she had nightmares. She felt haunted for years that her mother's head would be found in a garbage can.

Three days later, Henrik strolled into the house. Fallon was sure he noticed the look of fear on their faces, but he simply went downstairs to the basement, put away his things, and came back up to the kitchen where Rachel was waiting.

"Not that I care, but where have you been? We had a court date?" Rachel trembled inside but tried not to show her fear. She had to show strength against this cockroach.

"My attorney knew where I was. I told him I had an emergency at the farm."

"Is that so..."

"You don't believe me?"

"I don't believe a word out of your mouth. Oh, by the way, I got a call from your friend. He said I would find my head in the garbage can! This isn't a joke."

Henrik moved closer to Rachel. "I don't know what you're talking about!"

"Lower your voice, the girls will hear you!"

"I don't care!!"

"You're causing our girls psychological harm!"

"YOU DON'T KNOW WHAT YOU'RE TALKING ABOUT." Fire

flew from Henrik's mouth. "Besides, you should be worried about the psychological damage I'm gonna do to you!"

"Don't try and bully me with your stupid goons and I know you throw cash their way. Don't forget who is watching you, Henrik!"

"God? I bet you God could be bought if the price is right!"

"You are so sick. Forget about going to a doctor. No one will be able to help you!"

Henrik glared at her. "You've been the loser with this divorce and these court hearings for the last two years, and you're gonna stay the loser!"

He moved to the kitchen table and slammed it into the wall, denting the drywall.

"You're never going to get *anywhere* with these attorneys. If you want a settlement you will go through me! Understand?"

It was useless to argue with Henrik when he was in a brain meltdown. He was always meaner, louder, violent, and more calculating. Rachel kept a blank look on her face as she walked into the basement rec room to sit near Soraya and Fallon. They wouldn't know until much later that Henrik was seeing another woman named Maryann Gallo. He was seeing many different women at the same time, Millie, Sherry, and countless other whores, but he took a special liking to Maryann. Maryann had dark long hair, and the first time Fallon saw her face, she thought Maryann would look perfect with a witch hat and broomstick.

They would later learn that Maryann used to show up at the house when Rachel and the girls were in Spain. The neighbors saw and identified her as a woman with long, thick, dark hair with thin calf muscles. They told Rachel that Maryann would show up at the house completely nude except for a fur coat. The neighbors were disgusted and let Rachel know of other women who would show up at the house, but the dark-haired Maryann seemed to be a favorite.

Henrik had met Maryann in the circle of attorneys that he was seeing on a regular basis. In later years Rachel would learn that Henrik showed up with her during work hours, and she made many appearances at the hardware store.

Weeks went by and Soraya and Fallon were on a two-week trip to the farm with Henrik and their cousins. Rachel always worried herself sick about leaving the girls with their father, but she had no choice. If she argued about him taking them, he would just threaten to take her back to court for his parental rights. He promised to make her hellacious life worse.

The girls knew not to tell Rachel about Henrik's behavior at the farm. He would leave them for hours and hours, telling them that he was doing something at another farm or had to go into town. Later, they would learn that he was with local country prostitutes.

But it was the middle of summer and along with their cousins, the girls spent hours in the pool and played with the horses and ponies. Fallon was seven and a bit scared to do it, but she would take long walks in the back forty acres to watch the sunset: an open field with a fireball glow as if God had taken a moment in her life to tell her to never give up hope and that she would find her way. To Fallon, that sunset promised better days to come.

Two days after their return from the farm, Rachel received the letter for the new court date and was hopeful again. The court date arrived, and Henrik again was not there. This time his attorney gave the excuse that Henrik's father had to be taken to the hospital. The judge issued another continuation. Frustrated, she turned to Ward and again told him that Henrik was lying and that this was unacceptable. Given his breach, she now demanded full custody of Soraya and Fallon.

That infuriated Henrik, who did whatever he wanted. Two weeks after the court date, he took Soraya and Fallon on a ten-day trip to Florida before school started. Rachel had no say in this. He used the vacations with the girls as a power trip to control them and make Rachel feel miserable when they were gone. The trips didn't take the pain away, they only made it worse. If Fallon moved a shirt of his on the bed, or she put his glasses in the wrong spot, she would feel his wrath.

If he was in one of his moods, Fallon became his mental punching bag. It was as if a bomb was triggered and went off in his head. If you didn't seem grateful for a trip or something he bought for you, you would be shamed into thanking him a thousand times. Soraya and Fallon were conditioned from birth to listen to his bullshit, but eventually they grew to know that their father was a neurotic, violent, bully "with more issues than a cuckoo clock," they would say.

When they returned, summer was slowly coming to an end and Rachel waited for the new court date. She got a letter from her attorney's office stating that the new court appearance was in early September. The next day Rachel got a call from the hardware store.

"Henrik?"

"You Goddamn bitch. You want full custody of the girls."

"But Henrik."

"You will get those girls over my dead body, Rachel. You're too much of an idiot to navigate the court systems. Watch out, because you're gonna end up with nothing."

"Henrik I…"

"HENRIK WHAT? I WILL SEE YOU DEAD FIRST!"

"I just talked to…" Rachel couldn't get a word in edgewise.

"You just talked to *who*? You had better watch yourself because I'll be home in five minutes. You *Goddamn…*!"

At the other end, Rachel heard him beating the phone against the wall. She quickly hung up and found Soraya and Fallon.

"Girls. Come on, hurry!" Rachel searched for her purse.

"Mommy, what's going on?"

"Fallon, I'll tell you in a minute, just not in front of your sister. We have to go quickly to Maria's Grocery Store."

Rachel knew it took Henrik seven to ten minutes to get home from the hardware store. From Maria's Grocery Store, she would have a great vantage point. She could watch him turn off Irving Park Road and head down their street.

Leaving the kitchen radio on to fool Henrik for at least a few minutes, she grabbed both of the girls' hands in each of hers and they made a dash to the door.

She was no longer thinking straight but was smart enough to get them out of the house. They ran for the corner of Pittsburg and Irving Park. They crossed the busy street and continued running like a bunch of scared rabbits into Maria's store.

"Mommy. Why are we here at Maria's?" Fallon's stomach twisted in knots.

"We're hiding from your father!"

Fallon started trembling and shivering with fear, feeling sick. She took Soraya's hand, and they hid in the aisles of the grocery store. All three of them were tired of living in isolation and misery, but they had no choice.

Soraya spoke softly. "My tummy hurts too." She saw Fallon's hand on her stomach. They locked eyes, scared, not knowing what was happening.

Fallon peered around the corner where they hid behind the rows of canned goods. Rachel was on the other side of the store talking to Maria and looking nervously out the window.

Maria was behind the deli counter. Rachel reached across and grabbed Maria's hand.

"It's my husband! He's gone crazy again, he's out of control. I'm sorry to bother you but can we hide in your store for a little bit? He's driving home and he threatened me again. He hits me and yells at me and the girls. He tortures us." Rachel's lip quivered.

"Oh my God, Rachel. Do you want me to call the police?"

"Hang on Maria. I need to look out the window for him. I can see his car as he turns the corner."

Maria asked one of her coworkers to take over the deli counter for a few minutes. She walked over to Rachel and joined her at the window.

"Oh Maria," said Rachel. "Thank you again. Sorry for this bother at your store."

"No problem. I can't believe this. Henrik seems like such a normal friendly guy when he comes in here. He jokes and laughs and flirts with the girls. He's so charming."

"He fools everyone. It's almost like he has a split personality. Ohhhh, there's his car!" Rachel scanned the store quickly for Soraya and Fallon, waited a minute, and came to them.

"Fallon, Soraya, están bien, mis hijas?" Sometimes Rachel spoke Spanish when she was nervous.

"Yes, Mommy," Soraya said softly.

Rachel grabbed Fallon's hand and pulled her close to talk to her out of Soraya's earshot. Fallon was in deep, Rachel's first in command whenever it came time to deal with Henrik. Fallon was really all she had on a day-to-day basis.

"Fallon, honey. I have to go back by the window to see when your father leaves the house. If I must, I will go outside to see if his car is still there," she whispered.

"No, Mommy. Stay in the store with us. I'm scared! Sometimes when Daddy does this at home, I hide in my closet."

"Nothing will happen to you. Just stay here with your sister. I'll be by the window." Fallon reached out to hug her. Rachel took her in her arms and sighed before letting go.

All three of them had a separate vantage point of Henrik's violence. If Rachel didn't witness something, Fallon did. Even little Soraya saw things her brain couldn't understand. Rachel went back to the window and nervously watched for Henrik's car. A few moments passed, and she saw his car racing around the corner and heading back to the hardware store.

Rachel went to Maria's phone and called Mary.

"What's going on?" asked Mary.

"It's Henrik again. I can explain later. Can the girls and I sleep over tonight? I can sleep on your pullout bed and the girls can sleep in your daughters' rooms if that's okay?"

"Of course, Rachel, oh my gosh, you poor thing. Come over now if you have to."

"We're hiding in Maria's Grocery Store. We'll quickly go home, and I'll pack pajamas for the girls. We'll cut through Marge's backyard. I don't want Henrik to see my car in front of your house."

"The front door is open, and I'll make extra for dinner tonight!"

They stayed at Mary's house that night. Rachel knew that if there was some time between when the explosions in Henrik's brain, she might be able to reason with him. Rachel called Alice from Mary's house and told her the story. It was sometimes hard for Alice to help because she lived in the city but she was always a great support. She told Rachel that she would sleep over at our house when we returned from Mary's. "Thank you," said Rachel. "I'll call you in the morning."

Henrik frantically tried to find them. He first ran to the Kaffie's. Karin told him Rachel wasn't there. Immediately Karin called the house after Henrik left and no one answered. She was terrified that something had happened to Rachel and the girls. Then Henrik drove around the neighborhood and stopped at Edwardo's house and Lolli's house which were right across the street. Rachel and the girls were nowhere in sight. Then he stopped at Mary's house. Rachel always had a safety system in place. Mary Jenkins came up with the code name.

"Girls," she cried. "It's Operation Henrik. Find your hiding places! *Now!*"

Soraya and Fallon hid in Mary's oldest daughter's closet. Rachel ran into Mary's master bath and locked the door. Henrik rang Mary's doorbell.

"Hi Mary."

"Hi Henrik."

"Are Rachel and the girls here?"

"No, Henrik. I haven't seen them. They're not at home?"

"No! I can't seem to find them anywhere."

"Hmm, maybe they are at the Pickwick Theater. They love going there. Maybe they are at a movie?"

"Can I come in, Mary?"

"Actually Henrik. Now is not a good time. My husband's boss is here and I'm making dinner."

"If I find out that you are lying to me, you will be sorry."

"Excuse me, Henrik. I'll be what?" Mary glared at him. "I think it's time for you to say goodbye."

She slammed and locked the door, shocked at his response. When Henrik and Rachel finally argued about the matter, he made a promise that he was going to fight her for custody. He knew exactly what he was doing, putting Rachel into a constant tailspin of worry about losing her girls. Henrik could care less about what anyone thought about him. He never played by the rules. Henrik traveled the world, fucked whores, and did exactly whatever he wanted. He terrorized Rachel and the girls, they never had a moment of stability.

September rolled around and Rachel impatiently waited for her court date. Again, she called Michael Ward to make sure she had everything in order.

Rachel and Michael prepared for court with witnesses and all the necessary paperwork. Things were moving forward, and a lot was on the table with custody, division of assets, financial support, and alimony. Henrik once again was not at the court hearing and Rachel knew he was bullying and manipulating the system.

Henrik controlled everything, while she had sleepless nights and anxiety-filled days trying to take care of Soraya and Fallon. Henrik left her depressed, desperate, and insolvent, which is where he wanted her. He purposely brought her to the brink of insanity. No woman, she thought, especially one that had a wealthy husband, should be allowed to live on the verge of poverty while he gallivanted his way through life, mocking the system that was built to protect her. There was something evil and sinister going on with the court system. She had sensed it from the beginning. She just had to uncover the truth, if it even existed. The next court hearing came at the end of September. Rachel was at her wits end and pushing Ward who didn't seem to be doing much for her case.

The hearing was set, and Rachel and Alice headed downtown while Karin and Tante Annie took care of Soraya and Fallon. Mary Jenkins tried to get to court but had her hands full with work and a houseful of kids. Many of Rachel's friends made rotations, ensuring she would never go to court alone.

Rachel and Alice made their way into the courtroom and waved at Michael Ward when they saw him come in.

"Hello Rachel, Mrs. Tricocci." Michael nodded his head.

"Please Michael, call me Alice, we're all friends here." Alice chuckled.

"Okay ladies we're set. We just need to wait our turn, although I do not see Henrik here again. Rachel, did you have a talk with him about showing up this time?"

"A talk with him? The man is, how do you say this word, insufferable. You can't talk with him or reason with him, but to answer your question, I've talked to him every time he purposely does not show up. It does no good. He's a child!"

He looked at her, his face serious. "From what I know of this case, I've never seen anything quite like Henrik."

Rachel, Alice, and Michael waited their turn in court. She felt that everyone was playing a game, and she was one of the puzzle pieces. After forty minutes the judge called her case.

"Baumann versus Baumann case number 714556. Counsel, are both parties present?"

"No, your Honor. Mr. Damien Sherman, your Honor. I'm counsel for the defendant Mr. Henrik Baumann. I have an important letter stating the reason for his absence."

"Proceed."

Rachel leaned in toward Ward. "He did it again. This is never going to get resolved, is it? More bullshit lies."

"Let's see what the letter says."

Alice's eyes rolled.

Sherman spoke. "I have a written letter that my secretary typed up this morning and a letter from Henrik's doctor. I would like to address the court to explain the circumstances. I'm advising you orally today that Mr. Baumann is presently in ill health and is awaiting admission to the hospital."

"Lies," whispered Rachel and Alice.

Sherman continued. "Because of the doubt expressed by the plaintiff, I've obtained, enclosed herewith, a letter signed by Mr. Baumann's physician. Neither I nor Mr. Baumann have ever asked the court for a continuance in this case. We have always been ready for trial, and it has been Mrs. Rachel Baumann's requests for a continuance that have delayed this case. Therefore, the accusation that Mr. Baumann is doing something to avoid the court hearings is totally illogical."

"This is outrageous! More lies, more lies! He's not sick," Rachel hissed at Ward.

"Rachel, take a breath. This is a tactic to make you look bad."

"Michael, do something!"

"The judge is just going to file another continuance."

Sherman continued reading the doctor's note. "Mr. Henrik J. Baumann, a patient of mine, is suffering from an aggravated and severe case of cervical neuritis and chronic prostatitis. During the past two years due to neglect of necessary treatment, his condition worsened, and it is imperative that he be hospitalized immediately.

"This can be verified by my records and those of Dr. Reyes from the urology group on Wabash in Chicago, Illinois. Dr. Reyes has assisted in treating Mr. Baumann over the past six years. We recommend immediate hospitalization and isolation from stress. Sincerely, Michael Julian, MD."

Sherman addressed the judge. "Your Honor, this is all I have for today."

The judge hit his gavel. "We will reconvene at a later date; I will grant another continuance for Baumann versus Baumann."

"Michael, this is a joke! Henrik is turning this divorce into a circus! My two girls are suffering as this nightmare drags on. Alice. Did you see this shit? Can you believe it?"

"Henrik is a son of a bitch, Rachel. I wouldn't believe it if I didn't see it for myself. Call all the hospitals in town tomorrow," Alice spewed.

Ward didn't know what to say, except to apologize, "He's using every trick in the book."

The next morning, Henrik was nowhere to be found. Rachel called every hospital in a ten-mile radius to verify Henrik's story. She even called Saint Joseph Hospital off Lake Shore Drive in Chicago, where Fallon was born. Henrik was at none of the hospitals.

Next, she called the hardware store, and asked if they had seen or heard from him. Had they heard that he was in the hospital? They told her that they didn't know where he was.

She organized a brainstorming session with Mary and Alice to find yet another attorney. Mary and Alice came to the house and gathered on the couch. "Well, this scumbag husband of yours couldn't get any lower now, could he!" Alice said, taking Rachel's hand.

"He's gonna keep getting away with this and everything else he does," sighed Rachel. "I've lost weight, I can't sleep, and Henrik leaves me with less and less money. I barely have enough money sometimes for food."

"I've never seen a man like this," said Alice, "He must stay up twenty-four hours a day plotting all his evil shit."

Then it was Mary's turn. "I don't want to give you more than you can handle, but a friend from church told me that Henrik was spotted kissing an unidentified woman in the park near the high school at sunset. Who does he think he is, a teenager? Wait, I hope he wasn't with a teenager!"

Rachel gave a grim smile. "It wouldn't surprise me in the least. He has a new victim every week. He really should be locked up."

"I wonder why none of your attorneys are doing a darn thing, but his attorney seems to be a lying piece of shit just like him." Mary spoke as Rachel poured lemonade. "We need to find someone we can trust."

They sat, talked, and plotted all morning into the early afternoon. Alice made phone calls using her connections to find another attorney. In the meantime, Rachel fired Michael Ward.

Rachel now needed their help selling a few of her possessions to raise money for added expenses. They would start with her fur coats. Rachel opened up the downstairs closet. Alice made eye contact with her.

"I know those coats are some of your favorite things."

Rachel looked down at the floor. "I'll have to get a job soon," she added. "I've never had one."

"I'll help you with that," said Mary. "I thought Henrik was paying for all the attorney's fees. That's his job, you know."

"He pays for so little around here. If something gets broken around here it stays broken. I have a bicycle and some jewelry I can sell, too." Rachel's voice was haggard and exhausted.

Mary and Alice both looked at each other. Rachel didn't deserve one ounce of what was happening to her, but she was in survival mode and needed to push forward. First, she had to end the marriage and move on with her life and her girls. They would help Rachel borrow money when she needed it, or they would lend it to her. They would be there for her and see her to the other side. She simply needed to keep the faith.

Ten days later, Henrik sauntered into the house sporting a tan. "You were supposed to be in the hospital," she said, quietly. "Where did you get that tan?"

"I'm always tan and it's none of your damn business. Besides, you were dead to me the moment you asked for the divorce!"

"I don't want to be treated like crap, cheated on, and used as your punching bag! On top of that, the girls need a normal father and one that is around more than you are. You're sick in the head and you need help!"

"I don't give a damn about what you think. Besides, the girls are fine and leave them out of this!"

"Just be honest. Did you go to Mexico? More prostitutes?" Rachel spoke with sarcasm in her voice.

Henrik grabbed her arm.

"Don't touch me you filthy animal!" Rachel shouted.

She whipped her arm, freeing herself from Henrik's grip, fled to her bedroom, and locked the door.

"Oh yeah, you bitch! I'm selling your GTO, so I'm taking your keys. You can also kiss the cleaning lady goodbye."

Rachel yelled through the closed door. "Forget about the cleaning lady. What am I supposed to drive? I have to drive the girls to school and to the grocery store!"

"Don't worry. You'll get the car you deserve!"

Rachel went to her knees, then sat on the bedroom floor sobbing. She was embarrassed to ask her parents for money but there would come a day when it would become inevitable.

Within a week, her beautiful white GTO with black leather top was sold. Even though it was only a material thing, her heart broke to see it go. Henrik had driven up to the house with her new car, a rusty dark green Oldsmobile. She walked outside, not understanding what she was seeing.

"Is this another one of your jokes?"

"Nope…the car is fine. It runs well."

She sat in the front seat. "What is this smell?" she said. The stench on the cloth seats was musty and moldy with a hint of sewage.

"Apparently the car was in a flood of some sort," he said. "But they dried it out and it runs fine."

"I'm not going to take my girls in this car! It stinks and if there's bacteria it could be harmful for them. What on earth is wrong with you! You have money and you would put your girls in a car like this?"

"The girls are fine. Nothing is going to happen to them!"

"Get this car out of my driveway! I'm not going to drive this piece of shit. What do you think the judge is going to say when I tell him about the car that you are willing to put your daughters in! He knows you can afford it and you are doing this on purpose just to save money and get back at me!"

"You *ungrateful* little bitch!"

"Ungrateful…you took my car! It was fully paid for. I need something safe!" With that, Rachel walked back into the house, hoping she had made her point.

More than a week had passed, and Rachel had started over with a new attorney. Michael Ward had barely batted an eye when she told him she was finished. She was hopeful that this attorney would be the one that could turn things around. She prepared her notes and counted the days until their meeting. Meanwhile, Henrik took Soraya and Fallon to Grandma and Grandpa Baumann's for the afternoon.

Rachel heard the phone ring. "Hi," Henrik said, "just checking in with you. We're at Grandma Baumann's."

"I know. You just left here fifteen minutes ago."

"Okay, just wanted to let you know we got here."

"Okay...bye."

She was immediately suspicious of the call. Henrik had been uncharacteristically friendly. He was up to something, but she wasn't sure exactly what it was. She sat and thought for a little bit, and she felt God pushing her to go downstairs into Henrik's office.

She looked on the floor and saw a strange sight, one that she had seen before. They were empty jelly jars, some of them filled with quarters, dimes, and nickels. She wondered why a man who had money would spend his time hoarding jars of quarters. She almost laughed as she pondered the idea that Henrik could turn into Howard Hughes and start storing urine in jars. He was more volatile, eccentric, and batshit crazy than Hughes, and she was up for finding anything. She opened a few files, then headed over to the cabinet and opened some drawers, finding nothing.

She turned and looked at a stack of boxes in the corner. She began opening them. In the last box, she found a tape recorder and pulled it out. She hit the eject button and out came a tape. She put the room back as she found it and went upstairs to the kitchen. Tape in hand, she put it in the little white kitchen radio and hit play.

"Hello."

"Hi, just checking in with you. We're at Grandma Baumann's."

"I know. You just left here fifteen minutes ago."

It was their phone conversation. Henrik was doing a trial run with the phony phone call to see if tapping the phone lines worked.

The next morning Henrik came up from the basement looking for something to eat.

"Can I make breakfast for you?" she said.

"That would be great."

"Oh, by the way, I'm wondering why you have so many jelly jars of change in the basement."

"I want to give them to the girls for Christmas."

"Oh," she said, sweetly. "I'll be right back."

Downstairs, she retrieved the tape recorder and brought it into the kitchen.

"Here you go. Here's your breakfast." She placed the recorder on the table in front of him.

"What's this?" Henrik had a look of shock on his face.

"Don't play stupid with me. Did you want to hear our phone conversation from yesterday again? Don't worry, you won't find the tape anywhere. I'll be keeping that. Now you can go back to disconnecting the phone or any of the other little rotten, sneaky pranks that you do around here. And why would anyone give kids quarters for Christmas?

Henrik's face went blank, and he got up from the kitchen table and walked out the front door, still baffled at how Rachel knew what she knew.

He wondered how she discovered the recorder that was hidden away. For the first time in a long time, Rachel had a leg up on the situation, even if it seemed for only a moment.

12

Driven to Tears

The next morning, Rachel heard the phone ring. She was nervous about meeting yet another attorney and she had thought it was him on the other line to confirm their appointment.

"Hello…"

"You better watch yourself or you're gonna get hurt. You might have a little accident. You could even get killed… *You stupid whore!*"

Rachel slammed the phone down as the man on the other line began laughing. It was the same voice that she recognized from the other calls.

Rachel called Alice, her voice breaking into sobs.

"I know sweetie. What's wrong?"

"I got another phone call from Henrik's creepy friend."

"Oh, my Lord. I'll tell you Rachel, that man is going straight to hell! If I were a judge that man would already be behind bars serving a life sentence for what he's done to you. Please don't cry, you're making me sad."

"I just worry about my safety and what would ever happen to Fallon and Soraya with this monster, if I wasn't here."

"Don't you worry, you have good friends who love you. Trust me. Every time I see that man, I would love to give him a piece of my mind, but I don't. Rachel, I'm always worried that if I do that, he will beat the shit out of you when I leave. I couldn't live with myself."

"I do too. I keep my mouth shut most of the time, afraid of setting him off. But every once in a while, I lose it. I've done everything to kick him out of the house, but he won't leave. This divorce is taking too long. I go to bed depressed, and I wake up that way."

"Hang in there Rachel."

"Did I tell you that he tried to tap the phone line?"

"Are you kidding me? That pig will stop at nothing!" Alice sighed with frustration. "At least tomorrow you'll meet your new attorney, Andrew Sampson."

"Yes, but I have a few things to do in the morning. Henrik's insisting on taking the girls to school tomorrow."

"I wouldn't trust anything he does."

"I never do. I'll see you tomorrow around 10:30?"

Rachel gathered her paperwork hoping that the third time would be a charm. With each new attorney, she not only had to explain all the atrocities in her marriage but all the new horrifying and cruel stunts that Henrik had pulled. That night she tucked her girls into bed and prayed the Rosary before she fell asleep. Another night of tossing and turning littered with nightmares was right in front of her.

In the morning, Henrik emerged from the basement. Rachel knew he liked to make a good impression, and she was sure that was why he was taking her daughters to school.

Shortly after, she pulled out of the driveway to meet Alice and the new attorney. She started down the street, but the car refused to build up speed. She thought at first that she was doing something wrong, but she wasn't sure what, so she pressed harder on the gas. Suddenly, the car accelerated above the speed limit and kept accelerating. A stop sign loomed ahead.

Oh my God, she thought, and hit the brakes. The stop sign grew closer. Panicked, she started pumping the brakes. She pumped and pumped and screamed as she moved into oncoming traffic from Cumberland Road, a busy street on the opposite side of the neighborhood. Cars were flying down the street trying to get out of her way.

"Oh my God," she said aloud. "That's why Henrik took the girls to school!"

Time stopped. She turned the steering wheel to the right and jumped the curb, skidding across three lawns until finally, she came to a stop. Tears ran down her face and she put her head on the steering wheel allowing her mind to catch up with what had happened.

A man approached her window. "Oh my gosh, ma'am, are you okay?"

She opened her door. "I'm so sorry for what I did to your lawn."

"No, no. That can be fixed. Are you okay?"

"I think so. I don't know."

"Do you want me to call the police so we can report this as an accident?"

"No. Sure. Sir, do what you want."

Rachel got out of the car. She was dizzy, disoriented. With her hands on her knees, she leaned forward and vomited.

"Oh no! I think I need to call an ambulance."

"No, sir I'm okay!"

"But ma'am you just threw up. Did you hit your head?"

"Sir…call the police if you have to. I live in the neighborhood, and I will be back to have the car towed. I will have your lawn fixed, but now I have to go." Rachel wiped the side of her mouth and breathed heavily.

"But ma'am!"

"He's trying to kill me. He's trying to kill me!" Rachel grabbed her purse out of the car. She walked then began to run in her pink wedge heels.

"Who's trying to kill you? Ma'am!"

Rachel ran down the block, turned right and headed another six blocks to get home. She knew that no matter what was happening to her, she would trust in her faith, trust that God and the hand of favor and protection would always keep her safe. Seeing her house, she lost concentration for a split second, tripped on a tree root and fell onto Edwardo's lawn. She picked herself up and walked as fast as she could the last fifty feet.

She got in the doorway, fell to the floor, and cried until she ran out of tears. For a moment, she blamed herself for everything that was happening. She thought back to a time years ago when she allowed her ex-husband Alex to dictate that they abort her children. She had never forgiven herself for allowing her children to be taken from her body and she felt that now she was being punished.

She also blamed herself for not taking control sooner. She also knew that if she didn't fight as hard as she could, it would be too late. She got up and laid down on her gold brocade sofa in the living room, the one in which she had imagined she, Henrik, and the girls would settle in on cozy Christmas mornings. Once she felt better, she rinsed her mouth, and called Alice.

"He did something to my brakes. He's trying to kill me. This is for real!"

"I'll be right over! Give me thirty minutes. Where are you?"

"I'm at home. Can you call my attorney and cancel until next week? I'm too upset to go today."

"I'll be there, and I'll call him from your house. It will be okay Rachel. I'm on my way."

Rachel waited until Alice got there. She called Mary, Karin, and a few other friends to let them know what happened. Then she called the hardware store.

"Hello, Henrik there?"

"I'll get him Rachel."

"Hello."

"What did you do to my car?"

"What are you talking about?"

"Don't give me that. What did you do to my brakes?"

"I didn't do a darn thing." His voice was neutral.

"Oh no? Who did? Did you ever think, what if the girls were in the car with me?"

"Well, they weren't now, were they?" She was sure she could hear him smirking.

"You think you're so smart. You're the one who better watch your step now. If I end up dead, my family and friends know what you've been doing, and they'll come after you. I just finished writing letters to twenty-five friends stating that if I end up dead, they should find Henrik Baumann! Let me repeat myself, the letters all point to you! I sent them to Spain, Argentina, and to many friends and neighbors in the States, even our alderman. Everyone was given special instructions on what to do, in case of my untimely death. They will come after you, Henrik! One day your luck is gonna run out. You think with all your money and power you can try and kill me and make it look like an accident."

"You wrote letters?"

"Yes, I did! You think everybody loves you, when in reality, they know you are scum!"

Henrik was quiet. Rachel had just caused a small wrinkle in his plans.

"Go ahead and try to deny it, Henrik. You drove the girls to school on purpose. Thank God they're safe, but you are the most despicable human I have ever met."

"What are you gonna do? How are you gonna prove this?"

"Just get this damn car off the neighbor's lawn down the street and get it fixed. You'll be hearing from my new attorney soon enough. I'll have him bring this up to the judge. Maybe he'll file another order of protection against you."

"Oh really…let's see how that works out for you."

"Rot in hell…Henrik!"

"Remember, *money talks* and I've got all of it!"

The next day Rachel asked Mary if she could give her a ride to go pick up the car at the mechanic where it had been fixed. The owner of the auto shop knew Henrik so Rachel suspected if there was a coverup of sorts, she might never find out the truth. Mary and Rachel got out of the car and walked into the office of the repair shop.

"Hello Larry, how's the car?"

"All fixed up."

"What was wrong with it?"

"Just a loose wire, nothing really. All taken care of."

"Just a loose wire? Then how come I ended up out of control on my neighbor's lawn?"

"I'm not sure. I wasn't there."

"Just give me my keys and don't give me any of your bullshit. You might be able to bullshit another woman, but not me."

"Rachel, I have no idea what you are talking about."

"I'm sure you don't. Come on Mary, let's get out of here."

Mary walked over to her car and Rachel walked to hers. Just as Rachel was about to start her car another mechanic named Luke ran to her car window. He had known Rachel for a few years and had admired her from afar.

"Hi Luke…everything okay?"

"Please, you didn't hear this from me. I don't want to lose my job, but your brake line was severed. I saw it with my own eyes. That's why you lost control. They threw out the evidence immediately. I saw the split in the brake line. It was a clean cut, not normal wear and tear. I just wanted to warn you so you would be safe."

"Oh my gosh, Luke. Thank you. If Larry asked why you were talking to me, just tell him you were asking about the girls."

"I will Rachel, please be safe."

Rachel reached out of the car window and shook Luke's hand. She drove home weary, yet she was grateful for the people who loved her and were looking out for her. You couldn't buy love, true friendship, and the grace of God, but Rachel had all three.

Evil Web of Fate

By November, 1975, Henrik had stopped paying for food and gas, and Rachel had sold most of her jewelry and her fur coats to cover expenses. It had become clear that he took only pleasure in seeing her struggle. If he couldn't control her rejection, he certainly could control her financially.

Harder still was the fact that Rachel could no longer contact her family. Henrik had threatened that if he saw a single phone call on the bill, he would rip the phone from the wall. But Rachel vowed not to break under his will even though she no longer had a credit card, or access to checks or cash.

Henrik flaunted the fact that he had plenty of money to spend, especially on other women. He was now traveling wherever he wished with his latest conquest. He had no problem leaving her, sometimes as long as three weeks at a time, without a dime. She also knew she had to find a job fast, one that would allow her to pick Soraya and Fallon up from school.

Mary and Alice both worked for a large hotel chain ten minutes from our home, and they helped Rachel get a job serving tables in the hotel's banquet hall. As Rachel served prime rib and chicken cordon bleu, she smiled at the well-dressed couples and families. She thought of the days when she arrived at palaces in limousines, the sparkling dinner conversations, and the men who fell at her feet. Her crown had fallen and shattered on the floor, but she didn't care, as long as she was free from Henrik.

Soon, she was working full time, cooking, cleaning the house, attending to the girls' homework, and dealing with lawyers, judges, and a court system that favored men with money, all while dodging Henrik's clearly calculated abuse. She had her escape route. Neighbors she could count on. They had developed a system. She would turn on certain lights to signal she was in danger and that the neighbors should call the police. The neighbors said they would talk to the police or find out the police chief's name. What they didn't know was that Henrik had paid off everyone at the station, including the chief.

Rachel finally met with the new attorney, Andrew Sampson. A few days later, he called. "Mrs. Baumann?"

"Please call me Rachel. I can't stand hearing the name Baumann. I can't wait to get rid of it one day soon."

"After hearing your story and all the testimony so far, I completely understand. It sounds like your husband comes unhinged at the slightest provocation."

"It has been nothing short of hell for me and my girls."

"In all my years as a divorce attorney, I've never heard a story quite like this one. The abuse, mental torture, explosive temper tantrums, infidelities. Not to mention, he has quite a large estate and half of it belongs to you."

"I hope you can help me, Andrew."

"Well, I wish I had better news. I've been in contact with Henrik's attorney, and they're trying to get you and the girls kicked out of the house."

"What?"

"He's crazy if he thinks that's happening."

"You don't understand. He *is* crazy, and he gets everything he wants. Where does he think we should go?"

"He's trying to get you to relocate to the farms. His land in Wisconsin. Or he has a small apartment that you could afford."

"I can't afford anything and I'm not going to the farms. I just started a waitress job. You know on top of everything else, he's also a slumlord."

"I believe it Rachel."

"He probably wants me to live in one of his run-down apartments with the girls and pay him rent while he runs off with more of his whores to Mexico." Rachel tried not to cry.

"There's more." Andrew took a deep breath. Rachel closed her eyes and listened intently.

"Henrik has been all over the place with his demands and he wants to try and take the girls, too. He wants full custody. Henrik is telling his attorney that you have other men over at the house and are sleeping with them while he's gone."

"Is he crazy? I have no men at my house and if he thinks he'll take those girls, it's over my dead body. What if I leave for Spain with the girls? They can have a normal life there. We can move in with my parents. What about the illegal guns he has in the house? I told him to get rid of those things. Someone is going to get hurt or worse."

"Don't get ahead of yourself. We'll fight this."

"He's not fit to take care of my beautiful little girls. He will not touch them or take my house! After all this, he's trying to make me look like I'm an unfit mother! I can't believe this."

"Rachel! Please calm down, this is just one of his tactics."

"I'll fight him until my last breath! I also want that bastard out of my house and my life. He's still living in the basement."

"That has to be very difficult for you."

"It's hell, but I can do nothing. If I try, I'm worried that he'll become violent."

"I see you've tried the police and restraining orders many times."

"I've lost count. Please tell me you will help me and my girls. I worry so much about them. Especially my oldest daughter, Fallon. She has seen so much violence. She's having trouble in school, and she was such a happy baby. I'm starting to see the light in her eyes dim. I think it's about the unstable, what's the word I'm looking for? Sometimes my English is not so good."

"Environment?"

"That's it!"

"Well, I have some good news. Because the holidays are coming up, we can have our pick of court dates."

"I will tell you that court dates during the holidays will be horrible for him. Whenever he has bad news, he takes it out on me. I have the bruises to prove it." Rachel looked down at the now permanent dent in her leg.

"The quicker we do this, the faster he's out of your life."

"I don't think you understand this animal. He doesn't even show up for court."

"We will see about that. I'll subpoena him. I know this is a stressful time, Rachel, but don't forget about the retainer fee we talked about."

Rachel quietly whispered, "Yes," about a fee that she had no way of paying.

In the next few days. Rachel's work schedule was hectic. She lined up babysitters, had Karin and Tante Annie helping and sometimes Mary Jenkins and her girls. Soraya and Fallon loved it because they could play with their friends and the Kaffies were like family to them.

The best news was that Rachel truly enjoyed her work. Mary and Alice were good friends and she got to spend some time with them as coworkers. She also started meeting new people.

Meanwhile, Henrik kept a close eye on what she was doing and any new men in her life. He kept meticulous notes to bring up to the judge and create false accusations against her.

Rachel left for work one afternoon knowing she would be home late since all hands were needed on deck for a large wedding. She had entrusted

Soraya and Fallon with Lori, a high school junior who lived down the block and who was one of their favorite babysitters.

It was nearly midnight when she walked through the door, tired and ready to go to bed. But instead of Lori, she found Henrik sprawled across the sofa.

"Where's Lori? And what are you doing here? You said you were away."

"Well, I'm not and I still live here. This is my house."

"Where are the girls?

"Asleep, and I walked Lori home."

"What gives you the right? You are never home on Friday nights, and when you are, you come home at 3:00 a.m. and slither down into the basement."

"You should be grateful. I paid your babysitter and walked her home. It's always something with you."

"It's always something with me?"

"You know, Rachel, I can have two men come to the house anytime and have you taken to an insane asylum. Locked up forever and I will have the girls. No one will find you!"

"Don't threaten me, Henrik. And don't forget those twenty-five letters I sent. If something happens to me, my friends will come looking for you. You're gonna make a mistake one day and I'll be watching. Or better yet, Fallon. She hears almost everything you say."

"Don't give me that. Keep Fallon out of this. You're pathetic!"

"I'm pathetic… Look in the mirror, Henrik!"

"Oh yeah! Never mind."

Rachel couldn't hide the disgust on her face even in the midst of an overwhelming fear. She knew that he could make good on his threats. For a moment, she thought about Lori and felt that she was missing something from Henrik's story. Why did he have to walk her home when she lived kitty-corner from their house? She never knew what to believe when words came out of his mouth.

A few days passed. Rachel was still waiting for the new court date and a phone call or letter from her new attorney. When the phone rang, she was quick to answer it, but instead of her attorney, it was her neighbor Maggie who lived next door to Lori and her parents.

"Do you have a minute to talk?"

"Of course, is everything okay?" Rachel heard concern in Maggie's voice.

"I'm not sure how to tell you this. The other night, when you were working, Lori came over to babysit the girls…"

"Yes." Rachel mentally braced herself. "I hope Henrik paid her enough?"

"Well, about that. Henrik found out that her parents were on vacation in Miami and, well…"

"Well, what?" Rachel felt out of breath and her eyes widened.

"Henrik walked Lori home and when he got to her side door he went nuts and pushed her into her kitchen, started kissing her, pulling her shirt off, and touching her!"

"Oh my God, Maggie. I knew something happened that night! I could see it on his smug face."

"I'm so sorry Rachel! I didn't know how to tell you!"

"How did you find out!"

"Well, he pushed Lori to the floor, and she was so scared she could barely move or say much. She froze, then tried to stop him. Henrik shushed her and told her to leave the side door open. He would come back a little bit later when your girls were asleep. He left and Lori ran to my house. She stayed with us until her parents came home."

Rachel began to sob.

"Rachel, are you okay?"

"Yes…Maggie. I'm alright." Rachel wiped her tears with a dish towel.

"Poor Lori, she's seventeen years old. There is no stopping that disgusting pig!"

"I heard from Mary that the divorce proceedings have been unbearable. I'm so sorry for what you are going through."

"You have no idea. I'm so embarrassed for Lori and what do I say to her parents? Oh my gosh, he has destroyed so much happiness, mine and my girls', and now Lori's. I worry about my girls all the time, but so far, he leaves them alone."

"Well, Rachel, most of the neighbors know what Henrik is all about. When my husband and I see you standing out in the driveway, we're always on alert to run over and help you if you need it. I wanted you to hear this from me first."

"Everyone on this block has been such good neighbors."

"Henrik should get arrested for sexual assault or attempted rape. What's so strange is that he had most of us fooled. He's so charming and polite most of the time, and he seems interested in what we're doing. But when we turn our backs and someone vulnerable is in the picture, he's on the attack."

"The police never help me. He beats me up and they do nothing."

"Don't be surprised if you hear more stories like this. If he attacked Lori, he'll attack others."

"Nothing surprises me about this man. He's trying to kick us out of the house and if not that, he's trying to get full custody of the girls!"

"No judge on earth would give that lunatic full custody! I'll talk to Mary and let her know the details of his latest attack, so the judge can hear from other neighbors and witnesses. This might help your case. I know Mary is going to testify against him when you go to trial."

"I have other friends and neighbors, good friends of Henrik and his family that are willing to testify against him. I just don't know what good it will do. He seems to get away with everything."

"I'm a phone call away if you need anything. I promise to call Mary. Stay strong. You have a lot of people who love you."

"Thank you!"

Rachel sat on the floor staring at the receiver. Bob Dylan was singing "Shelter from the Storm" on the little white radio in the kitchen. "Come in, she said, I'll give you…" *If only I could find shelter from the storm*, she thought. *If only I could be released from this depression and anxiety eating me alive.*

There was no question that Henrik was engaging in riskier activities. He was bolder, more dangerous, and threatening. The more he got away with, the more uninhibited he was. Rachel did not say a word to Maggie, but she had heard from another friend that a similar incident happened with Gia Schumer, the daughter of two of Henrik's best friends, Georgia and Bob Schumer. Bob and Georgia owned the preschool that Fallon and Soraya attended, five buildings down from the hardware store. Henrik also owned the building that housed the preschool. Gia was only eighteen and Henrik forced himself on her. Gia managed to break away from him, and her father had put a stop to the friendship.

Thanksgiving came and went with more arguments, more tirades, and broken furniture. The holidays seemed worse for him. If Rachel talked to him, he would find a disagreement to start up. If she didn't talk to him, he would get angry at her for avoiding him. If she or the girls said something he didn't agree with, he would pick a fight. No matter what you did, you couldn't win. He was always better, smarter, faster, and more competent than anyone else. And yet, he had the capability of charming and manipulating anyone who didn't personally know him. He had no trouble picking fights with eight-year-old Fallon, yelling at her as if she was an adult, growing red in the face while she stood silently trying to understand what he was saying. He would get more furious when he saw his daughter inching toward her mother for protection.

And then, the notice from the attorney arrived. The court date had been set for December 5. Rachel borrowed $2,800 from Alice and Mary for the retainer to pay Andrew Sampson. She would pay them back with the money the abuelos sent her, money she needed for food, transportation, and clothes.

On the night before the court date, Rachel had finished another flurry of notices, petitions of divorce, injunctions, motions for support, alimony, and begging the attorneys to have Henrik pay their fees. She had lined up witness after witness to testify. She had letters to prove his abuse, infidelities, mental torture, and treatment of his children. She had no appetite and could not sleep before any court appearances. She was growing weaker. As the months and years went by, sometimes she felt as if she had no more tears to cry. Yet, she vowed to herself that when she arrived in the courtroom, she would never flinch. She would never let the judges or attorneys see her shed a tear. Hadn't she once been courted by kings?

The next day, she drove downtown. It was a chilly December morning, and she was worried about snow in the forecast for later that afternoon.

She spotted Andrew outside the courtroom. "How are you feeling this morning?" he asked. "Ready?"

"How would you feel if you had no money, had a crazy man for your husband trying to take your children so he could kick you out of your house and onto the streets?"

"Rachel…"

"I'm sorry. This has been going on for almost three years. This is not your fault. I'm tired, I'm not myself. Something doesn't seem right with all these proceedings. I feel like I'm drowning."

"I'm here now to make this better. Take a deep breath and let's head into the courtroom."

Rachel and Andrew walked into the courtroom and waited their turn as other cases were being heard. Rachel, with knots in her stomach, nervously looked around the room.

"I told you. I don't see Henrik anywhere," Rachel whispered loudly.

"We still have time yet. It's okay. Look, there's Mr. Sherman, Henrik's attorney. That's a good sign."

"That's another thing, Henrik is always with the same attorney. Over the past three years, I've had many different ones. It's always the same judge too."

"I thought you told me that you fired all of them?"

"Yes, because nothing was happening with the divorce. Nothing was moving forward. I had to."

Rachel and Andrew waited another forty minutes before the judge called their case.

"Baumann versus Baumann, case 714556." The judge's voice echoed in the courtroom.

"I told you! Henrik's not here again!" Rachel angrily and loudly whispered.

"I don't know what's happening," said Andrew. "I subpoenaed him and talked to his attorney to make sure he would be here today. We were in total agreement."

Sherman spoke first. "Your Honor, my client Henrik Baumann had an emergency with one of his buildings. He had a burst pipe that he had to attend to. There is water all over some of his tenants' units. I would like to submit another continuation."

Rachel quietly sneered in Andrew's ear, "He's lying. He does this all the time. Do something!"

"Your Honor, this is counsel Andrew Sampson. The defendant Henrik Baumann has lied to the courts time and time again, keeping my client Mrs. Baumann in a holding pattern. Mrs. Baumann and other counsel have been trying to dissolve this marriage for the past three years to no avail."

The judge interrupted, "Mr. Sampson. You're implying that Mr. Baumann is lying about the burst pipe in his building?"

"Yes, Your Honor. Mr. Baumann has delayed this process for years and shows a pattern of remaining absent on court dates."

"Counsel Sampson, that is a serious allegation. On what grounds? What proof do you have?"

"Your Honor, we have serious allegations here on our end. The defendant is accusing my client Mrs. Baumann of entertaining men at her home while her young children sleep under the same roof. The defendant is also trying to take the children with full custody and, if not, kick my client and her two small children out on the streets."

"Hearsay, counsel. Plus, the defendant is not present at the moment."

"But Your Honor!"

"Careful Counsel. I'm sure on this snowy day, you of all people do not want to be in contempt of court!"

The judge briefly addressed the court, snubbing Sampson, "Baumann versus Baumann, case 714556. I'm ordering a continuation. Next case please."

Andrew looked at the layer of frustration on Rachel's face as she spoke. "Now do you see what I'm talking about?"

"Yes, this is very strange. Talk about icing the kicker."

"Icing who?" Rachel widened her eyes.

"Forget it Rachel, it's a football term."

"I don't understand football."

"I know, Rachel. I'm sorry, it's just a phrase I use sometimes. I have this feeling that Henrik is stalling for some reason. I can't put my finger on it."

"I knew he was stalling years ago, but it could be for a hundred different reasons."

Outside the courtroom, Rachel and Andrew talked briefly about their next game plan. "I'll talk with my secretary," said Andrew. "We'll get another court date."

In the parking garage, Andrew watched Rachel fumble for parking money and paid for both their cars. "Keep the faith," he said.

For the first time in years, Rachel felt hope. Something about Sampson felt different and she felt she could tentatively trust him.

Days later, Rachel received a call from Lydia, Sampson's secretary. "Mrs. Baumann, we've set another court date for December 19 at 10:30 a.m."

"I'll make arrangements to be there, but it's so close to Christmas."

"That's probably why you got the date, otherwise you'll have to wait until next year."

Rachel hung up the phone and started to walk away when the phone rang again, "Lydia?"

"You really want to die, Rachel!"

Taken by surprise, she heard a man breathing on the phone and then a slight sinister laugh. She hung up quickly. Who had Henrik put up to this kind of behavior?

The new court date came and went with another continuation. Her despair deepened. Her parents didn't have the money to fly over because they were now sending money to pay for her court dates. She couldn't call them because Henrik was monitoring her calls and threatening to tear the phone from the wall. As the new year approached, her only wish was a quick resolution to her marriage.

January 1976 came and went. By the middle of February, there had been two more court continuations. She couldn't believe that this was happening to her so she decided to take matters into her own hands. She sent the letters she had collected to the judge who had been handling her case.

She reached out to Channel 7 News looking for anyone to find some justice or advice for her situation. Her father even wrote to Mayor Richard Daley of Chicago, making a desperate plea and describing in detail the brutalities and injustice that Henrik was putting Rachel and his granddaughters through. Not a word ever came back from the Mayor's office. Letters from Channel 7 told Rachel to get a good attorney but offered zero solutions.

At the end of February, Henrik left for Mexico. On the first Saturday morning he was gone, Rachel turned on the little radio in the kitchen. Led Zeppelin's "Ten Years Gone" was playing.

"I'm never gonna leave you," sang Robert Plant. And Rachel thought, *What if Henrik never does? What will happen to us?*

It was now the middle of March. Rachel had received another letter from Andrew with yet another court appearance. While she liked Andrew, Rachel was now growing frustrated with him.

"What if I don't go?" she asked.

"The judge can find you uncooperative and noncompliant. I know how hard this is, but we have to keep pressing forward so there's no room for mistakes."

Ten days passed, and Rachel found herself in the courtroom once again, this time with Alice by her side. Andrew, who was running late, walked into the courtroom a bit disheveled but animated. "Sorry ladies. I had a last-minute meeting with one of my partners, but I just saw Henrik in the hallway."

"He's here?" Alice scoffed.

"Necessary evil unfortunately, ladies."

Rachel rolled her eyes in revulsion at what was to come.

The judge called the case. Andrew discussed in brief the abusive behavior and infidelities brought on by Henrik Baumann. He then made a statement that the plaintiff wanted a quick settlement as the divorce proceedings had been going on unnecessarily for years.

Rachel only wanted the house and a cash settlement or alimony so that she could continue her standard of living while she raised the girls, but Andrew laid out a more ambitious agenda. She and Henrik would split fifty-fifty, four hundred acres of farmland, the multiple properties on the farmland, the hardware store, multiple apartment buildings, rental properties, stocks, and bank accounts. Andrew knew this would be impossible to split so he also offered that the plaintiff would be awarded fifty percent of those properties in a cash settlement. He also mentioned briefly the removal of the guns at the house and a move out date for Henrik.

Henrik's attorney abruptly cut off Andrew. "Your Honor, with all due respect, this is a load of horse crap. Before any settlement or division of property, we must discuss the character of the plaintiff. The defendant is claiming that the plaintiff is engaging in relationships with other men and brings them to the house."

Rachel pulled Andrew's sleeve and whispered loudly. "I don't have any men in my life besides this bastard. I don't have any men at my house with my girls!"

Andrew spoke up into the microphone and interrupted Sherman. "Your Honor, this is the interrogatory phase. There is no proof of any affairs."

"Counsel Sampson, I'll allow it."

Sherman resumed speaking. "Your Honor, may I approach the bench?"

The judge motioned Sherman with his hand. Sherman pulled some photos out of his briefcase and handed them to the judge. "These are photos of the plaintiff with a gentleman."

The judge motioned for Andrew to approach. He walked up to the judge then back to Rachel to show her the photos.

Rachel blurted out, "That's my neighbor Frank. I'm not having an affair with Frank!"

The judge rapped his gavel.

Andrew whispered to Rachel, "Defamation of character. Henrik is trying to cause trouble and portray you as a bad mother."

Rachel turned toward Alice, who was shaking her head in disbelief.

"Your Honor," said Andrew. "We're not at trial here. Is there any need for mudslinging? This is the plaintiff's neighbor."

Henrik suddenly shouted at Rachel, "What are you doing talking to Frank? Huh, *Rachel?*"

Sherman motioned to Henrik to quiet down while the judge sat quietly.

Rachel whispered to Andrew, "Did you see that? The judge did nothing." "I saw it."

She glanced at the judge and knew something wasn't adding up. The judge spoke, giving a sneering look toward Andrew. "Counsel Sherman, please continue."

"Like I said, Your Honor, the plaintiff, Mrs. Baumann, has been engaging in relationships with other men bringing them to her house which is detrimental to the mental health of the defendants' children. The plaintiff on many occasions gives the children McDonald's for dinner and is an unfit mother. If the plaintiff does not move out of the house, then the defendant would like full custody of the children. If the plaintiff wishes to stay with the children, the defendant asks that she leave immediately and move into an apartment. Or if she chooses, Mr. Baumann can make arrangements for her to live on the farm."

Rachel couldn't believe what she was hearing, even though she had known this was coming.

"Your Honor, these allegations are simply not true," objected Sampson. "Again, we're not at trial, we're trying to come to a settlement."

The judge spoke sternly. "Counsel Sampson, it's going to be a difficult settlement with such a large group of assets and property. I'll allow the character analysis. Please continue Counsel Sherman."

"Your Honor, furthermore, my client Henrik Baumann stresses the fact that he simply married the plaintiff as a joke."

The judge dimmed his eyes. "Counsel, did you say he married the plaintiff as a joke?"

"Yes, Your Honor."

"Your Honor, this is another lie!" Andrew blurted.

"Counsel Sherman, where are you going with this?"

"We're looking to have the plaintiff deported back to Spain, her home country, Your Honor."

"Deported?" Rachel cried, leaning toward Andrew.

Andrew leaned back toward Rachel. "I'm going to file a continuance. This is turning into a dog and cat fight."

"Your Honor," Sampson interjected. "We would like to file for a continuance so I can further advise my client in light of the circumstances and current climate in the courtroom."

"You want to file a continuance after years of continuances?"

"Yes, Your Honor, to further advise my client."

The judge slammed down his gavel. "Next case, please!"

Andrew collected his notes and Rachel and Alice followed him out of the courtroom.

Alice was exasperated. "That son of a bitch! Rachel, I'd like to take Henrik to Texas with me and have the authorities mistake him for someone on death row. Why didn't we think of getting your citizenship long ago?"

"First thing we need to do is file for your citizenship. Rachel. I never thought he would stoop so low as to have you deported." Andrew shook his head.

"I told you this man is beyond evil. He'll stop at nothing. Where do I have to go to get this taken care of?"

"The Department of Naturalization and Citizenship. Please Rachel, make this a priority."

The next morning Rachel knew that Henrik would be at the hardware store. She had heard from friends that Maryann Gallo was not only spotted at the house when she wasn't there, but was also showing up at the hardware store more frequently. With Mary and Alice, Rachel drove to the courthouse to pick up her application for citizenship. She didn't want to risk Henrik finding any papers in the house. It was a bittersweet feeling. She had always intended to go back to Spain, but her girls were her life, and her life was here.

She now lived in constant fear, worrying that when the girls were away at school, Henrik and his goons could come into the house and beat her or take her away. She worked as many afternoons as she could because she felt safer working than being home alone. She mixed in grocery shopping and other errands during school hours, so she wasn't alone. She had to be on her A game twenty-four seven.

By now it was the end of May. She had had enough of the guns in her home. They symbolized the terror she was living under the hands of a power-hungry control freak. The basement closet in the lower level was loaded with more guns, a powder keg of ammunition, and different sizes of rifles. In desperation to get rid of them, she called her old cleaning lady and asked her and her husband to pick them up and take them to their home for safekeeping.

If she had to endure Henrik's rage, the abusive arguments, at least her girls would be safe.

Another month passed. At the next court hearing, Henrik showed up with plenty of his vicious attacks. By the end of the day, Rachel refused the absurd divorce settlement offer that Henrik's attorney put before the judge. The slanderous comments that Henrik's attorney slung around the courtroom turned Rachel's stomach. Henrik was now calling Rachel a thief for the guns' unknown whereabouts and because of him the courtroom was up for grabs. She had asked Henrik plenty of times to remove the weapons for the safety of her children. Now he was telling lies, claiming she had stolen them and that she was an unfit mother.

"Who's the unfit parent now?" she threw back in his face. "You, Henrik!"

She started getting suspicious of Andrew. She couldn't put her finger on it, but she felt that he had fallen into a similar pattern as her other attorneys. She wasn't looking to fire Andrew but wanted to interview some other attorneys because of her doubts. She started asking other neighbors for names. She felt that she had exhausted possibilities from Alice and Mary.

Maya Hart lived down the street and came to Rachel's rescue. She had been Fallon's kindergarten teacher at the preschool she and Soraya attended. Maya and Bob Hart had four children of their own and were once good friends with Rachel and Henrik. Rachel was close to Maya but in recent years she had been in survival mode with the divorce, abuse, and bullshit kicked in her face by Henrik, and had not spent much time with Maya. Now, Maya and Bob tried to act nonchalant around Henrik but quietly supported Rachel. Maya made some phone calls and found Rachel a few attorneys whom she could interview.

Rachel and Maya drove into the city to meet one of the three attorneys that came highly recommended. His name was Lee Broward, and he was pleasantly handsome and charming. He had a kindness and softness about him that made Rachel feel very comfortable. Lee was instantly smitten by her. Her style, dark coloring, the way she dressed, her Spanish accent. He kept things as professional as he could and really seemed interested in helping her. Lee heard her story, which seemed to get worse by the day.

He read many letters from the Kaffies, letters from family and friends, letters Rachel wrote to the judges, attorneys, and Channel 7 News. All the beatings, infidelities, violence, brutality, and years of mental cruelty. He couldn't believe what Rachel had been through all those years and told her that after weeks of studying the case, he had never seen a defendant as horrific as Henrik and couldn't believe that he spent no time in jail for the atrocities he had dished out to the world.

"Henrik gets away with everything," she said. "He follows no rules, never pays for the consequences, and acts like he's above the law. He stalks me, showing up at work and hunting down new people that I have conversations with. Not only that, he sometimes uses private detectives and his own goons to pry into my private business."

Lee reviewed the affidavits of the witnesses that were at one time close friends of Henrik, who now wanted to testify against him. Lee was also concerned about her girls, wondering how they would grow up with such a monster for a father.

For the next few weeks, Rachel relaxed. She felt she had a new ally and legal confidant. Lee and Rachel had many phone calls, meetings, and he would even stop at the house. He knew Rachel was under so much pressure and stress and he didn't want her using her gas money to meet at his office. The oil crisis was still underway, and he understood that Rachel was trying to scrape up money for all the legal fees that Henrik refused to pay at times.

She couldn't believe that she had met the one and only kind attorney in all of Chicagoland. She didn't fire Andrew yet because of her overwhelming schedule, but she knew it was inevitable. She had struck gold with Lee. She believed for the first time that she had found someone that could finally conquer the beast.

The girls were home one Saturday in mid-June when Lee stopped over. They were used to his visits as he was over quite frequently. Rachel knew that her girls felt a sense of relief when he was in their presence.

The girls ran upstairs from the basement when they heard the doorbell ring. At an early age Fallon had become overprotective of Rachel and always tried to stand guard when her disgraceful father was around. She was relieved to see Lee.

"Hi Fallon… Hi Soraya. How are you girls doing?"

"Good." Fallon smiled.

"Girls, could you do me a favor and let me talk to your mom for a little bit?"

Soraya and Fallon ran back down to the basement to watch *The Brady Bunch* and Lee and Rachel sat in the kitchen.

"Can I make you coffee or something to eat?" Rachel felt the tension in the air and saw a hint of sadness in his eyes. "Is everything okay?"

"I don't know how to tell you this."

"Please..."

"A few days ago, I had a meeting with your husband's attorney. I had a feeling you were going to hire me, and I wanted to see what I was getting myself into. It's standard procedure to speak to the other attorneys and the other parties at times."

"Okay, and..."

"After that meeting I got a visit from your husband."

"I don't believe it…what did the son of a bitch want?"

"He handed me a large sum of money and tried to pay me off. Even before I officially took your case."

"I knew this was happening, but I had no way of proving it! Even if I did, Henrik would weasel his way out of it!"

Rachel pressed her hand against her forehead and held back the tears. After a moment, she got up and nervously walked around the kitchen.

"He told me what to do in court, how to stall, how to give the other attorney the edge. He wanted me to mess up the entire case for you so that he would win with all his demands."

"Oh my God. He's trying to ruin my life! Lee, my children are suffering!"

"Everything you said, all the letters and testimony I've read so far, it's all true. He's gonna try and deport you or put you in the nuthouse. He's trying to take everything away from you that is legally yours through marriage. He wants to kick you out of your home! He says he wants to take the girls but with his lifestyle I don't think he would want that responsibility. This man wants to completely break you."

"He's crazy. And I'm not going to let him take my girls. I'll take my last breath before that happens. I will fight to the death for my home too."

"I believe that Henrik is paying off the judges and all the other attorneys you hired. This is why this divorce has become such a joke."

Rachel sat back down and tried to steady her breath.

"Can he get away with this? Look at everything he's done. I'm a good mom. I never go out unless I'm at work or picking up my girls from school. I can't even think about dating someone else. He would destroy that, too."

"I did a private discovery on him, and it looks like he is about to buy a new home. Now, I don't know if this is a new rental property or if it is a new house for himself."

"He's buying a new home, and he is barely giving me any money for food for the girls."

"That may be a good sign. Maybe he's making plans to move out of this house. Which by the way, I can't believe he has the balls to stay here with you."

He grew quiet before carefully speaking again. "Rachel, in light of all of this with Henrik, I can't take your case."

"Ohh Lee! No." She put her head down on the table.

"I talked with one of the partners at my firm and we both agreed that this was very unethical and that I should walk away. I don't want to get disbarred. I've worked too hard for my career."

"I understand."

"I would never take that money."

"I know, Lee."

"I care about you too much and I worry about those girls."

"So now what?"

"Well, you should probably fire the other attorney that you have and try to find a new one."

"With you Lee, this makes four attorneys so far."

"I know, but I promise you that I will stick by your side as an advisor. Free of charge. I will be here to help you."

"I'm sad to lose you but I understand. I don't want to hurt your career."

"Gotta tell you, Rachel. A lot of corruption runs through Henrik's veins. Pure venom."

"The court system, too."

Lee shook his head in agreement.

After Lee left, Rachel came downstairs to the rec room. "Fallon, I need to talk to you for a minute."

"Okay Mommy."

"If you are ever asked to go to court or talk to a judge. Maybe an attorney."

"Yes Mommy?"

"Well, if they ever ask you who you want to live with. Please tell them that you want to live with me."

"Who else would I live with?"

"Your father!"

"No Mommy, please, I don't want to ever live with him. They can't take me away."

"I know, honey. They will never do it, but I'm worried. Just tell them you want to live with me. Everything will be okay."

"Mommy, Daddy's crazy, isn't he?"

Rachel nodded her head, then reached down and hugged Fallon. She would ask Fallon those questions many times over the coming months. And every time fear would claw at the pit of her stomach, attached to feelings that were much bigger and scarier. "They won't send me to jail, Mama? Will they?"

It broke Rachel's heart. She knew her girls walked from one lily pad to the next, their lives filled with so much uncertainty and fear for what the future held.

Summer was in full swing by now. Rachel had no choice as far as Henrik's right to spend time with her girls wherever he wished. And so, he took Soraya and Fallon to Florida for two weeks. They traveled to Marco Island, Naples, Miami, Key Largo, and all the way to Key West. Rachel always worried that he would lose his temper with the girls and implored them to obey him as much as possible to keep him from exploding. But how could they live up to his standards? Something as simple as laughing too much would set him off. However, they were used to it, and while it caused Rachel unending anxiety, the girls didn't know any better and thought all fathers treated their kids like he did.

Back at home, Rachel was on the hunt with her friends to find yet another attorney. Deep inside she knew that every attorney and judge could be corrupt from here on out, but she had no choice. She was more than exhausted and had to accept whatever came with this debacle. She had prayed every day of her life since she was a little girl, but now prayed harder and with a direct purpose: "Please help me get out of this. And please keep my girls safe."

Later that summer Henrik brought Soraya and Fallon to the farm. It was nearing July 4, 1976, the bicentennial. They swam in the pool, walked the land, roasted marshmallows, and played with their horses. Soraya and Fallon loved the farm, yet Henrik always had a way of letting them know that nothing was really theirs, making Fallon feel that she and her sister were not his real daughters. They were nothing more than second-class citizens when they were with him. It was a strange feeling. It seemed that everyone in Henrik's life was more important than Soraya and Fallon.

Everything he owned was his and he let the girls know it. Yet, at the same time, he always told them that they would inherit the farms one day.

They headed back home in the middle of July. Rachel, with Maya's help, had found another attorney who was supposed to be one of the best in the area. Roger Schofield was a heavyset man who came with great credentials. Roger and Rachel had many meetings and phone calls. Rachel also heard from Lee Broward who told her he had made a few phone calls and had sped up the time to get her citizenship squared away before Henrik could deport her. Lee made good on his promise and on July 27, 1976, Rachel became a citizen of the United States.

Rachel spoke gently to her new attorney Roger about the fact that Henrik had tried to buy her other attorneys.

"That won't happen again," Roger promised her. "Our law firm is too prestigious for him to break."

As August slid into September, October, and November, Rachel had two more grueling court hearing continuances and one more hearing with Henrik. She was given another settlement leaving her with almost nothing but more bills that she could not pay.

"I don't accept this settlement," she told Roger as the judge slammed down his gavel, and said, "This divorce is going to trial!"

14

A Divorce...
Of Course

PART I

Another set of miserable holidays came and went. Henrik was still living in the house and made sure Rachel and the girls all knew it was his, not theirs. Fallon's struggles in school increased and her grades were falling, yet Henrik found time to hypercriticize her for not being a perfect student like him. He relished the fact that he was superior to Fallon in multiple ways; she saw it in his big obnoxious face.

Rachel had secretly told Fallon's teachers about the violence at home, but they didn't investigate further. In that era, it was better to leave things at home and Rachel didn't know where to turn.

Spring of 1977 was in their midst and a number of songs from the album *Rumors* by Fleetwood Mac were playing on a new radio station called the Loop. Some of the lyrics from "Gold Dust Woman" made Fallon wonder: Who was this magical woman they were singing about?

"Rock on ancient queen," she sang. "Follow those who pale in your shadow."

It reminded Fallon of her mother. Everyone paled in her shadow, yet because she had rejected Henrik, he wanted to make her vanish. This song helped Fallon escape her impossible surroundings and she knew the haunting words and melody would follow her for her entire life.

Rachel was nervously waiting for any news on the trial. She called Roger many times to no avail. One afternoon, she received an envelope containing official documents sent to both her and Henrik. She found it to be a bit suspicious because Henrik usually had his mail sent to the hardware store. When she opened the mail, it looked to be foreclosure paperwork for the farmland. All the farmland, all four hundred acres.

She couldn't believe her eyes. She knew that Henrik only had a small amount of mortgage left until the farms were completely paid off. He had told her years ago that the farms would be left to their girls and then their children. It took her a few days to put it all together, but she suddenly understood that she was supposed to get these fake documents in the mail. Even though she and Henrik jointly owned the farms, he was setting things up so that she couldn't touch them. She put the fake documents on his desk in the basement and made sure her friends knew what was happening.

A few days went by, and Henrik called her from the hardware store.

"I'm gonna need you to come to this address tomorrow," he said. "Hang on, let me get it."

"What do I need to do that for?"

"It's a mediation about the guns, so we can get that straightened out."

"There is nothing to straighten out, I told you to get rid of them for the girls' sake. You wouldn't do it. What time, Henrik?"

"2:00 p.m."

"I have to pick up the girls from school at 3:15 and I'm working tomorrow from 10:30 through lunch. Why are you doing this at the last minute?"

"It's just a stupid waitress job and you always get people to pick up the girls for court."

"Yes. Wasted years driving to court and inconveniencing Karin and Tante Annie. What if I don't show up?"

"Then I'll take you to court for the guns. That is my property. I'll sue you for them."

"Who do you think you are? I can't get an attorney at this hour; I can barely get my attorney to call me back."

"You don't need an attorney. It's a quick mediation!" Henrik slammed the phone into the receiver.

Rachel felt so scared she couldn't even get the air out of her lungs to take her next breath. Her nightmares persisted. She'd had the same dream over and over. She was on a small boat; fog was everywhere. She was drifting from the shore when she heard Soraya's and Fallon's voices. They were shouting at her, but she was powerless to get back to them. She kept drifting further away until she was gone. She would wake up out of breath and hurry to their room to make sure they were safe in their beds.

The next morning, she found herself at yet another attorney's office. This time it was Henrik's attorney. She felt the dark, heavy weight of the room. Henrik and the two attorneys were stalling, talking legalese and trying to intimidate her as she looked over the paperwork. While her English had improved, the paperwork was difficult for anyone who wasn't an attorney.

"You're suing me for these guns?"

"Not suing yet! This is just a mediation, Rachel."

"I heard you the first five times about the mediation. I'm looking at it right here," Rachel blurted.

Sherman read off the list of guns and ammunition. "One .30-30 Canadian commemorative rifle. Two 20 gauge shotguns. One under shot muzzleloader. Three 16 gauge shotguns. One 12 gauge shotgun. One antique rifle. One powder flask. One powder horn. Two antique muzzleloader pistol kits. One munition molding kit. Two .25 caliber automatic pistols. One

.60 caliber musket. Five cases of assorted shotgun shells and small arms ammunition."

"That's right, Rachel. You took them. They're mine and I want them back. Or you are paying me for all of it!" Henrik pounded his fist on the table.

"Are you three years old, Henrik? Pouting like a little child because you don't get your toys back!"

"Don't play games with me Rachel. You were dead to me the day you asked for a divorce. I'm also keeping your fur coats hostage until you pay me! You know the ones that are in storage. I'm not paying to release those coats!"

One of the Sherman partners spoke up. "Let's try and just settle this, folks."

"I have to pay you $2,000 for these guns? Where am I supposed to get that kind of money!" Rachel's eyes widened in disgust.

"Maybe from your hostess or waitress job. Or whatever you do."

Rachel heard an off-color snicker in the background noise. "How dare you make fun of me. I'm trying to take care of my kids."

"They're my kids, too!"

"You don't care about them. All you care about is your bullshit and your money!"

Sherman tried to intervene. "Rachel, there's more." Sherman proceeded to read the next line item of charges.

"Rachel Baumann shall pay unto Henrik Baumann the sum of $1,290.76 to reimburse Henrik for the long-distance phone charges made by Rachel Baumann subsequent to the order of the court, commanding her from making long distance calls without first obtaining Henrik's written consent."

Rachel stood up. "You egotistical, petty control freak! These are calls to my mother and father!"

Henrik jumped out of his seat and flipped over the table. He ran to Rachel and grabbed the collar around her neck. Papers flew. The attorneys backed away and stood in shock.

"You sign these *Goddamn* papers Rachel! YOU'RE GONNA PAY ME WHAT YOU OWE!" Henrik shook Rachel's head and neck.

Rachel screamed, "Let go of me, you animal! I'm not paying you and I'm not signing anything. Do you understand! It will take me years to pay this off!" Rachel jostled herself free from Henrik's grip.

Sherman spoke with cracks in his voice. "Henrik, settle down, we will handle this the right way."

Rachel's makeup had smeared from her collar to the top of her dress. She sternly eyed Henrik and the attorneys.

"I'm not paying this, Henrik. One day your girls will know what a piece of shit you really are!"

Henrik lowered his voice into a menacing sneer. "You have been the loser these last few years and you're gonna stay the loser. I'm gonna win all the way. Do you hear me?"

Rachel slammed the office door, held back her tears, and walked down to her car. *I'm alive because I didn't keep quiet,* she told herself. *I'm stronger and braver than I ever thought I could be. I'm fighting so that my girls will never be treated like garbage. They will be respected, powerful, and educated. And they will thrive.*

A week went by, and Rachel, when she wasn't working or taking care of the girls, was busy talking to the friends who would soon be witnesses in her trial. Georgia Schumer called and asked for her to meet at the preschool so they could go to lunch. Elizabeth Conner also tagged along. Elizabeth was a good acquaintance of Rachel's. They had known each other from the hardware store. Rachel never looked for a spy, but she always had people who kept an eye on any surfacing drama. Elizabeth was a regular customer at the hardware store and knew things of interest.

"I can't tell you how good it feels to get out for lunch and live a little," said Rachel. "I can't wait until this nightmare is over."

"You look great as always," said Georgia. "And I love your outfit."

"Thank you. It's the last thing I spend money on, these days," said Rachel. "I sometimes don't have enough for food."

"Please," said Georgia. "If there is anything you need for you or the girls, let me know. I don't understand how this man can own every building on the block with his hardware store, the fish market, the preschool building, and everything. Yet, his wife and children don't have enough for their bills."

"That goes double for me. If we can help you with anything," Liz interceded.

"It's a complicated situation for us," said Georgia. "Henrik is one of my husband's best friends, or at least until that horrible incident with our daughter. They also do business together, so it's been very difficult."

Liz sipped her iced tea and added, "It's so hard to tell you what we know about Henrik's behavior. You already know what a dirtbag he is."

"I understand," sighed Rachel. "That's why I'm fighting so hard."

"We try to stay polite in front of Henrik to keep the peace. Then he puts on the charm, and we seem to forgive him, all the while knowing about the horrible behavior he's shown you."

"I understand," said Rachel, "But what are you trying to tell me?"

"I don't know how to say this."

"It's okay, you can talk to me."

"Do you remember long ago when you and Henrik got married? Do you remember his ex-wife, Carol?"

"Yes, of course."

"Well, Henrik was still married to her while he was married to you."

"No, I know he was divorced. I don't believe it." She felt the room spin. "I guess I do."

"Many of us knew her and we hated not telling you the truth, but it was a complex situation. Especially at first when there was more of a language barrier."

"So, you're saying that on top of everything else, he's a...I forget how to say this word."

"Bigamist?"

"Yes, that's it! Georgia, that's the word. I feel sick. I better let my attorney know immediately."

"Do you want some tea or Seven Up?" Georgia called the waitress over for some hot tea.

Rachel put her hands up to her forehead and her elbows on the table. "Why didn't anyone tell me?"

"I know sweetie, I'm sorry."

"He has no morals, no principles. He needs to be locked up in a hospital."

"I'm telling you this now because with all the stunts he's pulled, I'm worried about the trial."

"The trial?"

"He could use this against you."

"But, Georgia, he did this, not me! It could go against him. I could sue him for bigamy!"

"Some of your witnesses knew that he was married to you and Carol at the same time. Plus, you know how Henrik can twist things around to make it look like your fault. He is a master at that."

"I'm assuming Karin and Tante Annie knew about the bigamy but not Mary, Alice, and Maya?"

"I think you're right."

"There's more." Liz pushed her plate forward.

"Oh, geez Liz, I don't know how much more I can take."

"I'm telling you this because I'm your friend and you might be able to use this one in court, too. Do you remember me telling you about Maryann Gallo always hanging around the hardware store? I know your neighbors say they've seen her around your house."

"Yes Liz, so many sleazy stories about Henrik. It makes me sick to think I had two children with him."

Liz took Rachel's hand to comfort her. "This story is worse. I hate that this is coming from me, but the hardware store crew trusts me, so I hear things. Do you remember maybe six weeks ago, Henrik went to the farm?"

"Yes, I think that's when he was putting together the fake foreclosure papers for the land."

"Foreclosure papers? Well, I was told by one of the hardware store employees that Henrik took Tammy. You know, Tammy from the hardware store?"

"Yeah, I see the way Tammy looks at Henrik."

"He took Tammy to the farm and spent a few days with her there."

Rachel paused for a moment before she started speaking. "Tammy is sixteen years old! Where is her mother with all this? Oh my God, this girl doesn't know what she is doing!"

"Her mother pushed her to go to the farm," Liz blurted out. "From what I heard, Tammy's mom needed some money for bills and Henrik promised them extra money in Tammy's check. It's statutory rape! This man has to be stopped and Tammy's mother should be ashamed of herself. That is prostituting your daughter, so that you can pay the bills. He's a criminal!"

"We all know they weren't roasting marshmallows up there," said Rachel.

And as awful as it was, they laughed, breaking the tension. Henrik's sleazy affairs were the least of Rachel's worries. She was now preparing herself for bigger concerns such as losing her house, her girls, and half the assets owed to her. On top of that she worried that Henrik could indeed kill her, or even one day, her girls.

In early August, Rachel received a letter from her attorney's office. Her trial date was set for Monday August 8, 1977. She sat for a moment, then she called Lee Broward and her friends who were also witnesses. Lee also gave Rachel some advice to get an attorney from the public defender's office to watch over the trial. This attorney's name was Samuel Nelson. Rachel and Lee knew that Henrik was going to try and pull some of his stunts; she felt comfortable with a guardian attorney watching over things.

Per Lee's advice, Rachel hired Samuel without Roger Schofield knowing. Samuel secretly helped prepare witnesses for trial. He assisted in gathering information about appraisals of Henrik's land, properties, and real estate. Samuel would sit in court every day of the trial to make sure that things would go smoothly. Rachel and Lee thought they had an ironclad method to ensure checks and balances within the court system.

The court date grew closer. Rachel tried calling her attorney, leaving many messages. When Roger finally called back, Rachel knew that the stage was set. She had all her witnesses, paperwork, and petitions ready.

On the morning of the trial, Rachel dropped the girls off at school. Karin and Tante Annie were both testifying on different days, so she had an alternating pickup schedule. On the first day of the trial, Tante Annie was testifying, and she drove with Rachel. Right out of the gate Tante Annie was a great witness since she had known the Baumann family for over forty years and only knew Rachel since she had married Henrik. The witness schedule played out like a symphony. Most of the witnesses were Henrik's friends first and now they all had damaging testimony against him. The morning of the trial was beautiful and clear, yet Rachel was filled with dread.

When Rachel walked into the courtroom and sat next to her attorney, she looked around and smelled the corruption. She noticed Samuel Nelson making eye contact with her and breathed in a sigh of relief. Henrik made his way in with his attorneys, Damien and Drew Sherman; Drew was Damien's brother, whom Henrik had hired as an intimidation tactic.

Many of Rachel's friends were sitting in the courtroom gallery. Judge Bernard Malson entered and instantly Rachel's radar was on high alert. She felt apprehension in every cell of her body. This was a new judge.

The bailiff called, "All rise."

"You may all be seated," said Judge Malson, "Baumann versus Baumann, case number 714556."

Rachel made the sign of the cross as the judge briefly addressed the court with a quick synopsis of the case. The trial would consist of two sections, the first part was the divorce, or annulment, he said. The second part was the supplemental settlement decree.

"Annulment!" Rachel whispered loudly to Roger. "Where did that come from?"

Roger whispered back, "Don't worry. Henrik's never going to get an annulment with two kids and a ten-year marriage. No judge in the country would allow that. He's playing dirty like we thought."

Rachel caught glimpses of her friends shaking their heads with disgust.

Judge Malson called Rachel's attorney, "Counsel Roger Schofield, you may proceed with your opening statement for the plaintiff, counter-defendant."

Roger stood. "Thank you, Your Honor. Rachel F. Baumann is a good mother whose sole purpose is to take care of her children and be a loving wife to her husband, Henrik Baumann. She cooks for them, takes the kids to school, spends time with them. She's always at home, never goes out at night. She is a model mother and wife and from what I have been told…a great friend. She had the perfect life, until one day, years ago, Rachel started noticing behavioral changes in Henrik. He was becoming disrespectful, challenging, and abusive. She was noticing one affair after another with multiple women.

"Henrik would flirt with other women in front of her and they would carry on as if Henrik and the other woman were a couple instead of the other way around. Many friends and acquaintances of Rachel would witness Henrik's multiple indiscretions. It was degrading. On many occasions, friends and neighbors have complained about Henrik molesting and sexually assaulting two different minor teenage girls, and on other accounts Henrik was known to have consensual sex with a minor while still married to the plaintiff.

"Henrik began hitting, kicking, and beating Rachel. On a few occasions the oldest child was a witness and, in some situations, both Baumann children were present for the violence. Rachel filed for divorce immediately after the first beating incident, leaving her with a headache, bump on the head, and a bruised and bloodied leg. She knew this was an impossible existence for her young girls. Since the beginning of their marriage, Rachel had noticed many of Henrik's other dangerous qualities and wrongdoings. Even the very real suspicion of murder seemed to surround him.

"Then came tax evasion. Mr. Baumann kept three separate accounting books for his businesses and hardware store, forging Rachel's name on official documents and taking her name off multiple properties in joint tenancy and bank trusts. Henrik told Rachel that his hardware store was worth $20,000 when in reality it is worth $135,000 plus the building, which he also owns. Henrik sold guns illegally in Mexico and in his hardware store. Had multiple bank accounts in Mexico, Wisconsin, and in five other banks in the Chicago area, with much suspicion of money laundering.

"Henrik has made many attempts on Rachel's life. He cut the brake lines on her car, tried to drown her in a bathtub, dragged her up a flight of stairs by her collar to beat her in her bedroom. He threatened to deport her out of the country, attempted to lock her up in a mental hospital, and told another trial judge that he married Rachel for a joke. Many restraining orders and orders of protection failed to do their job. Squad cars and police officers were frequently at the Baumann's home leaving the daughters Fallon and Soraya scared and confused. Henrik also coaxed friends to place harassing phone calls, frightening her and threatening her life. At the hands of Henrik, mental cruelty spread like a disease throughout their marriage. Henrik is in fact a storm of deception, destroying all in his path.

"Furthermore, when Henrik and Rachel married in May of 1967, Henrik was married to Carol Baumann. Rachel did not know of the marriage until in passing Henrik told Rachel that his divorce with Carol was just about to go through. Rachel was in shock, but she trusted Henrik. She was also expecting a child."

Roger paused for a few seconds, cleared his throat, and continued.

"This is only a fraction of the many lies and atrocities committed against this woman and her children, Fallon and Soraya. Your Honor, may I approach the bench?"

Roger walked up to the judge with a small stack of papers in his hand.

"Your Honor, what I have here are letters written by many families, friends, and neighbors who used to be close to Henrik and are now sharing what they've seen perpetrated against Rachel Baumann. I also have a few letters from Rachel explaining in detail about the abuse, affairs, and mental domination at the hands of the defendant. All of these letters are a true testament of her great character and shed light on who she really is. I would like to place them in your hand as evidence for the plaintiff."

The judge took the stack of letters and looked at them as if they didn't matter.

"Your Honor, Rachel wants a fair divorce, a fair settlement, a safe home, and full custody of her children. She deserves peace and to move on with her life. This maddening life for Rachel and her children can be no more. I believe the court will look upon her with favor. You might say that some of this is hearsay, but I believe that you will find that Rachel's witnesses will bring clarity on the truth. Henrik Baumann is a compulsive liar, a narcissist, controlling, manipulative, and toxic, with an explosive temper. He will stop at nothing to make sure that Rachel and the children have no home or a dime to their name. All of this is for the sake of Henrik's money and in retaliation for Rachel asking for her freedom. Henrik wants you to believe that he is a good businessman and a good person, when in reality he is nothing more than a cunning and depraved criminal. All of these atrocious behaviors are at the epicenter of Henrik's true character. Thank you, Your Honor."

Roger walked back to his seat while Judge Malson announced Henrik's attorney, counselor Sherman, to begin opening statements. The courtroom was quiet from the unbearable tension and coolness in the room.

"Thank you, Your Honor!" Sherman's overconfident voice boomed into the courtroom. "This woman, Rachel F. Baumann, is a gold digger. Yes, a gold digger!"

The courtroom groaned as Sherman pointed his finger at Rachel. Samuel Nelson made eye contact with Rachel and shook his head.

"Rachel Baumann wants to help herself to *everything* that Henrik Baumann has worked for his entire life! This wasn't even a real marriage. Rachel knew from the start that Henrik was officially married to Carol Baumann. Rachel wants you to believe that she is a good woman. A perfect woman without any fault in this dilemma!" Sherman continued with his opening statement, throwing Rachel under the bus, one lie after another. Sherman portrayed Rachel as an unfit mother with false accusations. He told the court that Rachel screamed and yelled at her girls, that she would only feed them fast food and TV dinners, and that she never cooked. He told the court that Rachel had men over to the house. He was grabbing at anything that he thought would stick in the judge's ear.

Sherman continued with the opening statement, closing by saying that Rachel and her girls didn't need a large house on Henrik's dime. Rachel was capable of working and a small apartment would suit their needs. He was planting the seeds for the settlement trial once the divorce was granted. He repeated that Henrik was married to both Rachel and Carol at the same time, leaving family and friends in confusion as to why he kept pointing out the fact of the bigamy.

Once Sherman's opening statement was complete, Judge Malson directed Roger to examine his client. Rachel fidgeted nervously with her notes until Roger called her name. She was sworn in by Judge Malson and took her seat in the witness stand.

"Can you state your name for the court please?" said Roger.

"Yes, Rachel F. Baumann."

"Rachel. Where did you meet your husband, Henrik Baumann?"

"In Laredo…Laredo Texas."

"Was your courtship and marriage with Henrik ever happy?"

"Yes, at the beginning it was very happy. I have a stack of letters; love notes and postcards from Henrik telling me how much he loved me. Most of the letters are in Spanish because at the beginning I did not speak English."

"Your Honor, let the court know that I'm holding a stack of love notes written in Spanish by the defendant. We will need a court translator to read them." Schofield held up the letters and notes for the judge to see.

Judge Malson quickly yelled out, "Noted."

"Why are you seeking a divorce from your husband?"

"Well, I noticed within a few years of our marriage that Henrik had become very…it's hard for me to say this word with my accent. Cocky!"

"Cocky. Rachel, that's correct."

"Henrik was becoming very arrogant, trying to push me around, becoming very disrespectful. Almost treating me like a child. Then things got worse, and he thought I was blind to the fact that he was having multiple affairs, but I knew. Things got worse still, and he started beating me, and got bolder and abused me terribly in front of my children. He has threatened my life many times. My oldest daughter suffers the most from the violence she has witnessed. He's a compulsive liar, he cheats. He purposefully took my name off property that we bought together. He does sleazy things that are disgusting to me. No one should have to live under these conditions just to stay married. I could go on for another month about why I want a divorce, but this should be more than enough."

"At the time of your marriage, did you know that Henrik was married to Carol Baumann?"

Rachel moved her mouth closer to the microphone. "No! I thought their divorce went through."

Roger continued with his questioning for a while longer before he told the judge, "No further questions at this time, Your Honor."

The judge asked Sherman to cross-examine the plaintiff.

Sherman took the floor. "Mrs. Baumann, why did you really marry my client, Mr. Baumann?"

"At the time we fell in love, and we were going to have a baby," Rachel spoke truthfully.

"Mrs. Baumann, wasn't it more so that you could become an American citizen?"

"No, I loved my country of Spain."

"Wasn't it because you knew my client was wealthy and you knew that in divorcing him, you could take a lot of his money?"

Gasps, groans, and rumbles echoed throughout the courtroom. Judge Malson pounded his gavel.

"*No!* I had my own money in Spain and a good life. I didn't marry Henrik for the money!"

"Mrs. Baumann, did Henrik let you know a few months after you were married that he was, in fact, still married to Carol Baumann?"

"I thought his divorce was a done deal!"

"Just answer the question, Mrs. Baumann." Sherman knew the exact picture he was painting of Rachel in front of the judge.

"Yes!" Rachel winced every time she heard the name Baumann.

"No further questions Your Honor."

The court took a quick recess. Rachel got up from the witness stand and walked back to the counsel table. She felt uneasy and leaned over to whisper to Roger, "I feel sick to my stomach."

"Everyone feels that way when they're getting cross-examined. It's normal Rachel."

"Why are there so many questions about Henrik's marriage to Carol?"

Roger shrugged his shoulders and they both walked out into the hallway.

Court was quickly back in session and Judge Malson spoke, "I call to the witness stand Mr. Henrik J. Baumann."

Henrik was sworn in by the judge and Sherman started with his baseline inquiries. "Henrik, would you say that your wife Rachel knew that your divorce with Carol was not final when you married her?"

"Yes absolutely!"

Noise rumbled in the courtroom. Henrik was calm and on his best behavior in front of the judge.

Schofield interjected, "Objection, Your Honor. It was clearly stated in the testimony that Rachel knew after…"

"Overruled. Let the defendant finish his testimony." Judge Malson tapped his gavel.

Rachel whispered loudly to Roger. "He's lying…lying!"

The judge quickly interrupted. "Mr. Schofield, is there a problem with your client?"

"No, Your Honor, she just whispered a comment."

"Well, tell Mrs. Baumann to whisper on her own time. Not in my courtroom."

"Yes, Your Honor." Rachel and Roger glanced at each other, dismayed at the unfair reprimand. Samuel Nelson looked her way again, slightly shaking his head.

Sherman's questioning continued. Rachel sank down in her chair hearing one lie after another. Sherman questioned Henrik on how he treated his children. Henrik boasted about how close he was with his girls and that he had a great relationship with them. He talked about their travels and the places he took them, the only truth that came out of his mouth.

As Sherman's questioning continued, Henrik's testimony grew weak, distorted, and he was unsure of dates and facts.

Next, it was Roger's turn to cross-examine Henrik. Every question, the abuse and the numerous affairs, was met with a new lie, a new story. It didn't matter how many witnesses Rachel had gathered to testify against the cruelty, violence, indiscretions, and bigamy; it only mattered what the judge thought. Roger tried to catch him in many of his deceptions, Henrik always spun it around to make Rachel the one to blame.

The court took an hour-long lunch break. As Henrik walked out of the courtroom, he noticed next-door neighbors Lorraine and Rick Hallson, who had come to testify against him. Lorraine had rescued Rachel many times when Henrik was on one of his violent rampages. While Lorraine was another hero to Rachel, along with all the other friends and neighbors who came to her rescue, for Henrik, Lorraine would become another victim of his cruelty.

After the lunch break, court was back in session and Roger called the first witness for the plaintiff, Tante Annie Clemens.

"Mrs. Clemens, how long have you known the Baumann family?"

Tante Annie trembled. "About forty years, sir."

"How well would you say you know them?"

"Oh, our families have been very close. The best of friends for many years. I'm very close with Mr. and Mrs. Baumann too, Henrik's parents."

"But Mrs. Clemens, you are here testifying against Henrik Baumann?"

"Yes sir, this is breaking my heart, but I must do what's right. Rachel is a good woman." Tante Annie broke down in tears.

"Mrs. Clemens, would you like to take a short recess?"

"No sir…I have to get this out."

"Mrs. Clemens, when would you say the trouble started between Henrik and Rachel?"

"I would say midway into 1973. I believe things were bad before that time, but that's when Rachel came to us with the troubles."

The bailiff walked over to Annie Clemens with a box of tissues.

"Mrs. Clemens, please tell me in your own words some of the incidents that occurred between the plaintiff and the defendant."

"This is so painful…" Tante Annie was crying in between her sentences.

"Try your best."

"Henrik beat up Rachel several times just because she didn't want to sign some blank papers. We all didn't understand it at the time but now we believe it is because Henrik was trying to get a match of her signature so that he could forge her name to take her off many of his properties. Rachel was all black and blue with bruises, she was limping and still bleeding when we saw her right after that first incident." Rumblings could be heard in the courtroom from the reaction of Tante Annie's testimony.

"Where was she bleeding from?"

"Her leg. Years later you can still see the horrible dent in Rachel's shin bone and scarring from where Henrik kicked her!" Tante Annie sobbed, amidst more grumbles from the courtroom.

"Then what happened?"

"I told Rachel to go to Henrik's parents so that they could see what kind of son they have. Rachel went to Henrik's mother, Ethel, but she begged Rachel not to tell his father about the incident. Rachel came to me much later telling me that the reason why Ethel Baumann did not want to tell Henrik Sr. about the incident was because he would have put a stop to this violence."

The court gave Tante Annie a minute to let out her tears and catch her breath. She wiped her nose and continued.

"Rachel knew Ethel would never do anything about the beatings and violence. Ethel never liked Rachel much and wanted to send her back to Spain. Rachel said that this was a form of Ethel's manipulation. Rachel mentioned that she believed that Ethel was the anchor of abuse and discord in the Baumann family. Rachel told me that she learned a new phrase since she has been in this country, and she called Ethel 'a wolf in sheep's clothing.' I believe Rachel now. I don't understand how this family...these Baumanns can be so cruel to this beautiful woman."

"Your Honor, I object!" interjected Sherman. "This woman, Annie Clemens, is now saying disparaging comments about the defendant's mother?"

"Your Honor, this witness is simply painting a character profile for the defendant and if that has any involvement with his mother...I'd like to proceed," Roger Schofield quickly exclaimed.

"Sustained. Mr. Schofield, have your witness move on please."

Roger continued, "Mrs. Clemens, can you think of another situation where Rachel was in harm's way?"

"Yes sir...there were many. There was one day when Henrik hit her over the head, and she felt momentarily woozy. Out of sheer terror she ran with her girls and came over to our house and they slept over. The next day, she filed for divorce."

"How did that go over with Henrik?"

"Your Honor! Schofield is leading the witness!" Sherman barked.

"I'll allow it. Sherman, you will have your turn."

Roger continued, "Mrs. Clemens, you can answer now."

"It was terrible!" Tante Annie wiped her eyes.

"When Rachel filed for divorce, she was terrified of what Henrik might do to her and the girls. Rachel begged my husband and me to go over to her house. Rachel wanted us to stay overnight in the spare bedroom. Oh, this is terrible!

"When Henrik came home...he came after my husband and warned us of what he would do to us if we got involved. Henrik's personality changed instantly, almost to the point of insanity. He spoke violently and began throwing things that were in his way. Henrik told us in the meanest voice I had ever heard. 'I'm going to have to ask you to leave my house.'

"My husband told him, 'You will have to throw us out, then!' It was such a heated exchange. Most of the confrontations with Henrik are heated. I was sick to my stomach. All my life I've never witnessed so much turmoil like I have in the presence of Henrik these past few years!"

Tante Annie stopped for a moment to catch her breath. She told the attorney that this was too much for her. The bailiff brought her some water. Tante Annie continued, still wiping her tears.

"My husband and I stayed there and talked to Henrik for hours to calm him down. I don't recognize the Henrik that I knew as a child. I saw a few temper tantrums of his, but he is an adult now. I don't understand the violent way he behaves. What I'm saying here is God's truth! I don't understand why he would treat his beautiful wife and children this way! He tortures them!" Tante Annie's voice was broken up and she began to sob into her tissues.

Roger gave her a minute to collect herself. "Mrs. Clemens, how would you say Rachel is as a person, and how is she with the girls, Fallon and Soraya?"

"Oh my gosh. Rachel's home is always in perfect order. She is neat and clean. She is a good, honest person. She is a wonderful mother to her two daughters. She takes them to church, picks them up from school. She cooks for them and spends time watching TV with them. Whenever she can scrape up some money, she takes the girls shopping and they all love going to the Pickwick Theater in Park Ridge. It's such a shame, Henrik has so much money and Rachel has to beg him to do the right thing." Tante Annie picked up her tissues again.

Tante Annie turned to Judge Malson. "Please judge, someone has to help Rachel. This is terrible!"

Judge Malson slammed down on his gavel. "Mr. Schofield, please control your witness."

"Yes, Your Honor. Mrs. Clemens, did Rachel know that Henrik was married to Carol at the time of their marriage?"

"No, she did not, Mr. Schofield! The reason I know this is because quickly after we all met her, Henrik and Rachel were expecting a child and planning a wedding. It was a whirlwind. Our entire family, my niece Karin, and her husband, were all embarrassed, so we didn't say anything to Rachel about Carol. Everything happened so fast, and we thought the process of Henrik's divorce was underway. Rachel told us later that she knew that the divorce with Carol was a done deal. She believed in Henrik. We recently apologized to Rachel for our silence. We did not mean her any harm. We love Rachel!"

"Mrs. Clemens, how would you say that Henrik is with his girls? Does he spend a lot of time with them?"

"Just recently he started traveling with the girls a bit more and they go to the farm, but on a day-to-day basis he's never around. He works all the time and Rachel says he is even gone on Sundays. When Henrik does come home it's sometimes at 3:00 a.m. Henrik is not a huge drinker so what do you think he's doing at 3:00 a.m.? Any way you slice it, it just adds up to trouble. In my eyes, he's not a good father."

"No further questions for this witness Your Honor." Roger walked back to his table.

From the other end of the courtroom at the counsel's table, Henrik glared at Tante Annie as Damien Sherman took the floor.

Tante Annie begged the court for a break. They took a ten-minute recess. Rachel consoled and hugged her, knowing how hard it was for Tante Annie to put herself on the line to defend her. Rachel knew that the Clemens and Kaffie families had turned their back on this bully. They stood up for Rachel and the girls, they stood up for what was right. They put a spotlight on the ugliness and the darkness that shrouded their circumstances. They were heroes to Rachel for they spoke the truth.

Court was back in session and Damien Sherman was back in action.

"Mrs. Clemens, did you ever see Henrik Baumann kick Rachel in the leg?"

"What?"

"Did... you... ever... see... Henrik... kick... or... strike... Rachel?" His voice was loud, obnoxious, mocking, and intended to throw elderly Tante Annie into a panic.

Tante Annie put her head down on the table to catch her breath, then popped her head up like a gopher out of a hole. "Well, no, but I knew!"

"No further questions Your Honor."

The stunned and weepy Tante Annie stepped down off the witness stand.

Walking back to her seat, she couldn't help but look at Henrik's face. She thought to herself, *Real men do not beat their wives, terrorize their children, and leave them begging for necessities.*

None of Henrik's witnesses showed up that day and instead of adjourning early they found a court officer who could speak Spanish and interpret the love letters that Henrik had sent to Rachel. Roger called the court officer up to the stand and she was sworn in like the rest of the witnesses.

The letters read, "Rachel, I love you more than you will ever know and I can take you away from everything and we can build a life together in our beautiful new home in Chicago."

Henrik's face nearly melted off when he heard almost thirty private letters being read out loud in court. He couldn't believe that Rachel had kept them. Each of those notes confirmed that he had been in love with her. And with that, court was adjourned for the day.

Rachel, drained and exhausted, held Tante Annie's hand as they walked out of court.

In the hall, she briefly talked with Roger. "Why can't I sue Henrik for bigamy again?" she asked.

"Because we're trying to get a larger divorce settlement."

"Can't we send him to jail?"

"Listen, if he goes to jail, he won't be able to pay you."

Rachel caught a glimpse of Roger as he walked back into the court-room. She was too tired to ask, but it seemed strange, and she wondered why he headed back there. They would have a long day tomorrow, but she was comforted to know that Mary, Karin, and Alice would be in court in the morning and that Tante Annie would pick up the girls from school.

15

A Divorce... Of Course

Later, after the trial that evening, Rachel picked up the phone and confided in Lee Broward. They talked about all the things that happened in court and he sounded optimistic about what he heard.

Rachel did not see Henrik pull up to the house, but he got out of the car and walked next door to Lorraine Hallson's home. He rang her doorbell, and she stepped outside, a bit puzzled as to why he was there.

"Lorraine," he said, slowly and deliberately. "That is my house next door and I'm going to live there for a long time, so I don't want any trouble with you two." He moved closer.

"I don't know what you mean?"

"What I mean is I don't want to see you in court tomorrow, or ever again. Do I make myself clear?"

Lorraine instantly felt sick to her stomach, and suddenly she fully understood the depth of fear Rachel had experienced all these years.

"I know where you work, and I will personally get you fired from your job. Do you understand? Your job will be gone. No questions asked. When I want something done, it happens. Do we understand each other?"

Lorraine was now shaking. "I'm telling my husband."

"What is your weak, sick fuck husband gonna do? I told you once, mind your own business, and that goes for your husband, too!"

Trembling, Lorraine walked back into her house and watched Henrik drive away. She knew she couldn't go to court, and she didn't know how she would tell Rachel.

The next morning court started late because Henrik was not on time. Rachel was growing suspicious. Something wasn't right with this trial. And why was Henrik showing up all of a sudden? Roger had also shown up late and barely said a word to her. It seemed odd, but she was now days without sleep and needed to trust him.

The moment Henrik walked into the courtroom, so did Judge Malson. "All rise," he said, and the second day of the trial began.

Roger took the floor first and called Karin Kaffie up to the stand.

"Mrs. Kaffie, when did you start noticing any issues or incidents between Henrik and Rachel?"

Since Karin and Tante Annie lived together on separate floors, she shared many of the same stories Tante Annie had shared the day before. Karin also had a no-nonsense, straightforward approach that was hard for any attorney to wrangle. Her voice was full of power and conviction, and she was focused on the job she had been called to do.

Karin's similar testimony boded well for the trial and gave Tante Annie much credibility. Karin reiterated a lot of the abuse and psychological damage that Henrik inflicted on Rachel. She confirmed the fact that Rachel and her girls slept over from time to time out of fear of retaliation from the violent Henrik. She also made clear that Rachel did not know about Henrik's marriage to Carol until it was too late.

She had validated that her entire family, her husband, Onkel Paul, and

Tante Annie, had all begged Henrik not to do Rachel any further harm. Rachel was a great person and loving mother, and Karin made it clear that she wanted justice done with this debauchery.

Roger continued questioning Karin, who began sharing some of Henrik's disturbing dispositions.

"Tante Annie, Onkel Paul, and I sat one day with Henrik at our home, and we talked to him about his outrageous temper and uncontrollable rage. We told him that it was not normal for him to go from completely calm to erupting into a violent explosion within seconds, throwing things, destroying property, and smashing furniture; not to mention the violence and abuse against his wife!"

Sherman rebuked, "Objection, Your Honor! Do we have any proof that this violence even happened? Do we have any pictures of the smashed furniture?"

"Counsel Schofield, do you have any pictures of this smashed furniture?" Judge Malson questioned sarcastically.

Roger nervously looked around the room and locked eyes with Rachel, and then looked back at the judge. "No, Your Honor. Not currently."

"Have your witness move forward. Please redirect."

"Yes, Your Honor. Mrs. Kaffie, can you please continue without any indications of smashed furniture."

Rachel couldn't believe that Roger did not object. Henrik was famous for flipping over tables, throwing chairs, and hurling paperwork in every direction. She noticed that Roger didn't have as much of an edge today. She could sense that something was off, something was different with him.

Karin continued, "Well, you can ignore the fact that Henrik violently destroys furniture and everything in his path all you want..." Karin knew exactly what she was doing. "...But I told Henrik that I feel sorry for him, and I think he needs a doctor. I've seen a change in Henrik, or maybe I never looked that close before. I told him that the way he treats his wife, children, and my family has to stop. It is like Henrik is a bag of hot air, shutting everyone down, firing insults faster than a machine gun. He also has to let everyone know how smart and educated he is, always needing and demanding acceptance and praise from everyone. Henrik is always talking everyone's ear off. You could hook him up to a wind turbine and he could power an entire city with his incessant blabbering." The courtroom suddenly burst into laughter.

"Your Honor, I object! This is classic defamation of character!" Sherman shouted. Henrik squirmed in his seat and shot a nasty look toward Karin.

Roger interjected, "Your Honor…"

Judge Malson responded, "I'll allow it! This sounds interesting."

The courtroom momentarily turned into the Wild West. Karin didn't flinch. "Thank you, Your Honor and Mr. Schofield, I was saying that Henrik talked everyone's ear off, didn't let anyone get a word in edgewise, took over all conversations. Almost like he is a supercharged talking machine."

The courtroom continued with momentary laughter. Henrik glared at Karin.

Karin continued, "Anyway, what I'm getting at is that this rage, these behaviors of Henrik are manipulative, controlling, and very abusive. Henrik has some sort of self-inflated self-worth. Some kind of disturbing personality disorder."

"Your Honor! I object! Is this witness a psychological expert who understands personality disorders?" Sherman roared.

Giggles and rumbling erupted again. Judge Malson tapped his gavel. Rachel had a momentary sparkle in her eye and smiled at Karin steamrolling Henrik in her testimony.

Sherman continued, "Your Honor, I asked that this witness be excluded from the courtroom!"

Roger smugly spoke, "No further questions, Your Honor."

Judge Malson sighed like he couldn't be bothered and let Karin walk off the stand and back to her seat. Rachel looked around the room and was confused about the way all the officials, the judge, and the attorneys in the courtroom were acting. She couldn't quite put her finger on it, but she was sure that they knew something she didn't. There was no sincerity. Things were sloppy, and the trial seemed to have a phony structure around it. Still, she was cautiously optimistic about what Karin had said on the stand.

Hours moved forward until finally one of Henrik's friends was called to the stand. Chuck Gibson had narrow eyes, an odd-shaped head, and brown greasy hair. Rachel knew Chuck was addicted to cocaine and she had pegged him as the type of guy that she would never ever leave alone with her daughters.

Chuck owned a cement company and had a second home in Mexico, which he later sold to buy a house in Florida. He had a lot of dealings with Henrik working on projects for his apartment buildings.

Sherman started his baseline questioning and then probed deeper into Rachel and Henrik's relationship. Rachel heard Chuck tell one disheartening lie after another, with many inaccuracies and carelessness in dates and times of events. Shockingly she did not hear one objection from Roger as the untrue stories unraveled in the courtroom.

Roger took the floor. "Mr. Gibson, can you please clarify how you know that Rachel was, in fact, aware that Henrik was married to Carol at the time of their marriage?"

"Rachel was over at the house on Pittsburgh with Henrik. I think it was Rachel's first time there. I happened to be pouring the cement for their new driveway and…"

Roger interrupted, "What was the date on that?"

Chuck fumbled with his notes. "Uhm…yeah, it was January 8, 1966."

"You mean to tell me that you poured concrete in January, in Chicago? That's almost impossible. Concrete doesn't set up in that weather."

Rachel mouthed to Roger, "He's lying."

Chuck was antsy. He fidgeted in his seat and mumbled, "Uhm…uhhh, sure it does."

"May I remind you, Mr. Gibson, that you are under oath. Judge Malson, let it be noted that my legal team will verify the weather on that date in January."

Roger resumed, "Mr. Gibson, please continue."

"Uhhh…yeah, well, I was at the house pouring the cement and was walking through the property with Henrik and Rachel. We all walked through the master suite and bath, and I noticed Rachel opening up the bedroom closet. She looked inside and saw women's clothing."

Rachel was deliberately shaking her head. "No."

Roger interjected, "So, Mr. Gibson, what you are saying is that you think that Rachel automatically knew that Henrik was already married because she saw women's clothing in the bedroom closet?"

"Of course!"

"May I remind you again, Mr. Gibson, that you are under oath!"

The lies continued until Roger was finished with this witness. Rachel noted that Judge Malson never reprimanded Chuck Gibson once.

The morning turned to afternoon and Henrik was out of witnesses for the day. Rachel's friends lined up. Maggie from across the street came to testify for all the times that she saw Rachel run for her life out of her home and stand in the middle of her driveway. Maggie knew firsthand that Henrik was a sexual predator when she talked to Rachel about the attack on Lori, the Baumanns' babysitter. Rachel thought that if they painted Henrik in the light of who he really was, the courts would, of course, side with her.

After Maggie was examined by Roger, then cross-examined by Sherman, Rachel's friend Dorthey was next in line. All who testified were coming to her rescue against the dirty lies from the defendant's team. At the end of the day Roger put Rachel on the stand in rebuttal to Chuck's comment. Rachel clearly said that she hadn't known that Henrik was married until after she married him, and she was brought up with good manners and would never have opened the closet.

The next morning, day three of the trial, Soraya and Fallon saw how the trial was wearing Rachel down. They could hear it in her voice and read it on her exhausted face as she prepared to leave.

"I may be tired," she reassured everyone. "But I won't roll over and die under Henrik's hands."

In the courtroom, she watched Henrik come down the center aisle, his face filled with anger and menace. As he passed her table, he sneered, "Any day now, Rachel, I will have two illegitimate bastard kids from this annulment!" Mocking and laughing in her face, he walked to the counsel's table.

Alice Tricocci took the stand first. She and her husband had known Henrik for years and had met Rachel when she came to live in the downtown apartment. During Alice's testimony she got so spicy with the judge and both attorneys that she was reprimanded multiple times and almost in contempt of court.

Between questions Alice blurted out, "Judge, this man, Henrik, is nothing but a lying, cheating, beating shit."

Malson slammed his gavel, threatening jail time for the spirited redhead, but Alice didn't care. She went into the courtroom, guns blazing, telling it like it was and demanding justice.

The next hour Edwardo testified on how many times the police were called. Edwardo raised his voice and was in tears when it came time to talk about the girls and the unfairness and cruelty they faced at the hands of Henrik. He described in detail the day they showed up at his front door in their socks after running out of their basement, away from the crazy lunatic and into the safety of his home.

An hour passed. Nathan, Henrik's cousin, was ready to take the stand.

Rachel found out just before the trial, Henrik had sold Nathan the hardware store for a dollar. She had learned that Henrik paid Nathan to keep his mouth shut when Henrik took the hardware store out of Rachel's name and put Nathan on the quitclaim deed.

The grueling and strenuous days of the trial all seemed to bleed together. Rachel heard an echo in her brain. *Roger promised that I'll win this trial,* she thought. *I've done everything right.* Yet as the long days went on Roger grew more distant and aloof. He started to give her one-word answers and seldom made eye contact. She could feel a change on every level. Things looked to be going her way on the surface, yet behind a mysterious door lay the ugly truth: puppet strings were being pulled.

On Thursday, August 11, Maya Hart was first on the agenda, and she asked Roger if she could read aloud a letter she wrote about Rachel's heartbreaking marriage. Maya wanted the judge to hear the full story. Roger told her to begin, but Judge Malson slammed his gavel.

"Mrs. Hart, the court doesn't have time for such nonsense! Please answer the questions from Mr. Schofield."

Maya turned toward the judge. "But Your Honor!"

"Mrs. Hart, if you would like to be in contempt of court and have your letter confiscated, continue reading."

Maya's face grew red with disgust. "Your Honor, Rachel has been grossly railroaded by Henrik Baumann for years. This isn't fair!"

Roger quickly interjected, "Your Honor, I will move to redirect."

The trial commenced with cross-examination by Sherman and then the next witness for the defendant. This witness was another friend of Henrik's named Patrick Zellner. Rachel sat through more lies and careless testimony launched throughout the courtroom. Patrick lied about Henrik's whereabouts and timelines, covering for Henrik on the many nights he stumbled home at 3:00 a.m., telling the courts that Henrik had been with him.

Rachel knew better. But she didn't understand why, when her or her friends testified, they all were reprimanded. When Henrik's friends took the stand, the judge was silent. Rachel also noticed that Henrik's parents never came to court in support of him. It seemed to Rachel that Henrik's parents, the senior Baumanns, were in complete denial of Henrik's true criminal demeanor.

The rest of the afternoon Rachel had three more witnesses lined up to testify. Roger allowed only one of them to speak and sent the others home. It seemed he was in a rush to get out of court early, yet he never gave Rachel a reason why.

The last day of the trial, August 12, 1977. Rachel felt a bit weak and tired from broken sleep. She hadn't touched much of her food during the last few days. Her support system, Mary Jenkins, Alice, and the Kaffie family made sure to check on her to see that she was doing okay. They had also arranged their schedules to pick up Soraya and Fallon from school and prayed each night for their safety.

In a final act of grace, Mary had picked up some of Rachel's banquet shifts so she could focus on the trial. Mary was now up for her testimony. She would be the last witness before both attorneys made their closing statements and Judge Malson arrived at his decision. Mary also had a lengthy letter stating many facts about the case and she turned to the judge to see if her statements could be read. Again, Judge Malson opposed the letter and both attorneys began with their cross-examining. Mary fought hard for Rachel, knowing and understanding this case from its inception, she would have the last words the judge would hear in this trial. After that, Rachel's fate would be in God's hands.

Rachel's friends all knew the sheer gravity of this case, and with no gain to themselves, they were not only fighting for Rachel, they were also fighting for Soraya and Fallon.

Henrik's friends who had testified were nowhere to be found on that last day, yet the courtroom was full of many who had testified on behalf of Rachel. Seeing them warmed her heart. With the strength of their presence, she knew that God would always be there in dark times.

Sherman and Roger commenced with their closing statements. Sherman fired off that Rachel was nothing more than a gold-digging opportunist who knew about Henrik's marriage to Carol Baumann and who wasn't the picture-perfect mother portrayed in court. Roger gave marginal closing statements that appeared to be less than his incredible opening argument, lacking the vigor and substance he promised. Still, Rachel held her head up high even as she longed to vanish into the walls of the courtroom.

Judge Malson was now nearing his final decision.

"Counselors Sherman and Schofield, I thank you for your closing statements and for your enduring duties in this trial," he said. "I would also like to thank all the witnesses who took their time and effort to be here."

Rachel sat emotionless, thinking, *I'm moments away from a divorce I've longed for.*

Judge Malson continued, "I would like counsel to accompany me to my chambers where I'll bring my summaries of the case. We'll make our deliberations, and, after a short adjournment, I'll render my verdict."

Rachel turned to the bailiff. "How long will this take?" she asked.

The bailiff told her it could be an hour or two, he wasn't sure. Alice, Mary, Maya, and a number of neighbors waited in the hallway, chatting and happy to be momentarily out of the stuffy courtroom.

Deflated, Rachel knew that Henrik was using his guerrilla warfare tactics of ambush and sabotage, but there was nothing she could do.

The minutes seemed like hours. In a daze of anxiety and fear, Rachel heard the clock on the wall in the hallway outside of the courtroom: tick-tock, tick-tock. She stared into space thinking of the abuelos in Spain. She saw their warm loving faces, and longed to be back where she was cherished and cared for. The ticking of the clock grew louder until it was all that she could hear. Forty-five minutes had passed. Alice startled Rachel by grabbing her arm.

"It's time to go back."

"Okay." Rachel grabbed Alice's hand.

"Listen, Rachel. No matter what happens with this asshole, everything is going to be alright."

Rachel nodded her head and whispered. "I know."

At the table, Roger sat in silence. Everyone took their seat until Judge Malson walked into the courtroom.

The bailiff called out, "All rise."

"Take your seats please," Judge Malson addressed the court.

"With my deliberation," he began, "I've taken this matter seriously. I have reviewed witnesses, summaries, letters submitted as evidence, allegations, and all the dates, times, and facts of this case. There were very clear lines as to who is in favor of my ruling. Will the defendant and plaintiff please rise with respective counsel."

"Rachel, we have to stand," said Roger.

Henrik stood like an assassin ready to defeat his prey. Judge Malson continued, "We know that this trial was bifurcated into two sections. First, the trial of the divorce versus annulment, and the second part stating the terms of the settlement. In conclusion of the first part of the bifurcation, I would like to read part of the memorandum."

Judge Malson cleared his throat. "The question at hand here and I will begin to read as follows. The issue of whether the counter-defendant entered into a marriage with the counter-plaintiff in good faith and without knowledge that the counter-plaintiff was at that time married to another. The court, considering all the evidence on all of the matters before it, and being fully advised in the grounds, finds…"

Rachel stood stone-faced, trying to process what he was saying.

"That the counter-plaintiff has proven the allegations contained in his counter-complaint and that the alleged marriage between the counter-plaintiff and the counter-defendant is void."

Rachel quickly turned to Roger. "What?"

Gasps and rumblings erupted throughout the courtroom.

Judge Malson continued, "On motion of Counsel Damien Sherman for the counter-plaintiff, it is adjudged and decreed that a decree of annulment of said alleged marriage by and between Rachel F. Baumann, counter-defendant, and Henrik J. Baumann, counter-plaintiff, is hereby granted to the counter-plaintiff Henrik J. Baumann."

Judge Malson quickly slammed his gavel. Rachel turned again to Roger. "What happened Roger?"

Roger quickly responded, "The judge just announced in favor of Henrik's request for an annulment."

Rachel's breath grew shallow, then vanished from her lungs. Spots filled her vision, and her sight went blurry. Her knees buckled. "Thud!" Rachel collapsed to the ground.

Mary, Alice, and Maya rushed to Rachel's side. "Bailiff!" called Maya. "Can you get some water?"

Anger bubbled through the courtroom. People were shouting, "This trial is a travesty! The court is corrupt!"

Mary, Alice, and Maya kneeled on the floor next to Rachel, holding her until she came to, breathing heavily. Roger stood in silence.

"Order! Can I please get through this memorandum without any more interruptions!" Judge Malson looked out at the courtroom as if to scold the entire congregation.

"Where was I?" he continued. "That the complaint for divorce of the plaintiff Counter-Defendant is hereby dismissed and that the plaintiff Counter-Defendant is hereby found *not* to be entitled to alimony and that she is barred from same. The court will hear matters of custody, child support, visitation, property rights, furniture, and attorney's fees on September 12, 1977, at 10:00 a.m. The court grants the plaintiff, Rachel F. Baumann, the right to an appeal."

Judge Malson alerted officers and marshals in the courtroom, then addressed Roger, "Counsel Schofield, please approach the bench."

He handed Roger the annulment decree for Rachel to sign. Roger walked back to the counsel table where Rachel was now trying to get her bearings.

"You need to sign these," Roger coldly told her.

"I'm not signing these," said Rachel. "I deserved a divorce, not an annulment." Rachel looked toward Judge Malson and spoke again, a bit louder, "I'm not signing these!"

"Mr. Schofield, please inform your client that if she doesn't sign the annulment papers, she will be in contempt of court. Mrs. Baumann, do you see these court officers? They will happily take you to jail."

Rachel was numb, speechless, and shocked at the injustice. Henrik had gone for the jugular. She felt her tongue getting heavy as if she were about to vomit. She nervously looked around the room and caught the astonished looks on the faces of her friends and witnesses, powerless to help her. This was the greatest betrayal of her life. Tunnel vision set in as she mechanically signed the annulment papers. In her mind, she heard Henrik's vindictive voice as he boasted, *"I'm gonna have two illegitimate, bastard children,"* crushing his daughters' hearts in the process. Rachel was a woman of faith, but even that was tested on this day. For the first time she wondered why God would let such a horrendous thing happen.

She didn't understand how Henrik could get away with an annulment and leave her with no alimony whatsoever. She also wondered how in the world would this vile man with all of his criminal wrongdoings get away with bigamy on top of everything else. There were many layers of this inequity. She felt she was swimming in a cesspool of criminals, but she wasn't going to let them win. Even now.

"This court is adjourned."

The final slam of the gavel was deafening. In the name of greed, Judge Malson changed her and her girls' lives forever by excluding them from what was rightfully theirs.

Roger left Rachel without saying a word, followed by a smirking Henrik, and the Sherman brothers slithered out of the courtroom and under the nearest rock they could find. Rachel stayed in the counsel's chair dazed and not understanding how this could happen. She was in shock and would be for days and weeks to come. She needed time to process this sham.

People were filing out of the courtroom. The judge had already left when suddenly Alice shouted, "This is an outrage! She's gonna appeal!"

As they helped Rachel out of the courtroom and drove her home, her friends, who had proved so loyal, tried to console her. "Look at it this way," said Mary Jenkins, "you're finally free."

Little did she know how wrong she was.

16

Meet the Deceit

The trial had been over for a few hours when Rachel, mentally and physically drained, arrived at Tante Annie and Karin's house to pick up Soraya and Fallon.

"It's impossible," said Tante Annie. "He can't get away with it."

"He'll be hearing from us," echoed Karin.

Rachel looked at her beautiful girls, with dark eyes so much like hers. "I lost," she said.

"No, Mama," Fallon replied. "You have us."

It was a painful conversation, but Rachel sat Fallon down alone for a few moments and explained what Henrik had done. She explained as best as she could about the annulment and illegitimacy. The words that made it back to Fallon's ears broke her heart. She let Fallon know that Henrik forcibly put them in a grave situation. Henrik abandoned them for the sake of money and revenge against her, and that it had nothing to do with them. She wrapped her arms around Fallon and hugged her close before taking the girls home.

Ten minutes after they walked through the front door, Henrik was on the phone with Rachel, speaking in a harassing tone.

"I want the girls to be ready. I'll be there in half an hour to pick them up."

"You got your annulment, and you want to pick up the girls tonight? I don't think so, Henrik. You are done playing with our lives. I'm exhausted and you are not taking the girls anywhere."

"We'll see about that, YOU GODDAMN…!"

Rachel could hear Henrik beating the phone against the wall. She knew he would drive like a bat out of hell to get to the house. She had to think quickly, and she needed a man to step in. She was sure that Henrik could kill her, take the girls, and put them in an orphanage. She called Bob and Georgia Schumer. Bob picked up the phone and told her that he knew about the annulment. Word had spread fast.

"I was just about to call you," he said.

"Henrik's gone crazy again! He's madder than hell. He's on his way to pick up the girls. I'm afraid, Bob."

"Over my dead body! I want you and the girls to pack a bag. Georgia and I will be there to pick you up. Give us twenty minutes. Don't let the girls leave with that piece of shit! You can stay at our house for a few days."

Rachel grabbed an overnight bag and packed as fast as she could. She told Fallon what was happening, and that Bob and Georgia were picking them up. Fallon's insides started quivering and she felt numb everywhere. Within fifteen minutes, Henrik slammed open the front door. They heard him dump out the laundry basket sitting by the steps to the downstairs basement. He hurled it, denting the drywall leading upstairs.

Fallon peeked out of the bedroom door and saw dirty clothes everywhere. Rachel ran to their bedroom. "Girls, grab your dolls and an extra pillow. Don't leave your room until Mr. and Mrs. Schumer get here. I'm going to do my best to stall your father."

Fallon was ready to tell him that they would not be going with him. She didn't understand what was happening, but she showed her sister her hiding place in the closet, and they stayed there until they heard Mr. Schumer's comforting voice.

Fallon was trying to figure out whose voice was through the buffer of the closet. Mr. Schumer seemed very angry, and it felt good to have someone speak up for them.

"You are not taking the girls, Henrik."

"They're *my* daughters!" Henrik blurted.

"You better watch yourself, Henrik. You've gone too far. Who do you think you are, giving Rachel an annulment? And then you think you're going to take the girls. Oh, no you don't!"

Henrik was always cowardly in the face of another man who stood up to him. Rachel grabbed the overnight bag and called the girls downstairs.

Then the girls heard Mr. and Mrs. Schumer telling them it was okay. They were scared, but they walked downstairs and out to their Cadillac.

"*Girls*...don't you get in that car...DON'T GET IN THAT CAR!" Henrik shouted.

But we ignored him.

"Henrik, leave them out of this." Bob Schumer spoke in a calm yet scolding voice, trying to minimize the trauma. "They're too little for your bullshit!"

"Henrik, I promise," added Rachel, "the girls will find out one day who you really are!"

"Oh yeah? You bitch!" Henrik threw his keys as Rachel ducked her head.

In the back seat of the Schumers' Cadillac, Soraya hid her face behind her doll. Fallon held her tears in and saw that Mr. Schumer's face was red and steamy. This pulled out the grenade pin on his friendship with Henrik.

The Beatles' "The Long and Winding Road" was playing as they drove to the Schumers' home. Fallon turned around to look out of the back seat window and she saw her father's manic face behind the steering wheel of his car as he followed them for miles. By now her entire body was shaking and she just wanted to be that little happy carefree girl she once was. She seemed so far away, and Fallon hadn't a clue as to how to find her again. Maybe she never existed.

Safe within the Schumer home, while Mrs. Schumer prepared dinner, Rachel called all those who hadn't made it to the trial. She believed there was power in numbers, and she needed every single friend she had. Her last call was to Lee Broward. "Even with Samuel Nelson watching over things," she said. "Corruption was everywhere."

"I'll look into what I can regarding disciplinary action," said Lee. "I'll do everything I can, but my hands are tied."

He advised her to wait for the settlement hearing and to see what that would bring. But Rachel was even more worried about losing her girls and the house in the custody battle to come and getting thrown out on the streets.

The next morning, Rachel called her parents in Spain and told them she needed them. Within three days they flew to the States. When the abuelos arrived, she finally slept. She was now safe, loved, and cared for. The musical notes of Spain filled the house as did the aroma of tortas and rice with rich roast chicken.

Two weeks had passed, and Rachel was now getting ready for the settlement hearing. Rachel's friends and witnesses had written a barrage of letters to Judge Malson and all the corrupt attorneys involved in the case, threatening disciplinary action toward the counsel if justice was not done.

Rachel had no time to find another attorney, so she was forced to use Roger Schofield. She called his office multiple times but never heard back. She knew that Roger and Judge Malson were both in Henrik's pockets but she could do nothing against the bribery. She also knew that she had to ride out the storm even if the other end of the tunnel was saturated in poverty. She would take those odds rather than spend one more minute with that parasite. All this time even after the annulment, Henrik still refused to leave the house. He was never around much but was still living in the basement. It sometimes felt like an oppressive prison with him around. There was not a judge, cop, attorney, neighbor, friend, or family member who could make him leave until he was ready to go. He bullied everyone, even the abuelos. The abuelos tolerated Henrik as best they could to keep the peace for Soraya and Fallon, and for Rachel, too.

On September 12, 1977, Rachel left for the hearing that was to begin at 10:00 a.m. Mary Jenkins took Soraya and Fallon to school before working Rachel's banquet shift. Maya Hart went with Rachel to the hearing. Rachel never heard from Roger Schofield in the weeks between the annulment and the settlement hearing, and she wondered if he would even show up. Rachel and Maya walked into the hearing, and everything seemed very quiet. Henrik was nowhere to be found.

Roger and the Sherman brothers were lingering at the back of the courtroom and talking with each other. Roger avoided Rachel, even seeming to laugh in her face while idly chit chatting with the other attorneys. Rachel and Maya sat politely and patiently. Moments later Judge Malson entered the room and spoke briefly with the attorneys. Roger, the Sherman brothers, and Judge Malson left for the judge's chambers. Maya was aggravated and walked out into the hallway to ask if anyone could shed light on the holdup. No one gave Maya a concrete answer, so she walked back into the courtroom and sat near Rachel.

"Do you believe this garbage? No one seems to know what is going on."

"I bet Henrik knows what's going on. I guarantee you, Maya, Henrik is pulling all the puppet strings."

Within a half hour the court clerk approached Rachel and told her that the hearing was postponed until the first week in December. "This seems like a never-ending hell," she whispered to Maya. "What if I lose my children? What if I lose their home? Now I have to wait another three months to find out my fate with this violent *cabron* still living in the house!"

"You're not going to lose those girls. It will be over my dead body. Every one of your friends will storm your home in protest. We will bully the bully."

Rachel smiled as they walked out of the courtroom. Weeks went by and Rachel got a notice of the settlement hearing from Roger. By now Fallon's tenth birthday in October had passed. Halloween and Thanksgiving were soon in the rearview mirror. The abuelos were very busy with the girls. They went to church with them, cooked, and took care of them while Rachel prepared mentally.

Rachel dreaded the settlement hearing coming up December 6, but knew she had to forge forward. The night before the hearing, she prayed like she never prayed before. She prayed and fought for the two most important things. Number one, her girls; number two, her home.

The hearing was a little less formal than the trial, but Rachel still felt like throwing up, never knowing what misconduct Henrik was up to. Alice and Karin, who had accompanied Rachel, took their seats. Then, Alice got up and walked over to the counsel table where Henrik was awaiting the hearing.

"Henrik," she whispered loud enough for Rachel and those in the front row to hear. "You're gonna burn in hell for what you're doing to this beautiful lady!"

She returned to Rachel with a big smile on her face. The redheaded firecracker always knew when to get a dig in. Henrik didn't care, he was anticipating a win. The bailiff announced Judge Malson.

"All rise."

"Alright, let's get right to this. Please take your seats." Judge Malson looked through his paperwork.

"Baumann versus Baumann. This cause coming on to be heard on the issues of the supplemental decree, complete settlement, custody, child support, visitation, property rights, attorney's fees, and miscellaneous. A decree of annulment having thus far been entered on August 12, 1977. As we already know, this trial was bifurcated, this settlement being the second part."

The judge went on discussing the terms of the settlement memorandum.

"The court has heard the evidence in the case with respect to the remaining issues and arguments of counsel. We will commence with property rights to begin this hearing. It is therefore ordered, adjudged and decreed as follows…

"Miss Rachel Baumann shall execute and deliver a quitclaim deed conveying all of her rights, title, interest, or waive a claim against Henrik for the following properties…"

Rachel bowed her head, shaking in disgust at the word "Miss" connected to the name Baumann, the name she had taken when he had married Henrik in good faith, the name she had given her daughters.

The judge read on:

"7751 Roscoe Street, Chicago and 5660 School Street, Chicago.

"Rachel Baumann shall execute and deliver a quitclaim deed conveying all of her rights, title, interest, or waive a claim against Henrik for the following properties…

"4539 N Central, Chicago 10-flat building and 390 Ontario, Oak Park 20-flat building…

"Rachel Baumann shall execute and deliver a quitclaim deed conveying all of her rights, title, interest, or waive a claim against Henrik for the following properties…

"967 Belmont Street, Chicago, 596 Addison Street, Chicago, 3945 Oriole Street, Chicago, 6237 Olcott Street, Chicago."

Rachel leaned over to Roger and whispered, "What's happening?"

"You just lost half of the estate and buildings that you had joint tenancy with Henrik."

"Well, you're my attorney! I know my name was on all of these properties!"

Judge Malson continued the slaughter.

"Rachel Baumann shall execute and deliver a quitclaim deed conveying all of her rights, title, interest, and is barred from any interest in the following properties and businesses...

"7464 Addison Street Chicago (hardware store). Eight buildings, 7238 through 8324 Addison Street, Chicago. This is noted as an entire city block of properties.

"Rachel Baumann shall execute and deliver a quitclaim deed conveying all of her rights, title, interest, and is barred from any interest in the following properties...

"Real estate located in Monroe County, Wisconsin, which constitutes three farms, referred to in these proceedings as farm number one and one A, approximately 125 acres in Ontario, Wisconsin; farm number two approximately 165 acres in Norwalk, Wisconsin; and farm number three approximately 85 acres in Cashton, Wisconsin."

"I don't care about the farms," she told Roger, "But my name was on all of them! I don't understand this."

"Rachel Baumann shall execute and deliver a quitclaim deed conveying all of her rights, title, and is barred from any interest in the following bank accounts, stocks, bonds, trust funds, investments, and life insurance with the following institutions:

"Cotter & Company; American Growth Fund; Farm Producers; Commonwealth Edison; Cashier's Co-op Dreyfus Fund; South American Bank, Mexico; Norwood Park Savings and Loan; Columbia National Bank of Chicago; Exchange National Bank of Chicago; Pioneer Trust and Savings Bank; Banco de Comercio, Mexico; Bank of Sparta, Monroe County; Bank of Ontario; Mutual of Omaha, MetLife, Government G.I., and Prudential Life.

"Henrik Baumann shall transfer to Rachel Baumann, simultaneously with transfers to be made by Rachel which are set for in the next sections that follows…

"The improved realty commonly known as 7240 Pittsburgh Street, Chicago, Illinois, and its legal description. Rachel, as owner of said realty shall be fully responsible for insurance, taxes, bills, and maintenance of her property; with a stipulation that Rachel will have to sell the property within five years of this supplemental decree. Within said date Rachel and daughters will have to vacate the property or be penalized with an interest tax per diem.

"Henrik Baumann shall vacate the property commonly known as 7240 Pittsburgh Street, Chicago, Illinois, no later than April 8, 1978."

"Rachel, you got the house and Henrik's got a move out date," Roger said, his voice free of any emotion.

Rachel knew that she was losing most of Henrik's estate, but her only concern was the wellbeing of her girls.

Judge Malson continued, "This next section will cover custody, child support, and visitation. Rachel Baumann shall have full custody of the two minor children, namely Fallon Baumann and Soraya Baumann."

Rachel caught her breath.

"Henrik Baumann will be granted reasonable rights of visitation. Henrik Baumann shall pay Rachel Baumann the sum of $300 per month for child support. Henrik Baumann shall be entitled to claim the minor children as exemption for state and federal income tax purposes."

Alice was standing in earshot of Rachel. "Petty-ass!" Alice blurted out under her breath. Rachel softly smiled.

Judge Malson continued, "This last section will cover the attorney's fee and miscellaneous expenses. As attorney's fees go, $10,000 of equity of said realty which Henrik Baumann is causing to be deeded to Rachel Baumann shall be in full satisfaction and discharge of Henrik Baumann's obligation to pay Roger Schofield the sum of $10,000 for Rachel Baumann's attorney's fees and costs. Roger Schofield shall have a lien impressed against the aforementioned realty in the sum of $10,000. Rachel Baumann shall thereby assume the sole obligation to pay Roger Schofield his attorneys fees which have been incurred from the commencement of this lawsuit."

Rachel whispered, "What?"

Judge Malson concluded, "Looks like miscellaneous is left. Rachel Baumann shall pay the sum of $3,290.76 to reimburse Henrik for long distance phone charges subsequent to the order of the court. Rachel Baumann was ordered to obtain Henrik Baumann's written consent before making these calls. The remaining $2,000 is for the reimbursement of the said guns listed in this decree. That will conclude this settlement hearing. Will both counsel approach the bench for this decree to be signed and approved?"

Roger walked back to the counsel table where Rachel was numb and sitting quietly. "Rachel, you have to sign this decree."

"I'm not signing my life away. I got almost nothing from my husband's estate and now I have to pay thousands of dollars with this settlement."

"You got the girls and the house."

"Yes, I have to take good care of them. How can I do that nearing the poverty level?"

"Miss Baumann, this again!" boomed the judge. "May I remind you, if you don't sign those papers, you'll be in contempt of court. Another thing. If I find out that you took those girls to Spain without consent from Mr. Baumann, you will again be in contempt of court and heading to jail."

Henrik stood coldly looking at the judge, throwing his shadow over the courtroom. Rachel pondered the idea that this could be more than money motivating the unbearable corruption that swallowed her and forced her hand. Reluctantly, she signed the papers and turned to Roger.

"What happened here? I got nothing that I expected to get from you.

I'm happy to have my kids but can you explain the rest?" Alice and Karin stood side by side next to Rachel.

"No Miss Baumann. You get no alimony or any of Henrik's properties. You are only entitled to child support. If you are looking to appeal this, I really don't have time for you."

"I don't want to go through an appeal. The same thing is gonna happen to me. I've been going through this for years; I have no more strength for another trial. I'm exhausted! How can I pay you this money when I have nothing? My husband has to pay you."

"That's why we put a lien on your house, Miss Baumann, and since Henrik got an annulment, he was never your husband in the first place." Roger closed his briefcase and walked abruptly out of the courtroom.

Alice yelled out, "You'll be hearing from the disciplinary board! Look at what you've done to this woman, she can hardly talk!"

Both Alice and Karin hugged Rachel and told her, "It's over." They grabbed their purses and coats and walked out into the cool December air.

Funny thing about deceit is that sometimes you don't know how many layers it comes in. One understanding of deceit, betrayal, and precalculated schemes is that they all come from the same place, insatiable greed. But for Henrik, it was more than greed. It was Rachel's rejection of him that made him seethe in rage. He wanted to take the very air from her lungs to make her pay for leaving him.

What was done to Rachel…what was done to all three of them, was beyond the boundaries and thresholds of wrong. It was one of the greatest cases of obstruction of justice, witness tampering, and immoral conduct that was never spoken of beyond the walls of the courtroom. What Rachel didn't hear in court were the facts of what the neurotic Henrik did with his properties, land, businesses, and investments. Henrik had a plan B in case something slipped up with the judge.

He had sold the hardware store for a dollar to his cousin Nathan, who testified against Rachel. He had put all of the farms in a state of fake fore-closure and sold most of his buildings and rental properties to his family. He had forged Rachel's signature multiple times to get her name off of any other monetary proprietorships. He was insuring and hiding all of his assets. He had his greedy pig knuckles wrapped around everything. Rachel had a stack of letters from family and friends vouching for her character. The court took these letters and had all of them destroyed, silencing her once again.

Rachel fought like hell, walking away with her home only by the grace of God. Henrik, disturbed as he was, loved fucking people over for money and fucking people out of their money. This form of intolerable behavior was his compass and sick way of navigating through his life. Thankfully, Fallon and Soraya took a completely opposite path, never coming close to following his template of stench.

From Lee Broward's tip-off, Rachel knew that Henrik had paid off Judge Malson, the Sherman brothers, and Roger Schofield. Henrik used his money like a powerful muscle, yielding him women, property, and people. He got whatever he wanted with force and the almighty dollar. It would take a while for Rachel to find out that the judge alone got an extra $10,000 in manipulating the divorce trial and granting an annulment so that Henrik would only have to pay Rachel peanuts. Henrik could not have cared less if Soraya and Fallon found out they were bastard children. He didn't care if it hurt because he had no conscience whatsoever.

It would also take Rachel a few years to find out that Henrik was fuck-ing Judge Malson's secretary, the dark-haired manipulative Maryann Gallo. You could almost see Judge Malson's erection under his judicial robe as he knew payday would come soon. Rachel felt as if she picked up a rock and discovered a new breed of cockroaches. In all of Rachel's life, she had never been around so much filth and sleaze. Maryann Gallo was doing double duty making sure that Henrik got away with most of his estate during the trial. This secretary had a vested interest in Henrik's estate. Although by this time Rachel and the girls had heard whispers for years about her from neighbors and hardware store acquaintances, they had no idea how she would become part of their lives.

As far as the estate was concerned Rachel knew she was entitled to half of Henrik's properties and investments. Instead, Henrik beat her, cheated on her with multiple whores, committed bigamy, annulled the marriage, gave her no alimony, placed a lien on their home for over $10,000, made many attempts on Rachel's life, boasted about calling Soraya and Fallon bastard children, and had a never convicted criminal rap sheet a mile long. The problems with Henrik rolled in like multiple tsunamis of crashing waves, one after another, never stopping until the adult child got what he wanted: everything!

Henrik took a lot more from her than money and property on that fateful day in court. He sealed her financial fate with years of sacrifice ahead of her. He took her faith in people, justice, and that the righteous will always win in the end. He took her peace; he took her belief that the law was supposed to fight for the underdog. Most importantly, he momentarily took her belief in God. She wondered where God was on that day.

Internally, Rachel felt as if she was an expensive vase that slipped off of a shelf and shattered into a million pieces. How would she ever put her life back together? She thought she lost that day, and wouldn't realize for years that what Fallon saw was a woman gaining her strength and pushing the boundaries of courage. A woman of valor who wouldn't give up, a fighting soul even in the face of hopelessness. A woman who had slayed the dragon and protected Soraya and Fallon before herself. A woman that stood her ground and wouldn't back down from this premeditated plot. Fallon witnessed a soldier protecting her with her shield. A warrior that fought for her home with her last breath and would protect her children against this insufferable serpent, confronting this parasite head-on. Externally, Rachel buckled and swayed like an oak tree against the storm…yet she never broke.

A few days had passed, and Rachel was trying to catch up on some needed sleep as the settlement hearing took its toll. In between work and taking the girls to school, Rachel had many get-togethers with her friends and Lee Broward; she had a collection of letters that they typed for the Attorney Disciplinary Commission. She was trying to file a complaint of misconduct against her attorney Roger Schofield and expose what seemed to be a very corrupt section of the legal system. She would have loved to file a complaint against the judge and Henrik's attorneys, but had no physical evidence documenting the payoffs.

Since most of the letters were about the annulment, Rachel asked her women friends to put an addendum about the horrific settlement and fees that she owed. In the beginning when Rachel met Roger, he promised her a divorce and that she would get a great settlement. He later told her that no judge in the country would ever allow an annulment in her situation. She had ended up with almost nothing and her name was on all property in joint tenancy with Henrik. She ended up with exorbitant fees and never got her $2,000 retainer fee back from Roger.

It was understood that Henrik was supposed to pay all attorney's fees and refused. Rachel was supposed to get the retainer fee back and pay Mary Jenkins who loaned her the money in the first place. Rachel finally paid her back when the abuelos gave her some money. Rachel was never made aware of the extortionate attorney's fees until the final slaughter in the settlement hearing. The fees popped up in the documents like a jack-in-the-box. The court basically shut Rachel down; she had to sign the documents under duress or face further penalties and jail time. Roger knew beforehand about the annulment but neglected to inform Rachel. It was a bait and switch in this twisted wormhole.

Roger discovered Samuel Nelson was secretly observing the trial and confronted Rachel. At first Rachel denied the truth about Nelson for fear that Roger would drop her case. When Rachel made the disciplinary complaint against Roger, he made a big stink about Samuel Nelson, calling Rachel a liar because she did not disclose the truth about adding extra counsel.

The craziness is that this entire trial was based on nothing but lies sprouting from Henrik Baumann and his corrupt legal team. Rachel had Samuel Nelson as a check and balance to ward off any illegal wrongdoings. Rachel knew that with Henrik, the wolf was always at the door.

Roger told Rachel that she lost most of the settlement and Henrik was granted the annulment because she did poorly on the stand. He also stated that her witnesses were vague and not believable. This could not be further from the truth. Roger also never backed Rachel up when Damien Sherman accused her of being responsible for all the continuances with the hearings. Rachel sadly learned that Roger had turned this entire story around for the sake of money! An attorney's job is to find justice…instead, each attorney Rachel sought out would find that they were sitting on a wad of Henrik's cash firmly planted up their ass.

Again, deceit can happen in layers. Henrik made sure those layers were fully paid off, from the judge to the lawyers, and all the way down to the Disciplinary Commission. Rachel had a stack of letters that went unread. Not one of her complaints ever received a response. Rachel was duped, tricked, and stifled. She had no voice among this band of white-collar criminals. They thought they could silence her, but they were wrong.

The holidays came and went. The abuelos were still in town helping her rebuild her life. They insulted Henrik's character behind his back, but in front of him they tried to keep the peace so that Soraya and Fallon wouldn't suffer any more trauma. Rachel never gave her parents the full story of what Henrik did to her because she knew that her aging parents couldn't handle the outrageous acts. They only knew bits and pieces. Soraya and

Fallon knew their parents were no longer married but their father would not budge from the house.

April 8, 1978 seemed to take forever to show up. When it did, Rachel felt a lightness in her step. Henrik would finally be out of her life. Soraya and Fallon didn't have the tools to understand the depth of their father's illness, but they too couldn't wait for him to be gone. Rachel saw how hard it was for the girls to verbalize their fear. They had been conditioned to take his abuse with no way to navigate around the poisonous fabric that enveloped their lives. No one told her she could have called Child Services for help. Even if she had, surely Henrik would have found a way to pay them off.

But here it was, move out day, gloriously sunny with a chill in the air. Soraya and Fallon were playing in the backyard. Mary Jenkins had packed up and taken most of the bar trinkets and glasses that Rachel had brought from Spain.

Rachel had braced herself for Henrik's refusal to move out. But here he was with a white truck and one of his friends to help him load up. He packed up all of his personal items and then started on the rec room furniture where the girls played every day. He took out the wooden barrel-shaped chairs with their leather upholstery and bar stools. He took the ornate doors that enclosed the now-empty gun rack. Next, he took the couch from the rec room.

Rachel ran downstairs. "Henrik, this is where the girls and I watch TV, the girls play down here. You can't take their couch. What are you, the Grinch?"

"Get the hell out of my way."

"Stop! You're taking furniture you're not supposed to!"

Henrik took a box of items and threw it against the wall in a rage, smashing all the contents.

When Fallon heard the disruption, as if by instinct, she walked from the backyard to the basement and stared through the screen. *"Get out of my way!"*

Fallon heard Henrik's voice rising, shaking the walls. "*I paid* for all this Goddamn furniture and I'm gonna take what I want."

"But this is stuff for your girls!"

"Go to a secondhand store or a garage sale for all I care! They don't need anything fancy!"

Rachel could do nothing. Henrik and his friend had already loaded up the couch and headed up to the bedroom. Fallon walked into the basement and looked at her mother.

"I'm sorry Fallon, your father took the couch."

"Why?"

"Because he's crazy. Don't worry, I will get another couch. We will find one this week. Go watch your sister out back."

"Okay, Mommy. Yell out if you need me."

By now Henrik was stripping the king size bed upstairs and Rachel ran up and confronted him.

"Put down that bed! This is where I draw the line! Where am I gonna sleep?"

"I really don't care bitch!"

"I'll call the police, or I'll tell the judge. You can't take my bed! You got almost everything and now you are gonna take my bed? This bed is not in the decree for you to take!"

"Go ahead, tell the judge! What a *joke*!" He took the mattress and bed frame, threw it sideways, sending it slamming against the dresser. Part of the frame hit the floor and Henrik stormed out of the bedroom.

Rachel followed him outside onto the driveway where the truck was parked. Henrik saw Tony, one of their neighbors who lived on the next block. Tony always said hello and was friendly with Rachel. Henrik started flailing his arms and threw a shaving kit into the neighbor's bushes. He was now moving closer toward Tony, shouting, "You *asshole*. Who do you think you are? Get out of here! I KNOW YOU ARE SLEEPING WITH MY WIFE!"

Tony was startled by Henrik's sudden assault. "What are you talking about? I'm not sleeping with your wife." Tony quickly walked away.

Rachel followed a few feet behind Henrik, still keeping her distance.

"Are you crazy Henrik? I'm not sleeping with him or anybody, and I'm not your wife."

Rachel knew something worse. Henrik was actually having an affair with Tony's wife. Henrik was a master at playing the blame game. He loved blaming people for things he did. Henrik packed up the rest of the truck and was gone.

That night, Rachel made fried hamburgers for dinner and together she and her daughters sat on the beanbag chairs. Later that week, Rachel found another couch at a local garage sale. They sat on it, celebrating their new-found freedom.

NUESTRA PORTADA

Esta bellísima señorita se llama Faly Vázquez, y ustedes, sin duda, habrán admirado más de una vez su espléndida hermosura durante las pasadas fiestas falleras. Se trata de la representante de Galicia que formó en la corte de honor de nuestra fallera mayor. ¿Verdad que es guapa? En las páginas centrales publicamos las fotos de la corte de honor de la fallera mayor.

(Foto Valentín Pla)

17

Disoriented Sunlight

—— FALLON'S STORY ——

Everyone understands that there are two sides to every story. As for Henrik, in all my years on this planet, I have never seen another human being cheat, pillage, embezzle, demoralize, extort, and degrade humanity the way he did. What he did to Rachel, Soraya, and me was worse than his crimes against others.

Henrik wanted to destroy Rachel, not understanding or caring what that would do to Soraya and me as we suffered years of consequences and pain due to his actions. Everything Henrik plotted against Rachel was to paralyze her mentally and financially. In finding clarity in my life, I would grow to know every illegal, disgraceful, immoral, criminal act that my father was capable of perpetrating. I would eventually see it for myself. What he didn't understand was the ultimate price he would eventually pay for his greedy, sleazy, selfish decisions. From the first moment I witnessed violence at the hands of my father, I believed in my mother Rachel. She was only one truth, but it would take a lifetime to put the shattered pieces together.

May of 1978 settled in, and Soraya and I were in a visitation routine with Henrik every Wednesday and Sunday. We had no choice in the matter. Sometimes we enjoyed going with him because we did fun stuff. Once in a while we would see a blockbuster movie like *Jaws*, *Star Wars*, and *Smokey and the Bandit*. Yet, it was always in Henrik style. If things were not done to his high standard of perfection, there was hell to pay. He would yell at me for the simplest things like dropping a kernel of popcorn on the movie theater floor. He was grooming me to be his new victim, to believe that everything was my fault.

Soraya and I didn't consider it to be unusual at the time, but often, on our days with Henrik, we worked long hours in the hardware store, for which he paid us pennies. He had bought a new fixer-upper home and we hammered, tore out drywall, painted, spackled, cooked, and cleaned until we fell over. I splattered some paint with my brush on his floor and he knocked my knuckles with a screwdriver, bruising all of them. I hid my hand from my mother until the bruises healed.

He opened up his own fencing company and we dragged fencing panels like longshoremen until our shoulders bled. Henrik was a workaholic which meant that Soraya and I had no downtime when we were with him. In the winter months, we painted all of his tools, with me in the lead and little Soraya handling her fair share. Henrik said that he could see his tools better when he worked outside if they had a coat of paint on them. Years later I would understand this to be more of his manipulation and control over us.

I was having more trouble in school. We worked on homework until I couldn't take it anymore. It was always more of an interrogation session. Many times, Henrik locked me in his office until I had completely finished my homework. I couldn't take a break or even go to the bathroom. Grilling me about my schoolwork was just another way to punish me.

The homework sessions turned into yelling matches. Henrik barked orders at me, his expectations reaching into the stratosphere. One night, for fun, Henrik locked me out of the house and screamed at me through one of the bedroom windows because I didn't finish an assignment properly. I could hear my sister yelling at him to let me in; it was cold outside.

For fun, we would go out into different alleys and root through garbage, searching for aluminum cans. We would crush them and would make five cents a can. Once, when one of Henrik's customers, a neighbor, saw us picking through trash, he came out. "Henrik," he yelled. "What's wrong with you! Don't you have enough money, now you have to crush cans with your daughters in the middle of this alley? Poor people do that shit because they have no choice."

"I'm trying to show them a good work ethic!"

"Yeah, I've seen them in the hardware store too. You work those girls to death."

The man walked away. I could tell my father was momentarily embarrassed by his comments because his face turned red and he grew quiet. The man was correct, we worked day and night for our father like dogs. It was all part of his control and pathological manipulation. We never mentioned things to our mother for fear of retaliation. We also worried in silence that if we told our father we didn't like seeing him, we would still be picking drywall out of our skulls. Henrik had an abusive, militant chokehold on us, indefinitely.

Summer was inching closer, and Rachel was making new friends through Alice, Mary, and many coworkers. She liked her job as a banquet waitress at Marriott Hotel, yet sometimes it was tough carrying big heavy trays. Still, she had found some happiness, freedom, and flow in her life. She wanted to celebrate her divorce and scraped up enough money to throw a party in early June.

Rachel knew that a ripped up marriage license would not keep Henrik on his best behavior. He was now even more hyper-interested and consumed by what she was doing. He followed her after work and when she went out. He showed up at movie theaters and at church. Soraya and I were always frustrated when he stalked us. We really didn't understand what stalking meant back then, but we always felt uncomfortable around our father's aggressive behavior and bad energy. Rachel still felt trapped and isolated under his surveillance. This upcoming party was no different. Rachel invited all her neighbors, friends, and new coworkers. Lee Broward showed up hours ahead of time and took us all for a ride in his RV. It was huge and had a kitchen and a bathroom with a shower.

So many familiar faces came to celebrate with us. It always felt great to be surrounded by friends who brought us through many difficult years. Later in the evening my mother turned on her favorite Bee Gees album, *Saturday Night Fever*. She played it over and over. Rachel still loved her rock and roll, but disco seemed to take over for the time being. The party was moving along, and Rachel did not find out for a while that Henrik was there. He was laughing and talking people's ears off as though nothing had happened. A lot of the partygoers were a bit buzzed and didn't want to cause a scene, so they kept things friendly. Mary Jenkins approached Rachel.

"Why the hell is Henrik here?"

"I have no idea. The house is wall to wall with people and I'm still making desserts!"

"He's blabbing people's ears off about all of his accomplishments, and I overheard him saying some nasty things about you. You should call the police to get him out of here."

"I already confronted him and asked him what he was doing here. Do you know what he told me?"

"What!"

"He got in my face and said that he built this house and can do whatever he wants."

"We should call the police."

"Do you really think he's gonna listen to the police? This asshole is above the law." It was always funny to hear my mother swear with her accent. She looked around the party and told Mary. "I don't see Maya and Bob Hart anywhere."

"I heard that they might be going through a divorce."

"A divorce, that's crazy! They have four children. Why didn't Maya tell me anything?"

"Some people withdraw when they go through tough times."

Summer moved forward and we went back to the farm. Henrik told Rachel that he got the farms back by paying the balance for them in full. Rachel knew that Henrik was a pathological liar on top of all of his other great qualities, but she had to pick her battles with him. She really didn't care what he did as long as he left her alone.

The rest of the year went by slowly with school starting up and my mother working just to break even with her bills. Winter came in with the blizzard of '79 in Chicago. We were off from school for ten glorious days with our free and happy mother.

In early spring, Mary Jenkins and family had moved five miles away just down the street from the Pickwick Theater. Rachel still saw Mary all the time at work and still spent time with her on weekends. By now Maya and Bob Hart were divorced. Bob bought a house and moved with some of his kids to Des Plaines, Illinois.

The Friday before Memorial Day weekend, May 25, 1979, I stayed over at the Jenkins home and my eyes just happened to catch the news. I couldn't take my eyes away from the TV and I saw the horrific crash of Flight 191 American Airlines; 271 souls on board. It was an enormous loss for the Chicago area.

In late summer, Rachel was invited to a party at Marge's house to celebrate before all the kids went back to school. It was a low-key party in the backyard and Rachel usually had all the single neighborhood men checking her out. She had dated a few men whom she met through mutual friends, but nothing serious. When Henrik found out about them, he usually would get their information to cause trouble and tell them fabricated stories about her.

An hour or so into the party Bob Hart noticed that Rachel was there. For many years when Rachel was good friends with Maya, Bob stayed quiet and in the background. Bob had silver hair, was of medium build, and was the definition of a good human being in every aspect of his life. He was a great cook and had a good job with one of the large phone carriers. That evening Rachel comforted Bob about the breakup of his marriage, and they talked about their kids. "I still love Maya," he said. "And we love our children, but we just weren't meant to live together anymore."

Before the night was over Bob asked Rachel for her number and if she'd like to go to lunch the following week. Rachel said sure and they picked a day. They met in a little café in Park Ridge and talked for over an hour.

"Can you believe Sally is getting married and Bobby is planning on moving to Virginia for his work?" Sally and Bobby were Bob's two eldest children.

"Time flies," sighed Rachel. "If you think about it, we have known each other for a little over ten years now."

"I wanted to talk to you about something. You never met my older brother George, have you?"

"I don't think so."

Bob's eyes began to well up in tears. "George was on the DC-10 flight 191 that crashed in May. He lived in California and was in town on business. He was heading home."

"Oh my God, Bob. I'm so sorry! I had no idea." Rachel moved to the other side of the booth, hugged Bob, and held his hand.

"I needed to let this out. I needed to talk to someone. You always seemed like a great person, especially from what Maya has said about you."

"Of course, Bob. I'm here for you."

They continued talking until Rachel had to pick up Soraya and me from Mary Jenkins's house. Bob came over on his birthday and Rachel made him homemade fried calamari. He was now coming over more often and Rachel thought it was a good, strong friendship. But Bob wanted a bit more.

In addition to his ongoing relationship with Maryann, Henrik was seeing multiple women. It was never fair, but these other women paled next to Rachel. One by one these women showed up at our doorstep during our visitation days with our father. Rachel had had enough and let Henrik know.

"When you get the girls to spend the day with you, please keep your prostitutes away from them." She spoke to Henrik, but she looked at the woman on his arm. "Do I make myself clear? I don't want your sluts around them."

Henrik made a nasty comment under his breath. He wasn't about to cause a scene around the new flavor of the week. In later years I often thought how lonely it must have been for Henrik, a serial womanizer, to call these women family. It was clear they were in the game for his money. Soraya and I could smell it.

Summer turned into fall, and I started having my own visions and dreams. I didn't understand what these visions meant even though Rachel had talked about hers since I was a little girl. I could see things; I would know things that I couldn't explain. It would take me a long time to wrap my brain around my insights. They happened randomly and later in life they would become clearer in a more precise succession. At times my telepathy would scare me, and I kept my thoughts about it to myself.

One night I had a horrible nightmare. I knew I had a baby brother in the dream and only saw the severed arm of this sweet child. I was on the farm. I saw a rainbow and trees swaying in the wind. I woke up in a cold sweat. I knew whoever this child was, he would not survive. It haunted me for months. I couldn't make sense of it. I also knew in reality that I didn't have a baby brother and tried to convince myself that it was only a bad dream. I wouldn't find out for a few years later but Rachel would have a simpler vision about this very child.

Halloween and Thanksgiving were behind us, and Henrik formally introduced us to Maryann Gallo. We could tell by the scowl on her face that Soraya and I bothered her. I could sense her agitated vibe a mile away. From the start Maryann would tell me if my clothes were too loose or too tight. She would make fun of things I ate, how my hair looked, or if I wasn't wearing any makeup. I was twelve years old, and it was a difficult age for girls. More judgment from an adult that I did not care about was most certainly not welcome, but I had to keep my mouth shut and take whatever she said to me.

I remember her in the front seat of my father's car as Soraya and I sat in the back. She laughed at things that I was talking about with my father, and she would make fun of me and call me stupid. I never understood why I was her target, but I believe she saw me as a threat. A possible threat to their relationship, to my father's money. I was never sure and could not prove it. One thing we knew for sure, Maryann looked at Soraya and me as trash that needed to be removed even though my father made me give her the ceramic cups and bowls I made at school.

"Thanks Fallon, but I have no use for this," she would say, handing the bowl back to me. It was awkward, confusing, and embarrassing. I had tried hard to make a work of beauty. My father would say nothing, but insisted I give her another ceramic creation or a greeting card the next time an occasion arose. It was a sick game he played, and I knew it. He watched as she rejected my gifts as if she was rejecting me, knowing I had seen through her and didn't want to give her anything or have a relationship with her.

No matter who his latest girlfriend was, he insisted I kiss their ass. As I got older, I refused and the fights with him became edgier.

That year we spent Christmas Eve at Gallo's house and Christmas Day with Rachel. Bob came over to help cook and our house filled with warmth, good smells, and laughter.

On New Year's Day, 1980, Rachel got a phone call from Margie across the street.

"Rachel! Turn on the news right now!"

Rachel rushed to the TV and grabbed the phone downstairs. She couldn't believe her eyes. Henrik and Maryann Gallo were on TV. They were the first couple on New Year's Day, Tuesday, January 1,1980, to get a marriage license in Chicago. They not only made the news but also made the front page of the *Chicago Tribune*.

"Fallon," Rachel shouted upstairs. "Your father's getting married to Maryann Gallo!"

"What? How do you know?"

"I just saw it on the news! This will be his fourth marriage."

I was hurt that our father felt so little of us to not tell us about this news in person. I was disgusted at the same time. I had this sixth sense that Maryann was trouble. She loved to make rude comments about me every chance she got. The next day was Wednesday, and Henrik was due to pick us up. I wasted no time in confronting him.

"So, Dad, you and Maryann are getting married?"

"Yup!" Henrik pulled out the newspaper with the picture of him and the Bride of Frankenstein on the front cover.

"Why wouldn't you tell us this first before we saw you on TV?"

"I thought you'd be happy for me," he said, his voice betraying the truth. He simply didn't care if his daughters were hurt or confused by his actions.

Within three months, Henrik and Maryann were married and Rachel would soon have an unlikely ally. Maryann Gallo's mother hated and loathed Henrik to the extremes. She knew Henrik was a bad apple from day one.

Mrs. Gallo was smart. She had so many suspicions about Henrik that she knew her instinct had to be right. She asked me for my home phone number and knew that Rachel would be the perfect person to find some insight on her new son-in-law.

Rachel and Mrs. Gallo talked frequently and secretly. Soon Mrs. Gallo knew everything about Henrik. She also shared the fact that Maryann was Judge Malson's secretary. Mrs. Gallo told Rachel that Henrik had shared with Maryann that Soraya was not his baby. The lies and deceptions kept coming and many new pieces of the puzzle were coming together. From the beginning Maryann knew exactly what she was doing. She could sniff the money in my father's wallet from the other side of the room and soon quit her job. Maryann was forty-five to my father's fifty, never married, and had no children.

One night, Mrs. Gallo called Rachel in a panic. Maryann had gone out. While she was out Henrik went crazy and shoved Mrs. Gallo down a flight of stairs, trying to kill her. Luckily, she had fallen on her knee, breaking her fall. He then pushed her into a closet and was about to strangle her until he was startled by the phone.

"Promise me," said Rachel, "that you will never be alone with him again. Next time, he'll kill you and make it look like an accident. He wants you out of the picture."

Summer came and went. Maryann was pregnant and we wouldn't find out about it until she was showing.

Rachel wouldn't tell me her visions until later, but she knew Maryann was pregnant before it was a reality. Her vision also told her that the baby would not be healthy. Rachel and I both saw this in our minds, but nothing could prepare us for the real-life heartbreak that it brought.

At the end of January 1981, Mary Jenkins was expecting her fourth child and Maryann was a few weeks away from delivering our half-brother. Jenny Jenkins and I were giddy with excitement, We were going to have new baby siblings. In the interim, Mrs. Gallo reached out to Rachel and let her know a few things that Maryann had made clear. After she had her baby, she would do everything in her power to take every penny away from Soraya and me. Henrik's fortune would be for her and the new baby.

But Soraya and I didn't know any of it. All we knew was that we couldn't wait for the arrival of our baby brother. On February 15, 1981, John Henrik Baumann was born. Henrik waited a few days then picked us up to visit him. We sat in his car and listened to what he had to say. He told us that baby John was very sick. They were running some more tests, but they believed that he had Werdnig-Hoffmann disease. It was also called floppy baby syndrome. He told us that it was a type of spinal muscular atrophy syndrome.

"Prepare yourselves, girls, for what you're about to see."

He waited for a while to let us know that babies with this type of syndrome would not live to see a year of their life. We were sad about the news but still elated to see him. We drove to Lutheran General Hospital in Park Ridge and put on scrubs for the intensive care unit.

For two months, we drove back and forth to the hospital with our father. I heard "Red Barchetta" by Rush playing constantly on the car radio: "My uncle has a country place that no one knows about. He says it used to be a farm before the Motor Law."

It was the first time I thought of a song as a story. I could identify with this story and wished that I could drive off free with the wind in my hair. The song was an escape and soothed me as I watched my brother suffer.

It seemed to rain every day, and I prayed and prayed for my brother's survival. I begged God not to take him. After two months a miracle happened. Maybe it was my prayers, I thought, but my baby brother got to go home. It was a strange setup; my father lived in his house and the baby lived at Maryann's.

May rolled around and Henrik brought John to my eighth-grade graduation party. It was one of the first times that I held him outside of the hospital. He was very fragile and could not move around much or pick up his head. He made a gurgling sound when he cried, and Maryann had to suction out his throat and mouth constantly. Rachel tried to prepare Soraya and me for the worst. I told her and everyone that he would live, that he would beat this.

In July we took an abbreviated trip to the farm, and when we came home, baby John was back in the hospital. For the first time in my father's life, I don't think he knew what to say. His quiet demeanor would not last long but for now he seemed a bit somber. He told me that my brother's eyes were turning gray. I asked him if that was bad.

"Yes," he said quietly.

Our father came by to get us to visit baby John on Sunday, August 2. Soraya and I were always happy to see him. I made him a card, drew a rainbow on it, and got him a new pajama top. When we arrived at the hospital, I looked into my brother's little lost eyes and knew he was saying goodbye. I held his hand. I noticed his shriveled tiny arms; I told him to fight and that I would see him soon. He had an oxygen tube in his nose, and he kept making his gurgling sounds.

Soraya and I gave him a snuggle hug before we left. I taped my rainbow card behind him on his bed and walked out the door, shielding my eyes against the bright August sunlight.

It was still summer break, and my father came by our house unannounced on Thursday morning, August 6. He walked in the front door. I sat on the steps with Rachel and Soraya.

"Baby John passed away yesterday morning," he said abruptly.

Tears slid down my cheek. I hid my face and hugged Soraya. "I'll give you an hour to get ready," he continued. "We are doing the wake and funeral all in one day." He sounded cold and callous.

I ran upstairs. It was too much for me to hear, so I cried in the shower. When we got to the wake, I couldn't bear to see John in that tiny little casket. Friends and family were all around us, but I was numb. I asked my father where Maryann was, and he told me that she couldn't be there. I understood. It was time to close the casket. Grandma and Grandpa Baumann, Henrik, Soraya, and I said goodbye. I kissed John's forehead and let a tear fall onto his cold cheek.

My father and I carried the tiny casket, the size of a cooler, to the grave. When the pastor finished his final prayers, I walked away disoriented into the sunlight. I wandered aimlessly into the cemetery feeling hollow and lost. I wore the sadness and heartbreak, felt it pulling on my face. The pain of losing such an innocent soul broke my heart. I sat alone with my thoughts. Too much had happened in my first thirteen years of life. How could I have been a pallbearer for my baby brother? So much was always asked of me. How could I stand there as they lowered his tiny coffin into the ground? And, for the first time, I was angry at God for so much sadness and cruelty.

It was gut-wrenching to watch a baby die, and I didn't understand any of it. No one but Rachel seemed to understand how I was feeling. No counselor at school, no friends, no clergy, no family. Almost no one said a word of comfort. It was as if my baby brother didn't exist. Rachel and I wouldn't realize it for years but her vision and mine about my innocent little brother had come true.

"Fallon, one day we'll all understand why God took your baby brother. I know it's difficult, but God has a reason for everything. He's in a better place."

Rachel told me that Henrik had pulled the plug on baby John. Rachel always wanted me to know the barbaric things that Henrik did. He had also told the nurses to stop helping baby John when he couldn't breathe. The bills had piled up at the hospital. I hoped baby John hadn't died alone. I would never know for sure, but I also didn't want baby John to suffer and live on machines. What I couldn't understand was the fact that my father never shed one tear for his son.

A few days went by, and I saw a rainbow in the sky. Golden-yellow monarchs would find Soraya and me. Neighborhood cats would walk in our direction and rub up against us. I believed these were signs that my baby brother was safe and no longer in pain.

I started high school. Within a few weeks of the beginning of the new school year, Henrik picked Soraya and me up to work with his fencing company. "Stop with the glum faces, you two," he yelled. "Your brother is gone. Grieving is a sign of weakness, and I won't have it! Let him go and move on!"

I sank deeper into myself and kept quiet. I knew my father's deplorable, cruel behavior would return. And just like that, it did.

Rachel and Bob had been a couple for over a year at this point. He was often at our house. I liked Bob and was glad to see my mother happy for once.

By now Maryann had gone into a terrible state of grief and depression, verging on psychosis. She told Henrik that baby John was flying around her room in his white christening gown. Mrs. Gallo was also beside herself. Nearly two months had passed since baby John's death and Mrs. Gallo called Rachel.

Her voice bordering on hysterical, she told Rachel that Henrik and Maryann had been sitting in her basement rec room on barstools. Henrik had been arguing with Maryann and then started screaming, "Stop crying about the baby, you bitch. I'm sick of it and he's never coming back!"

In a rage, Henrik punched Maryann off the bar stool and onto the floor. Mrs. Gallo hobbled downstairs with her bad knee as quickly as she could and told Henrik to get the hell out of her house.

"This is terrible," said my mother. "But Maryann is better off without him."

Rachel was sure that Henrik was being punished for all he had done, but I was confused. "Why are Soraya and I being punished?" I asked. "What did we do to lose that little baby?"

"Honey, only God can answer that question and one day you'll understand."

"I'll never understand why God would take an innocent little boy," I replied.

Maryann filed for divorce shortly after and we never saw her again. But Rachel and Mrs. Gallo secretly stayed friends until Mrs. Gallo passed away years later.

The painful months passed, and I knew that I had to move on. John would always stay in my heart, but for a long time, all my thoughts were with my sweet little brother who never had a chance. Something about losing him made me feel more isolated than ever.

By now Rachel and Bob were together most of the time and happily living their lives, yet there was no talk of marriage or moving things forward. Rachel was content with the way things were. Bob was the opposite of Henrik in every way, yet Rachel was apprehensive about another marriage.

Bob loved making us cinnamon rolls and having us over for dinner with his kids. Bob always told Rachel that he could pick us up from school and take care of us when she worked. He was just an all-around good guy whom we knew for most of our lives from our home on Pittsburgh Street, and Soraya and I felt comfortable with him.

Yet, for Rachel and Henrik, the fights and turmoil continued. He felt Rachel slipping away from him one day at a time and he couldn't stop or control it. As far as I was concerned, I could do no right in Henrik's eyes. Everything was laced with an argument. He made sure I knew that everything that didn't go the way he wanted was my fault when in reality it was because his own mind was filled with insecurities, self-doubt, and drama.

In the absence of Rachel and Maryann, it was now clear that I was his number one mental punching bag.

18

Hart to Hart

The summer of 1982 came in with travel, and in June, Henrik, Soraya, and I flew to the Cayman Islands. He demanded that we show gratitude for everything, including a simple glass of lemonade.

One day on Grand Cayman, we drove to Seven Mile Beach. Soraya and I were in the back seat in our own little world, whispering and laughing about school and our friends. Suddenly Henrik started shouting, "Why are you both ignoring me? I want no secrets between us! You are to include me in your conversations! UNDERSTAND!" -

He pulled the car to the side of the road and in a rage, said, "Get out!" He sped off, leaving us stranded, alone, scared, and miles away from the hotel.

Dumbfounded, Soraya asked, "What are we gonna do?"

"I don't know," I said. "Let's start walking."

The roads were narrow and dangerous. I went into survival mode and tried to calm Soraya. We walked for over forty minutes in the hot sun… fifty minutes…sixty minutes. We were sweating, thirsty, and demoralized. A car drove by and backed up. A man leaned out and said, "Want a ride?"

Soraya and I were lucky they were scuba-diving friends from the hotel. It would take me years of contemplation to understand that my father had put both of our lives in danger because of his temper. Our lives could've been compromised if God and our angels weren't watching over two young girls stranded on the side of the road. My anxiety ran continuously like a rollercoaster for the rest of the trip.

Henrik pulled a similar stunt and explosive tirade in Acapulco and in Miami, blaming me for ruining the trip. We never told our mother for fear of retaliation. It wasn't all bad, I reminded myself. In fact, we were able to tell her that we bumped into a Beatle, Ringo Star, at our pool bar.

While we were away, Rachel flew to visit her friend Theresa in Houston, Texas. Theresa and Rachel had a great time shopping, going to lunch, and talking about days past. There was a great shift for Rachel, and she could feel it. The two ladies got to talking and Theresa told her that she had someone in mind for her to meet. Rachel said that she was seeing a man back home whom she cared about, but things did not seem to be moving forward much.

"I think he's happy the way things are," she sighed.

"Are you exclusively dating?" asked Theresa.

"Well, yes, but the relationship has gone nowhere."

"Then, meet my friend. If nothing else, you'll have a nice chat."

The next day Theresa set up a lunch date. The minute that Charlie Malley walked into the restaurant and spoke, Rachel instantly felt she remembered him from a past life. Charlie was transfixed by Rachel. There was an immediate spark and chemistry between them. It felt as though he could look right through her.

Rachel, Theresa, and Charlie talked, laughed and had a great time for the rest of the afternoon. Rachel opened up about her past. Charlie explained that he had two kids and that his divorce was about to become final. Charlie talked about owning a successful construction company that built custom homes around the Houston area and how he played football in college. Rachel and Charlie spent the last three days of her trip together. They felt like they lived a lifetime, as if two souls from the past had found each other. They exchanged contact info and Charlie drove Rachel to the airport. Rachel didn't know what to do and Charlie couldn't wait to see her again.

When Rachel landed in Chicago, she felt something stirring inside of her. She felt that she could be happy after all that had happened. She felt hope, she felt options, she felt that one day soon she would have a decision to make. When she walked outside of the terminal, Bob Hart was waiting for her.

During the next weeks and months Charlie called Rachel every day. He also wrote to her and sent airplane tickets for her to visit every chance she could. She hated lying to Bob but told him that Theresa kept inviting her to visit. Thanksgiving came and Charlie flew in for a special dinner. He was staying at the Marriott Hotel where Rachel worked and wanted to show some of her friends the ring he had bought her.

Through the grapevine, Henrik found out Charlie was visiting and called Rachel.

"I heard that Charlie's in town!"

"Yes, Henrik. So?"

"I know you're at home cooking, so I'll run over to the Marriott to pick him up, I'd like to meet him."

"Over my dead body! Just leave it alone!"

"I'LL DO WHATEVER I WANT!"

"No! Just stay out of my life!"

The phone slammed down. She was at a loss and terrified. There was no stopping him, and she knew it. An hour and a half had passed, and Henrik pulled up to the house with Charlie.

Rachel felt as though she would faint when she saw both men talking up a storm. Oh God, she thought and rushed outside to see Charlie walking toward her.

"You won't believe this," said Charlie, giving her a knowing look. "He just told me five-hundred reasons not to marry you."

"What?" Rachel glared at Henrik.

"Yes, this man told me that you're a gold-digger and other awful things." He turned to Henrik. "I wouldn't listen to you if you were the last human being on the planet. I love this woman and I'm going to marry her. You don't even know her and how kind she is. Why don't you get the hell out of here."

"Fuck you," mumbled Henrik, got in his car and drove off, screeching down the quiet street. Charlie had scared off the bully.

At dinner Charlie pulled out the diamond ring and asked her for her hand in marriage. Rachel said yes, already knowing that when the holiday was over, she would go to Bob's home and explain the circumstances. She hated hurting Bob but was clear about her decision. She told Bob that he never made a move to take their relationship to the next level and that Charlie had actively pursued her. She explained that while Bob had a piece of her heart, Charlie had offered to take care of her and her girls. Charlie was much more ambitious, made things happen, and had a plan for his and Rachel's life.

I felt terrible for Bob and could see that he was heartbroken. Bob was distraught over Rachel's decision and tried to talk her out of marrying Charlie, but Rachel's mind was already made up.

In April 1983, Grandpa Baumann passed away, a man who to me had been full of class, much gentler than his wife. By now Bob Hart had spent months begging Rachel not to marry Charlie and told her she was making a mistake. Rachel and Charlie had fallen in love, but she was torn in so many places. She worried mostly about what was the best decision for us girls, yet at the same time she wanted happiness for herself. She asked herself if she was running away. She also knew that Bob was a good man. Bob never thought he was going to lose Rachel. It was a mental tug of war. Charlie could take her away from ten years of past hurts, disappointments, and cruelty that kept her in a mental prison. Charlie would love her and be a great provider.

Charlie's place was a beautiful million-dollar home with a built-in swimming pool and a jacuzzi tub half the size of our kitchen. Rachel, Soraya, and I flew down to Houston's sprawling suburbs with our dresses, and while Soraya and I had mixed feelings about living in Texas, we were excited for this new venture in our lives. The wedding was perfect and took place in the great room in Charlie's home. We flew back to Chicago and Rachel took care of the painstaking details of selling our home on Pittsburgh Street.

It was perfect timing. Newly married Rachel put our home on the market just as Henrik was breathing heavily down our necks to sell. She would get one last surprise from Henrik. The total amount of the lien was now up over $15,000 and would have taken a lifetime for Rachel to pay off. Henrik was also making good on tacking daily interest to the principal of the lien. Rachel was tired of living under Henrik's thumb and scrutiny. She wanted out, far away from him and his poisonous reign. Moving to Houston would get Henrik out of her way.

Things in our home were being sold, thrown out, donated, and given away. Christmas ornaments were crushed, lost, and destroyed; our beds were sold because we would have new ones in Texas. The little white kitchen radio was lost in the move. It would take me years to appreciate what it meant to me. It was peace amongst the chaos, it was strength against madness, it was an escape to something better. I didn't realize it then but the music that I heard from that little radio would follow me my entire life.

Our house sold fast, the closing and move out date would come at the end of June. Rachel quit her job at Marriott Hotel and with the profit from the sale, our father received his $15,000 and some change in lien money.

Charlie flew up from Houston to help with the move. My head was spinning; I was heartbroken at the thought of leaving the only home I had ever known. Mary Jenkins was there to pick up Soraya and me. We would live with her family for a few weeks and then move in with our father before moving down to Texas. In the interim, Rachel would look for a school in Houston. Mary, Rachel, and I walked from the backyard to the south side of the house one last time.

"Mom, why do we have to leave?" I asked. My eyes filled with tears. My heart beat with hopelessness.

"Fallon, I know you won't understand this now, but your father wants his money. He's forcing my hand on this."

"Why did he do this to us?" My voice cracked with despair.

"I don't know honey. I don't understand your father. I never will. You'll see, change is good. Sometimes you have to let go of things that you love in order to move forward."

"I don't want to leave. It hurts to go!"

My mother hugged me. "Everything will turn out okay, just have faith."

Soraya and I stayed with the Jenkins family for a few weeks and then the plan was a month with Henrik. Part of the custody ruling gave Henrik that amount of time over the summer with us. It was his visitation right and there was nothing Rachel could do about it. She knew the court systems wouldn't help her.

I looked at Soraya's sad eyes as we got into Mary's station wagon. All we had were a few boxes and some suitcases of clothes. Edwardo walked over and comforted Rachel as she stood on the driveway crying. When we drove off, I saw tears streaming down Mary's face. She felt the sheer gravity of the situation. She had been with us for every turn. She understood what Rachel had gone through at the powerful hands of Henrik. Now, she saw the magnitude of what Soraya and I had been through, the loss, mental abuse, the callous manipulation of two innocent girls at the hand of their father.

The sun was setting. I turned to face the window; my insides were trembling. I saw the house getting smaller in the rear-view mirror. Almost every memory I had was in that home. At that moment, all I had was that seat in the car. I felt a void in my heart. I had no idea where I was going.

I felt an ache and longed for my life to make sense. For now, my sister and I were in limbo. Our home was gone, our mother was leaving for Texas, and we dreaded staying with our father.

The next three weeks with the Jenkins family was a much-needed transitional period. Soraya and I hung out, stayed up late, and rode bikes with Jenny and Michelle who had become some of our closest friends.

On the day Henrik came to pick us up, we begged them not to let us leave with him, but he reminded us that we had no choice. We moved in with him and began a summer of travel like two lost gypsies. He had no idea how to take care of us; he might have been better at raising wild chickens. Soon we took off for the farm, then did the circle tour to Mackinac Island in Michigan. We came home and left for a dive trip on the island of Bonaire off the coast of Venezuela. Anything was better than staying at our father's depressing home that was nothing more than a bachelor pad and foreign to us. Although he had money, lots of it, sometimes he lived like a poor person. We missed our mother terribly. When we were in town Rachel called us every day. We knew wherever she was, so was our home.

When we got back from traveling, we visited baby John's grave and took a picture of the engraving of his name and dates on his headstone. He had only lived for five and a half months, and the pain of losing him still burned.

Henrik talked to Rachel from time to time and tried to guilt her and threaten her marriage.

"If you want your girls back," he sneered. "You have to move back to Chicago. The girls don't want to move to Texas! And I'm not letting them go!"

Henrik was causing more trouble and couldn't stand the fact that Rachel was married to a wealthy man who lived in a house five times the size of his. He told us that our mother needed more time in Houston and that we wouldn't start school in Texas until next semester. He was playing us with more of his tricks. Henrik knew if Rachel had settled down in Texas and us girls were still up north, he could now sling his web of chaos. He was always five steps ahead of everyone.

That fall, we returned to our old schools in Chicago. Henrik was now playing the doting dad, picking us up after class. But he fell quickly back into form. One day he started screaming at me about what I was wearing. While we wore school uniforms, one day a year we could wear what we wanted. I was wearing jeans and a T-shirt.

"You look like a slob," he said, his voice rising as he grew angrier by the minute. When we walked into the house, he went to the closet. Pulling out a wooden hanger, he shouted, "I'll show you what happens to slobs!"

He raised his arm. I flinched and then he smacked me with the hanger.

I used my arm to block him as I fell to the floor. The sting of the hanger sent shivers through my body.

"Dad, stop!" begged Soraya. "Please!"

He turned his head, and, in that moment, I got up and ran from him, closing the door of Soraya's and my tiny bedroom.

He left shortly after and I called Rachel. "Mom. Please, you have to get us out of here. We hate it with Dad! Since we moved in with him, he's thrown pennies at my face, screamed at me, and accused me of stealing bird seed from his bird feeder. Then, he slapped me for laughing and spilling milk on the kitchen floor."

"Oh my God, this man is completely crazy, but he never hit you when he was with me. I don't know how to fight the custody laws."

"Mom, I told him to get help and he told me that I needed help! He screams at us for everything. I have a bump on my head now."

"Honey, give me a few weeks and this will all be over."

What my mother didn't say is that she had discovered that Charlie had a drinking problem. She was worried that she had jumped from the frying pan into the fire. She heard Charlie coming home after work one night. He was loud, drunk, obnoxious, and slamming doors violently. She was scared and snuck out of a side door to one of the neighbors' homes while Charlie was in the kitchen.

She thought to herself, *What should I do? I can't bring my daughters down to Texas with another volatile man. Even if I'm not sure about Charlie's behavior, I can't take that chance with my girls. I can't put them through this again. And now Henrik is going to start trouble if I arrange flights for the girls.*

She knew that she couldn't repeat the last twelve years.

At the same time Henrik had done such a good job of lying to her. He had convinced her that we wanted to stay in Chicago.

With nowhere to turn, she reached out to Bob. He told her he would come and get her if she asked, and she was now considering his offer. She was also concerned about the ailing health of her father. It seemed like another whirlwind of chaos was circling her and she needed to simplify things.

She had to tell Charlie the truth. She thought the best way to diffuse the situation was to call Charlie's parents and have a sit-down talk with them first. She talked with Mr. and Mrs. Malley for hours before Charlie came home from work.

"I love your son, but I cannot bring my daughters down to Texas. If Charlie drinks and gets violent with my daughters, what will I do?"

"We understand but you're not giving your marriage a chance," pleaded Mrs. Malley.

"My ex-husband is very violent and is giving me problems about bringing my girls down here. I went through hell with this man for ten years. I can't bring them to another volatile situation. I don't even want to leave them up north with their father one more day. What should I do? Risk battling Henrik to bring my girls into another horrific situation? I can't do this to them or myself and I can't live without my girls."

They continued trying to talk Rachel out of leaving, but they were good people. "We're not happy about your decision but we can understand," they said. "You have to do what's best for your daughters."

When Charlie walked in, she told him the truth. She loved him, wanted the best for him, but she couldn't stay.

Back in Chicago, I missed my mother terribly and I didn't know where to turn. I was a fourteen-year-old girl who had seen so much violence, anger, and pain, and I carried a load of mental baggage. I was thinking about Houston as an escape away from my father, yet I didn't have the marbles at my age to know what I needed.

I had scars that had forged concrete barriers into my future. I wanted to erase all the sadness. I wanted to be happy and repair my broken spirit. When you grow up with abuse you sometimes do not realize it's happening to you, but the signs are there hidden behind a thin veil. Maybe I was to blame. Maybe it was my fault my father was so cruel. Maybe I shouldn't have fought back so hard. I lived wedged between two worlds: coping skills and fighting back. I was broken in so many places.

Luckily, I was social and was trying my best to regain the joyful identity in the center of my soul. But I had trust issues. How could I not? And so, I stayed quiet and kept to myself, remaining close to a smaller circle of friends. My grades suffered, my brain felt like scrambled eggs, and I had difficulty focusing. I stayed away from drugs and alcohol knowing that they would only beat my life deeper into the ground. I felt brainwashed and duped into thinking that I had no voice, no escape. I saw no way out. I started doing the only thing I could do. I fought back.

At the end of September, Rachel called to share the shocking news that

Bob was flying to Houston to get her. Rachel knew the best thing for us girls and the entire situation was to move back to Chicago and start a life with Bob.

Bob stayed in a hotel, rented a truck, and when Charlie was at work, they quickly packed up Rachel's things and drove north. Bob was in the truck and Rachel followed behind in her car. Rachel had made the decision to secretly leave Houston, worried that charming Charlie could have turned into another Henrik and could have done something irrational. Bob had a much more passive personality and avoided confrontation, but there he was driving ahead of her, not only coming to her rescue but doing so with no blame. In a whirlwind ping-pong match, Bob was overjoyed with his second chance. Later, they jokingly called the move back to Chicago "the Great Escape."

While I felt sad for Charlie, I liked Bob and the thought of staying in Chicago filled me with happiness.

When they got back, Rachel moved into an apartment with a month-to-month lease near Bob's home. She had a lot to straighten out with Charlie and asked him for a quick divorce. She still loved Charlie with all her heart, yet she knew this was the right thing to do. There was nothing easy about it. Charlie was heartbroken, distraught, and flat-out angry. Rachel kept all of her friends in the loop, Lee Broward being one of them.

Henrik put his foot down. "You won't get the girls back until you find a house," he said. "If you want, I'll take you to court, and you know how that will end." Henrik kept us unknowingly hostage and away from Rachel.

While Soraya and I focused on school, Rachel and Bob went into action. "Don't worry, my darlings," said Rachel, "soon we'll be together again. Bob and I are about to settle on a house."

The house was a beautiful bi-level in Des Plaines, larger than our home in Chicago with a built-in garage, and where Soraya and I would have our own rooms. Bob sold his house on the other side of Des Plaines. Rachel and Bob closed a few days after Thanksgiving.

Rachel was ready to start over, and bought us new bedroom and living room furniture, towels, plates, and silverware for the kitchen. I couldn't remember the last time she looked so happy or radiated such peace. By the time Christmas break arrived, Soraya and I moved in. Our Christmas tree was lit up. We shopped, baked cookies, and snuggled by our new fireplace.

The Jenkins family lived six minutes away and Bob's two youngest college-age daughters had moved in with their mother. We had a rotation of family and friends coming to visit our new home. For the most part, Soraya and I felt welcomed by our new stepbrother and stepsisters. We had known the Hart family since we were young children growing up on the same street. We knew that we would not live in the same household because most of Bob's kids were older and had their own lives. The oldest son, Bobby, lived in Virginia and Sally was married.

Everything seemed to be falling into place. Our lives had changed for the better overnight.

February 1984 came, and Soraya and I were busy helping Rachel plan for her wedding day. I also met Mike Daytona through Jenny Jenkins. He was tall, dark, hilarious, and would become one of my lifelong best friends. Rachel and Bob's wedding day, February 24, dawned chilly and bright. They married in the front foyer of our new home with their children and a few close friends as witnesses.

That should have been our happy ending. I started healing and finding my own identity, but Henrik was always in the background, doing his best to hang over me like a dark cloud that I couldn't shake.

19

Fabrications

The economy was booming in 1985, and the year brought more autonomy for Soraya and me. High school was in my rearview mirror, and I worked part time at Dominick's Grocery Store where I met another lifelong friend named Pina. She lived in Des Plaines and when I wasn't with Mike and our gang, I was with her.

In the fall I would start junior college and swim team, but for now I was busy with work and friends. It gave me a great diversion from Henrik who was always finding a way to latch on to Soraya and me.

On the opposite side of things, life with Rachel and Bob was serene. I constantly looked at Bob, wondering when he would explode or throw furniture at us. Each day I was pleasantly surprised that it never happened. He was kind to us and treated Rachel like the Galician princess she had once been. He bought her a new Cadillac, and together they planned trips to Spain.

They spent six glorious weeks on their honeymoon and found time to spend with the abuelos. After they returned, one busy morning, she received a call from Abuelo Alfonso. "I'm in a rush, poppa," she said. "Can I call you back?" It was the last time she talked to her charismatic, caring father who passed away a week later, leaving her devastated.

I was in California on a senior trip with Mike and a group of friends when she called with the news. I felt terrible that I wasn't there for her.

I told her how lucky she was to have had such a great father. I also said, "Look at the father I've got." She began to giggle, but I knew it was little comfort to her now.

The past year Henrik had jumped from one woman to the next. Some were nice, but to Soraya and me, most were skanks. Not surprisingly, he couldn't hold on to any of them.

In late summer that year Henrik bought an A-frame house on a wooded lot in Fontana, Wisconsin, a beautiful setting about two blocks off Lake Geneva. He had sold his hardware store, and this house was his new project. Like he had promised us when we were little girls that all the farms would be ours one day, he now promised us the house. I believe he wanted to use Lake Geneva as a lure to keep us in his life and for the most part, it worked.

The rest of the summer we helped him rip out old carpet, trim bushes, and haul stuff up to the lake house until we fell over. Soraya and I felt that we had a vested interest in the farms and the lake house because of the promises that he made. He was still a cruel asshole, in our opinion, but this land was turning out to be our legacy. And we would make sure it remained cared for and loved.

That fall, when I started at Triton College, Mike and some other friends grew concerned. They started seeing my struggles with my father. Every week brought a new argument or battle. It never seemed to stop. I would try and keep the peace, I would ignore my father, I would yell back. Nothing worked. His outbursts were always grossly disproportionate to the situation. When he fell into one of his violent tantrums, his brain would short circuit and implode, and I was his prime target.

Bob was equally concerned. He had stepped up to fill a void, talking me off the ledge when it came to a mushroom cloud of issues brought on by Henrik. He took the time to teach me how to control my breath and thoughts when my father came at me. Bob was well aware that the horrors of my childhood were rising to the surface. I talked to Rachel constantly about my father. She was the only other human who really knew what I was going through.

"Honey," she would say. "You'll never win with your father, ever! It's his way or the highway." She would try to say that phrase with her accent and would always mess it up. It was always funnier that way. And for that I was grateful.

I took yoga and I started seeing a counselor at school for bouts of anxiety and mild depression. I did my best to suppress my misery. All I wanted to feel was joy. But I didn't yet understand that I had been conditioned since birth and programmed for chaos at the hands of a man with a laundry list of undiagnosed mental illnesses.

The following Christmas, Soraya and I met Henrik's new girlfriend, Rosalie Lobo. She seemed sweet and friendly, yet I was always cautiously optimistic. Most women were trying to hook and reel in my father's wallet, but Rosalie was different from the women my father usually went for. She was pint size and a bit chubby, with short dark hair, and she had a great spark. There was something about her that Soraya and I liked. She was fun and light when our lives around our father were always difficult and gloomy. She owned a ladies clothing store and would find adorable clothes for us. She also had two kids a few years older than Soraya and me. Henrik seemed excessively obsessed with both of them, giving them presents and pushing Soraya and me aside to make room for the new kids in his life. When Rosalie's kids were at Lake Geneva, Henrik would shove us down into the basement to sleep on the pullout bed with all the spiders. We refused and Rachel got the phone call after the first incident. Soraya and I were tired of the second-class citizen treatment from Henrik.

In 1988 I graduated from junior college. That summer, when we came back from the farm, Henrik, Soraya, and I flew to Acapulco. Henrik was sulking from a bad breakup with Rosalie Lobo. They had gotten into a horrendous fight and Henrik called me at 3:00 a.m. to pick him up. Since I was living in Des Plaines and Rosalie's house was in the next town, it was a no-brainer. I found my father stomping mad in the middle of the street. He had walked about a half mile when I found him. I thought to myself, *He is an absolute child, he is incapable of having a normal relationship.* Fights, violence, and pounding his fists were always his answer. I was sad to lose Rosalie, but once she saw Henrik's true colors, she broke off all contact with him and us.

Like clockwork, Henrik found a new girlfriend, Joanne. Joanne had two daughters and I felt a bit sorry for them. They lived in a very dumpy apartment complex near the airport. One of Joanne's daughters told me that she couldn't wait to get out of their ghetto. I felt for her. I knew years ago that it could have been our fate if Rachel hadn't fought with everything to keep our home.

Time moved forward and Henrik was getting antsy. He started flying to Germany, but lied to Soraya and me telling us he had some kind of spy mission in Washington, D.C.

I told him he was lying. He threatened to hit me, and I told him that I didn't care what he did anymore, knowing that somewhere, someplace, he would have hell to pay. I only wanted to punish him by exposing his fabrications and bullshit.

Rachel was in the grocery store one day when she bumped into Joanne and asked how things were going. Rachel and Joanne weren't friendly from the start but had formed an alliance.

"Henrik and I broke up."

"I'm sorry!"

"I'm not! That man is absolutely crazy! Rachel, All I had to do was talk to a male friend and Henrik would go completely insane!"

"I would have loved to warn you about him but..."

"He screams at me, violently! I broke up with him three times and then he started harassing my daughters! I finally had to get a restraining order. I didn't know what else to do. This was going on for about a month. He would show up at my work, at my apartment. I thought he was going to break down my front door one night."

"Unfortunately, I remember those days being married to that asshole. Joanne, if you need anything, here's my phone number."

Like so many of Henrik's former girlfriends, Joanne would keep in touch with Rachel over the years.

In spite of all my confused emotions, I enrolled in and was accepted at Illinois State University where I devoted myself to my studies. "Get a good education, my darling," Rachel told me over and over. "You will become something. Promise me, and you won't be dependent on a man."

Not only did I promise her, I made the same promise to myself. I was lonely at first but made friends and had my fair share of boyfriends. I worked hard; I never gave up. And before I knew it, it was 1990 and I graduated with my bachelor's degree.

Soraya still had two years of school left. Henrik was now talking about a plan for us to open a small business once we both graduated. He would pay up front, help us get the business going, and when we made back the initial investment, we would repay him. Just like my memories from college, if Soraya and I did not follow Henrik's rules and what he said, he would revoke our college tuition. I could see the same things happening here. This business idea would have had the same repercussions. This was a way for him to dangle the carrot of success and control and manipulate us on many levels. Soraya and I agreed out of guilt and an obligation to our legacy.

Henrik had given us one solid piece of advice. "If you do nothing else," he said, "always remember to save, invest, and buy property." After all we had been through with him, at least I knew that he would leave us a legacy of property that Soraya and I would do our best to take care of. Now he was promising to invest in a business we could run. I didn't fully trust him, but it seemed the least he could do for us.

In the middle of June, Rachel, Soraya, and I left for Spain to visit our abuela. Since we'd lost Abuelo Alfonso, we relished every minute with our grandmother. Little did we know that Henrik had followed us and was on the Island of Palma de Mallorca, a puddle jump away from us, with another woman whom he'd met in Germany. We were in shock when he showed up at our hotel unannounced. Beside herself, Rachel said, "You have no right to be here. You're stalking us."

"I paid for the girls' plane tickets," he said. "So, I can show up if I want to! Besides, I was visiting my new girlfriend." He had indeed bought our plane tickets, but we had also earned them down to the penny through the work we had done for him in Lake Geneva. He had nothing to do with Rachel's ticket and she was furious to see him.

Rachel took a deep breath and called Bob. "Don't panic," he said. "I know all about Henrik. He's insane and vindictive. Try your best to ignore him. If he harasses you and the girls, let management know immediately. And if I have to, I'll get on a plane myself."

Secure in Bob's love, Rachel did her best to ignore Henrik, who stayed in our hotel for two nights and made sure we saw him everywhere we went. When we got back from our trip, eager to set out on my own, I began investigating different careers. Rachel jumped in, sending any lead she thought fit my talent. But Henrik, the Chicago businessman, ignored me.

I had learned a few things from him. I found a job in marketing and sales and saved up enough extra money to make a few successful investments in the stock market. I invented a round, water-resistant picnic blanket, and asked Henrik to help me patent it. I found it peculiar that he let me know he didn't have the money to do such a thing. I put my idea to the side and an ex-friend took the idea and ran with it. Mistake noted. I worked a second job to save for a condo. It was an opportunity to move out on my own and I closed on a two-bedroom condo in Prospect Heights in October of 1991.

As I eagerly moved into my future, the baggage I carried grew heavier. My anxiety flared intermittently and at times I sought help from different psychiatrists and counselors. I fought constantly with Henrik and relied on Rachel to be my mom, friend, and counselor in all matters relating to him. When I tried to talk to Henrik, he would explode in complete denial. Still, I thought I was moving on, but what I didn't understand was that things were about to get worse.

Her name was Mildred Helga Strauss, and she was Henrik's new girlfriend from Germany. At first, Henrik lied to us saying that Mildred was his cousin from the old country, but we knew better. Mildred didn't speak much English at first, and her voice had a growl that reminded me of nails on a chalkboard. She was methodical, calculating, and robot-like, very much an alien to Soraya and me. We joked that Henrik had disgusted so many women in the States, that he had to find himself some nasty imported pussy.

We wouldn't know for years until her English improved, but Mildred was the perfect manifestation of my father, shrewd and greedy with no filter. She could sniff cash from miles away and had already latched on to Henrik's wallet. We couldn't understand what Henrik saw in her. Maybe Mildred reminded Henrik of his mother, cold, calculating, and vindictive. To us, she had no style, no class, no charm. She was plain, boring, homely, and had an ugly emptiness about her. She looked like an old dusty rag, with her old hag shoes and blunt haircut, perfectly fitted for her Nazi helmet.

Mildred paled in comparison to drop-dead gorgeous Rachel. Mildred would soon have a seething case of jealousy toward Rachel as the natural beauty was adored by all that met her. At this point in his life, Henrik had settled for Mildred, and she had settled for him. Mildred became nothing more than a sniveling, soulless, black hole of a bitch that was content to stick around if only for the money. Her life would not be easy, but not even a catastrophic event could remove her ass from the golden egg she was about to sit on.

Henrik and Mildred carried on a long distant relationship for years. Soraya and I joked that she flew back and forth on her broomstick, and we hoped she would get tired of his bullshit. She had been dealing with her estranged husband. Now, Henrik told us that she was divorced, but I was sure he was lying.

I was equally sure that Henrik was forcing her to leave her husband and move to the United States.

Whenever Mildred was in town, he harassed me at work, wearing me down, asking me to come to Lake Geneva. He would convince me to take her to lunch, buy flowers, and shop with her so that she felt wanted.

"Go to hell," I told him. "I'm not dating that whore. It's your job to take care of her. I don't like her, and I can't speak to her because she's not interested in learning English."

Every week the nagging phone calls came. If I didn't do what he said, then I was the problem child. I told him to stop bothering me at work because I could get fired. He never listened and he never stopped. He was nearing retirement and had nothing else to do but to harass me. One week's call came in and I was fed up.

"Fallon, the Jamisons are having a graduation party, and I would like you and your sister to show up."

"I don't know them and I'm going horseback riding this weekend."

"Fallon! Enough already! You need to do some things for me when I ask you! You *will* be there! You have to show your face, I will not take no for an answer."

"I said I'm going horseback riding!"

"YOU ARE NOTHING BUT DEFIANT!"

Every week there was a new tactic, guilt trip and manipulation of my time. I was overwhelmed.

That holiday season, Henrik started a new tradition. He would celebrate Christmas with Soraya and me three weeks early, and then fly to Germany to see Mildred, whom we now called Broom Hilda. We didn't really care about the holidays with those two because we preferred spending them with Rachel and Bob.

By early summer, 1993, Mildred was back in Germany and Henrik was having a small party up at the lake. He insisted that Soraya and I be there. Reluctantly, we agreed, and I arrived at the house on Friday after work. I called hello and went up to the guest room where I set my overnight bag and sweatshirt on the edge of the bed where I sat taking off my sneakers.

Henrik came in and saw my overnight bag. Suddenly he burst into a rage. "How many times do I have to say it? Do *not* put your bag on the bed! It's dirty and it will contaminate the comforter!"

He threw the bag and my sweatshirt on the floor. The bag rolled to the wall spilling clothes everywhere. Then he kicked my shoes.

"Are you serious?"

"YES, I'M SERIOUS! NOW PICK UP ALL THIS SHIT ON THE FLOOR!"

"My bag is not dirty. What's wrong with you! All you ever do is yell!"

I began to pick things up. My face slumped while he scolded me like I was a dog rubbing my nose in my own piss. I knew my self-worth, but around Henrik I felt like a constant failure; I could never measure up. No sooner had I finished picking up my clothes, Henrik started in on me again. His vile aggression was always rooted in shame.

"Why are you wearing sweatpants again?" Henrik used belittlement to control me.

"Excuse me?"

"You heard me!"

"Because I left work and I felt comfortable in them!" I looked away and continued picking up my clothes.

"LOOK AT ME WHEN I'M TALKING TO YOU! You should wear tighter clothes, so you know whether you're gaining weight or not."

"My weight is fine! If you're going to continue to talk to me this way, I'm leaving."

"You and your smart-ass mouth! You're just like your mother."

"Why? Because I stick up for myself, and so did she?"

"You, your mother, and your hate program for me."

"Hate program? Maybe you should think about how you treated us."

"Oh yeah? Don't challenge me!"

"You know Dad, you are sick! You need a psychiatrist, medication, or something. There is no peace with you, only bullshit!"

"*You* are the one that needs a psychiatrist, Fallon, not *me*!"

He launched himself into another tirade, shoving the lamp and picture frames off of the bedroom dresser. Some glass broke, a lightbulb busted, and the shade dented in on one side.

I was smart enough to know when to leave. I gave him a look as if I wanted to spit on him. "I'm leaving until you calm down." I walked out and up the road to my girlfriend Regina's home.

Besides the violence, he never missed an opportunity to maliciously judge and criticize me. "You're stupid," he would say. "You can't even speak fluently in Spanish. Come here, tonta…*tonta*!" Tonta meant stupid in Spanish. He told me that my cooking was horrible even though I was a single girl who ate salads, cereal, and peanut butter and jelly sandwiches like all the other single girls I knew. My hair didn't look good, my clothes, my grades. It was constant ridicule.

Nothing was ever good enough for him, I was used to that. But jabbing me about my weight was taking things too far. I wasn't a string bean, but I wasn't fat at all. I enjoyed the attention of men and had received compliments about my looks for most of my life. I had a different style but my face and coloring were identical to my mother's. I knew he hated that I looked a lot like her. I knew my father was manipulative, yet it still hurt, and I couldn't get him to stop. If I was upset, then I was too delicate. If I yelled and fired off a sarcastic counterblast to his insults, I had an anger problem.

I could have told him that he had a big fat ugly nose right in the middle of his pathetic face, but I didn't need to shoot off insults to make myself feel better. Henrik would fire off insults anytime he felt the need. He fired off insults to everyone around him because of his self-loathing. He fired off with violence because anger was all he had inside.

When Soraya arrived, I did my best to stay out of my father's way. He had organized a party on Sunday for family, friends, and neighbors. As the party moved into full swing, Soraya and I occupied ourselves at the badminton net in the front yard.

We were in the middle of a volley when I noticed a strange girl arrive. Soraya and I had never seen her before. She was about my age with bad teeth, greasy blonde hair, and acne near her chin. She looked like she was high on something. Her tiny red car was badly in need of a paint job, with a spare tire on one of the axles that made it look lopsided. With all the clean-cut partygoers, the girl stuck out like a sore thumb.

I asked her who she was. She gave me a smart-ass chuckle and walked away, setting my radar on high alert. The party was winding down, but before I drove home, I stopped at my friend Regina's. An hour later, I was on my way, turning the corner past my father's house, when I noticed that the red car was still in front. *What the hell*, I thought, and parked behind it.

I got out, ran up the front walk and opened the door. "Hello," I called.

I heard them upstairs. They were loud, and the bed was thumping against the floor. For a moment I was convinced that the bed would crash through the ceiling.

"Dad, what the hell are you doing?" I shouted. "Fucking that meth head, crack whore? I'm sure Mildred will love to hear about this!"

I heard him jump out of bed and jostle his belt buckle, then a pause. The air grew quiet.

"Fallon," he suddenly shouted, "I was taking a nap!"

"Yeah, and I was born yesterday! I know that girl is upstairs, Don't lie to me! Her car is out front!"

"What?"

"You better pay her and tell her to get out of here. I had better never see her here again!" I slammed the front door and left. I thought to myself that there was not a big enough can of Raid to kill this cockroach.

Our father-daughter relationship had failed on many levels, yet for once I felt on top of the world. I had vaporized my anger and helplessness. I had confronted a small fraction of the injustice that plagued our family. As I drove home, I had a good laugh and wondered if Henrik's dick was dripping like a faucet, in need of some penicillin. I stopped to visit my mother and told her the ridiculous story.

Summer was behind us, and the falling leaves of October were everywhere. I had tried my best to put my grudges with my father behind me. When he called to say that he had some business to attend to at the farm and that Soraya and I needed to be there, I was suspicious. But Henrik reminded us that the farm would be ours one day. We loved the farm and had not been there since we started college, so we went. Little did we know what he was planning behind our backs.

Regarding our father, we had evolved our behavior to engage as little as possible. He was well aware that he was an outsider. He had done it to himself and would never be welcomed into our world. Soraya handled our father by staying quiet and trying to keep the peace, while I jumped at the chance to rip his head off.

We had no idea what business Henrik took care of that weekend, but in a few years to come we would slide down the face of that mountain into another valley of betrayal.

20

Land-Scam

Grandma Ethel Baumann was now ninety-one. I was twenty-seven, engaged in my own life, and really didn't care much about her. To me, she was as nasty as her son. But Rachel held compassion for her. During the last years of Grandma Baumann's life, Rachel would bring her lunch and sit with her. She also brought her an emergency contact wristband in case something ever happened.

One day, Rachel got a call from Lutheran General Hospital in Park Ridge. Grandma Baumann had been picked up wandering two miles from her home, scuffed up, disheveled, dirty, wearing old pajamas. After work I took Rachel to the hospital to pick Ethel up.

"It's okay, Ethel," Rachel said gently. We brought Ethel back to Rachel's house where she gave her a bath, fed her, and washed her clothes. In the meantime, I called Henrik. I knew Mildred was in town and that he was spending all his time with her. "You need to get your mother," I said sternly. "The way you take care of her is pathetic."

Rachel and I looked at each other. Over the years, we had grown closer, and the fact that I could tell Henrik off only made our bond stronger.

Grandma Baumann was diagnosed with dementia. She was still living in her home and needed regular care but Henrik refused to pay for her healthcare. A record-setting heat wave had engulfed Chicago and Rachel went over to make sure she was okay. To her surprise, Henrik answered the door.

"Get the hell out of here, Rachel."

"No. I'm here to see your mother. You know I come by a few times a week to check on her."

"I told you to get out of here!"

Rachel noticed that all the windows in Ethel's home were shut, and she had no air-conditioning.

"You have to open some windows. It's stinking hot in here. Your mother will suffocate."

"I SAID GET OUT!"

Rachel walked to her car, shaking her head in exasperation. She sat behind the wheel, pondering for a moment, and wondered if she should call the police. She was sure Henrik had closed all the windows in Ethel's home on purpose. *He won't go* that *far*, she reasoned, but then she knew. She saw the events unfold before her. In her mind she saw the windows shut to seal Ethel's fate. Henrik would keep all visitors away and Ethel would not be allowed to have water. With her brain smothered in dementia and the temperature reaching 105 degrees outside, Rachel's prediction came true. Ethel Baumann was dead in thirty-six hours.

There was nothing Rachel could do or say. We all knew the truth and wondered if in the end, Grandma Baumann saw who her son was.

The year of 1997 was busy. Rachel and Bob came back from their annual six-week trip to Spain. I got engaged to my boyfriend Sam and we were grieving the unexpected death of his sister, Lisa. Sam and I wanted to be happy with our engagement but felt the gut-wrenching pain of losing her. We felt lost, but knew we had to move on. At the same time Henrik was about to marry Mildred, to me the Witch of the Berlin Wall.

Rachel sat down with me to express her concerns. "I have good reason to believe that Mildred could take everything away from you girls," she said.

"I'll try talking to Henrik," I sighed.

He was becoming more difficult to speak with, more arrogant and impatient, walking around and bragging that he was moving to Lake Geneva with Mildred. Soraya and I couldn't understand what he was doing with Mildred. She was unattractive and severe. But maybe that's exactly what he needed to enable him to sleep with his whores while keeping an air of respectability. We knew if we shared our thoughts, a bomb would go off in his head and we would be the victims of his wrath.

A few months before he got married, I sat with him at the lake and told him I was concerned about the farms and other land. "I'd rather you give your money to charity than have it go into a different family," I said.

I politely explained that Mildred was thirteen years younger than him. If something happened, she could get remarried, and his entire estate could go to another man or her daughter. I reminded him that he had made promises to Soraya and me.

Things went worse than I had anticipated. "How dare you speak to me that way?" he said. "Your inheritance is none of your damn business!"

In that instant, I knew with utter certainty that Soraya and I were now marginalized out of the equation. Henrik knew I was onto him. We couldn't prove this, but Mildred made Henrik promise that we would get nothing from his estate once they were married. I had never asked him for anything. Still, I was surprised that when I talked civilly about a woman who was not in love with him and who was clearly only marrying him for his money, he would not listen. He laughed in my face as he dismantled his promise and severed the roots of my existence; and I had no way of stopping him.

Soraya had her own experiences with Henrik and Mildred. Once they were in downtown Lake Geneva and found themselves in Soraya's favorite boutique. She saw a jacket she liked and wanted to buy it but she had forgotten her wallet. "Dad," she called. "Can I borrow some money from you to buy this jacket? I'll pay you back when we get home."

"No sorry, Soraya, I don't have any extra money with me right now."

Soraya was puzzled but believed him. As she was browsing through the store, she noticed Mildred whispering in his ear. A few minutes later, she found Henrik and Mildred at the cash register. Henrik had pulled out his wallet and was paying for the jacket Soraya had shown him. He was now asking the clerk to cut the tags off so Mildred could wear it home. Mildred glanced at Soraya and put on the jacket.

Soraya's mind went blank.

"Don't look at me like that, Soraya," said Henrik. "I couldn't buy the jacket for both of you."

"I thought you said you had no extra money?"

"I don't. There was just enough for Mildred, and you have enough jackets, anyway."

Mildred deliberately ignored Soraya as she casually put on the jacket and admired herself in a mirror by the cash register, a blatantly rude and callous power play, showing Soraya who was in command of Henrik and his money.

Soraya and I had many similar stories. From the time I was a little girl, I had been watching and listening to Henrik's behavior. It would take time, but this would fuel me to learn all I could learn about empowering my own investments, my career, and my faith. I carried the heart of my mother who never gave up and who held a strong faith and gentle soul. I would live to make my father regret every sword he had forged against Soraya and me. I owned my power because it was Rachel's power, and he knew it.

I didn't anticipate that Henrik was constructing a German army against me to seal the deal, headed by Mildred. A gang of putrid soldiers enticed by Henrik's cash to intimidate me, to shame and shoo me away. What they wouldn't realize is that I would stand my ground. Henrik would be the one to pay the ultimate price for Mildred's greed. He would lose his own flesh and blood.

I started receiving hateful, ranting phone calls from him, berating me about the damaging talk that we had. Next, he and Mildred began sending scornful letters in the mail. Now they were plotting and having Mildred's family take on the dirty deed. A week later I walked out to the mailbox and found a letter from Germany. It was Mildred's aunt tearing me to shreds about what I had said to my father about his estate, telling me to go to hell and to keep my hands off of what was my father's and now Mildred's. "You will have no inheritance," she said. "It now belongs to Mildred and how dare you talk to your father about things that no longer concern you."

Seething, I called Henrik who denied that he had told Mildred's aunt anything about our conversation. I asked him how she got my address, and how she knew what we were talking about.

"She must have guessed about everything we spoke of?" he replied coldly.

I couldn't believe the blatant lie right to my face. I told him this is war and if he didn't watch his step, he would lose his daughter and when his miserable wife had had enough of his bullshit and left, he couldn't come crawling back. I told him if "Team Germany" ever sent me another letter I would never speak to him again! I told him to remember who I was. As disgraced as I was to be part of his family, I was still his flesh and blood, and I wasn't going away just because his latest conquest wanted me to. I knew he was in his glory at home within a familiar cloud of misery, chaos, and rage.

I returned to the mailbox to find another letter, this one from Henrik himself. Pages of scornful rhetoric attacking me. I had forgotten who I was dealing with, a man who had no conscience, who had no concept of other people's feelings, no scruples. A man whose DNA structure was woven into strands of hatred. Henrik was a mindless machine with no delete button.

I sat on my front steps and cried. I felt broken and branded by animosity. I knew in my heart that I would always live on the other side of evil.

I called Rachel daily just to hear her voice. For weeks I sat in an empty church. I was suffering, and I prayed for resolutions. I begged God for a solution, a way out. I went back over the years to see what God would tell me, wondering if I was ever heard. I always looked toward the skies and stars for answers. My life that was encompassed by my father was in a state of complete collapse. I knew that he could try to mentally and physically beat the faith right out of me, but I held my ground. Sometimes as I sat there, my mind wandered, and I thought of times when I was in my father's hardware store and people would come up to me and tell me how wonderful he was.

"Did you know," they would say, "that your amazing father went out of his way last week to fix our broken front door hinge. We heard he can fix anything. Your mom is so lucky to have him."

I always gave them a dumbfounded look. I couldn't believe they were talking about the same man. I sometimes felt that I was trapped inside of a snow globe. There I was with my father in the midst of sheer chaos with no escape from his control. Outside the snow globe my father charmed and captivated people with a completely different persona. They had no idea that under that exterior lurked a sociopath. Looking in from the outside, they would smile at me, the dutiful daughter lucky to have such a wonderful father.

My mind came back to the present moment. The choir was practicing hymns for that week's service. I listened to their beautiful voices echoing through the church and wept. I prayed for peace, I prayed to find myself amongst the madness. I longed for my life to make sense and wanted to ask Henrik for a father-daughter separation. I didn't yet know there was a term for it. It was called emancipation. I didn't realize that it was possible to cut my father completely out of my life. I dreamt about it, and plotted in my mind how I would do it. I didn't need to legally emancipate myself;

I would just sever the connection. I didn't want to wake up one more morning dealing with the slop that Henrik threw at me. After what he had done to my mother, there would be no peace with him. Rachel told me over and over that I would make myself sick fighting him. "You won't win, cariña," she said, holding my hand.

I didn't care, I hated him, and the war was on.

Even though I was newly engaged, my father only thought about his own marriage. June arrived with a fragrance of blooming lilacs. Things settled down momentarily and I was sure he knew that I was on the brink of cutting ties. I was becoming stronger, wiser, and bolder, and I was standing up in the face of the bully. He seemed intent on stripping away any happiness I wanted for myself. Yet, I questioned myself constantly. Why was I letting this happen? How could I break free of the hell I was going through?

The dreaded day arrived. Henrik was about to marry Mildred, Broom Hilda, the Witch of the Berlin Wall. This hadn't stopped him from sleeping with every slut he could find, which only confirmed for Soraya and me that Mildred was only interested in one thing as far as he was concerned. We came for the ceremony but stayed away from so many family members who had arrived from out of town. Mildred wore dusty black shoes that looked like they came from a witch's closet and a bonnet that made her look older than she was. And then it was done. They walked past Soraya and me, the picture of unhappiness.

Katrina, Mildred's only daughter, had flown in and she had told me in so many words to leave Henrik and her mother alone. I was sure Katrina was after Henrik's fortune as much as her mother. But Katrina was conflicted, too. After the wedding, she shared a story that was straight out of Henrik's playbook.

One afternoon, Mildred invited her girlfriends over. Henrik noticed them laughing and having a good time. Slowly his rage grew. How could she have a good time and ignore him?

Later, while Mildred was taking a nap, Henrik, still furious, threw a full glass of water at her face.

She woke up stunned, not understanding what had happened. The weather had been warm, and at first, she thought that maybe she was sweating. And then she realized the truth. Upset, she called Katrina who called Henrik and told him that if he did something like that again, she would personally come back from Germany to pick up her mother, and he would never see her again.

She had also learned that in one of his rages, Henrik had thrown a television set over the twenty-foot balcony.

I told Katrina that Soraya and I had tried to warn Mildred not to marry our violent father, but no one would listen. Mildred had made her bed and now she needed to lie in it.

A few months passed and Sam, our friend Mike, Soraya, and I headed up to the farm for an October weekend. Henrik had told us for years that he had rented out the farmhouse so that it wouldn't lie vacant.

We went canoeing down the Kickapoo River and stayed in a bed-and-breakfast just outside of Ontario, Wisconsin. When we reached the farm-house, we took time to walk the back forty. It was raining that afternoon, and we were now driving on some of my father's land, giddy and jumping out of the car to take pictures of the soggy autumn landscape. What happened next was as if the hand of God pulled us toward the painful but necessary truth.

Sam, Mike, Soraya, and I walked happily in the sloppy soaked grass when a man appeared out of nowhere, aiming his bow and arrow at our faces.

"You're trespassing." He spoke crossly.

I put my hands up in the air. "Sir, can you put the bow and arrow down. This is my father's land. Henrik Baumann." I had turned white as a ghost and the blood had rushed to my feet.

"Baumann? That jerk off hasn't owned this land or the house in years. He sold it years ago."

"What are you talking about? My dad's owned this land for thirty years." Soraya's heart sank as she spoke.

"Well not anymore. You're probably the same idiots who drove all over my land and put tire tracks everywhere a few weeks ago!"

"No sir, we weren't here."

"Well, I tell you what, you better get out of here now before I call the police."

All four of us somberly got back in the car. Mike and Sam had no idea what was going on. Soraya and I made eye contact and shook our heads in disbelief. We were in shock and needed time to think. Mike and Sam knew our history with Henrik and knew this was bad. I told Mike to drive into town and that Soraya and I needed to talk to the banker's wife. She had been friends of our family for years and if there was a real estate transaction in town, she would know about it.

It continued to rain, and I felt my throat closing. I tried to control my breathing and started EFT tapping. I took my index and my middle finger and began tapping on the middle of my forehead. It was a stress technique that I learned in therapy and a great coping skill. It looked crazy but it helped in times of chaos. We walked into the bank soaking wet and found Mrs. Robinson. Both of our sad faces looked straight at her, tears streaming down our cheeks.

"Hi girls, I didn't know you were in town. What's wrong?"

"Mrs. Robinson, we need to ask you a few things."

"Of course." Mrs. Robinson had a concerned look.

I couldn't believe the words as they came out of my mouth. "Did my father sell the farmland, the house, and land around it? Mrs. Robinson, I need the truth."

Mrs. Robinson hesitated momentarily. "Yes girls, I'm sorry. He sold it back in 1993. I don't know what to say. I thought you knew."

"This can't be! The land can't be gone. This was supposed to go to

Soraya and me one day. We were never supposed to sell it. It was in our family, and it was supposed to be for our kids." My tears wouldn't stop.

"I'm so sorry girls."

I wiped my nose with my sleeve. "Can I use your phone?"

"Of course, I'll show you to the side office. You can use the phone there."

I was numb from head to toe, devastated and sick to my stomach. Soraya and I walked over to the phone. I called my father. My heart was pounding but yet again I was ready to go to battle for what was right. Henrik picked up.

"Dad?"

"Hi Fallon."

I paused for a moment. "You sold the farms. Don't try to lie about it. We know the truth about everything."

He grew quiet and I could tell he was thinking of something to say. "But there's still some farmland left. That piece was only empty fields."

"You sold the house and the land around it! That was family land, and you sold it four years ago and didn't tell us. I'm going to do what I should have done a long time ago. Don't call me, don't come over to my house, don't write me nasty letters! I'm not talking to you for a long time. This goes for Soraya as well. You don't give a damn about us and that sniveling greedy bitch you're married to will find out soon enough who you really are!"

I slammed the phone down as hard as I could and began to sob. Soraya and I hugged each other tight, both of us heartbroken. I found it hard to breathe from the anguish and treason, I felt suffocated by the layers of betrayal. It wasn't the land or the money. Our father had ripped at our hearts yet again and sold us out. We stood dumbfounded and alone like fools in a giant circus tent.

The next phone call was to Rachel. There wasn't much she could do but comfort me. Soraya and I wouldn't find out until later, but with the money from the sale of the farmland, Henrik paid off Mildred's condo back in Germany in full so that Mildred could fly back and forth from Lake Geneva to Germany in style.

Seven months had passed, and Henrik was trying devious tactics to get back in my good graces by calling other family members so that I would call him back. From then on, I was edgier, always had my guard up, and never fully allowed him into my personal life. I focused on my career, my friends, travel, and my upcoming marriage. I had a good life away from Henrik. My mom and I grew even closer; she was in her glory helping me with wedding plans.

The big day had almost arrived in October 1998. The church was bustling with family and friends for the rehearsal dinner. Everyone was there, Jenny, Pina, Mike, Regina and eighteen in our bridal party.

My father had manipulated, triangulated, and insisted on paying for the reception and demanded to walk me down the aisle. He had called everyone, including Rachel. I knew he was capable of ruining my wedding, sabotaging my friends, and that this was his pathetic way back into my world. But I was too afraid to say no. I gathered my strength and talked to him privately to ask if Rachel could also walk me down the aisle, as planned.

"ABSOLUTELY NOT!" he shouted. "All she's done is cause problems for me."

But at the rehearsal, I asked Rachel to join my father and me at the back of the church.

"I already said, *no!*" he jeered when he saw her.

"She raised me," I countered. "It's my wedding day. You're here. You got what you wanted. Why can't I have what I want? Why does everything have to be about you?

"GOD DAMMIT, RACHEL," he shouted. "Did you put her up to this?"

"Of course not, Henrik," she hissed. "I raised my daughter to have her own mind."

"Shh!" I said, "Stop causing a scene and ruining my rehearsal."

Bob had found us. "I don't want to tell you again, Henrik," he said. "Leave my wife alone."

My friend Mike's family was staring at me as the blood rushed down to my feet. Mike, who knew me so well, was now walking toward me. I stood there lost and outraged.

"Classic!" Mike giggled, glancing sideways at Henrik and pulling me away before hugging me.

"I told you Mike, this is what my dad does. He ruins everything."

"I can see that. In church? Who starts a fight in church?"

"Someone who's going to hell."

Mike laughed as we waited for the priest to show up. "Listen, you're between a rock and a hard place," he said. "We'll let the bully think he's having his way. If it keeps him quiet, all the better for us."

The morning of the wedding, Henrik called the house. Rachel answered the phone, and he informed her that he wasn't coming to our home to drive in the limo. He would meet everyone at the church. He slammed the phone down. I thought for a split second that I should ask Bob to walk me down the aisle, but I knew that would start World War III. Bob deserved to walk with me; Rachel and Bob were always there for me and the only voices of reason who completely understood what I was going through.

In the limo with my bridesmaids, I stewed momentarily about Henrik's chronic destructive behavior. But when we reached the church, glowing and candlelit, my mind relaxed. It was raining, drops tapping against the windows, but the church was elegant, regal, similar to a cathedral in the European countryside. Soon, I would be Mrs. Colucci, off to Maui, and finally rid of the tainted Baumann name.

We had 250 guests from all over and I had worked on the wedding for the last sixteen months. I kept my eyes on Sam as I walked toward him, my cruel father holding my arm, but my heart glowed as bright as the church.

After, in the penthouse ballroom with its chandeliers dripping light, I ignored Henrik, who was in rare form. He pretended to be a newscaster talking about the wedding as if it was the event of the century. It was not only a tactic to put him in the spotlight but by doing this stunt he avoided any emotional speeches he would be expected to give about his daughter.

21

Mental Bake Down

In June, 2001, Sam and I joyfully awaited our new baby boy and Rachel was over the moon with excitement. Tensions with my father zoomed and twisted like a roller coaster and the stress was more than I could handle.

I had a wonderful pregnancy but a difficult delivery, an emergency C-section; Sam was in the operating room with me. Jake Samuel Colucci was beautiful from head to toe. Rachel, Soraya, Sam's mom, and Mike were at the hospital immediately to see him. My father showed up fifteen minutes before visiting hours were over. The morning after my delivery, I sensed I was in a different world. It was as if my hospital bed had slid off the side of a mountain and I was nowhere familiar. Nothing looked the same. I sensed I was in some sort of fog, surrounded by a cement prison. I did all that I could to shake it.

A few days after we came home, I knew something was wrong with me; my brain felt like a bowl of spaghetti that had been dumped on the floor. I knew I was in trouble. I had horrible urges to hurt my baby, yet I would never make good on the impulses. I loved my Jake, and it was my vow as his mother to protect him. I thought if I ever said anything about harming my child, someone would put me away, so I kept the horrible thoughts to myself. I asked Sam to put our mothers and Soraya on a round-the-clock schedule. I had solid help night and day for over a month.

I wouldn't be made aware of this for some time, but I was suffering from a terrifying case of postpartum psychosis. Much darker, twisted and menacing than postpartum depression. I remember hearing my baby crying when my sister would tell me he was sleeping; I couldn't sleep or rest and had horrific bouts of impending doom. I saw giant shadows of my baby on the wall and fought with my delusions, forcing myself to understand that they weren't real. I ended up with mastitis and a 102-degree temperature. I laid down in the basement and had what I believed to be an out-of-body experience levitating off of the futon bed, while my thumb was the size of the room. I suffered suspended in midair and out of reality. I pushed myself every day to escape this horrendous depression, but I was in such a mist that I couldn't reach out for help. I felt my brain was ripped open and foraged by psychosis. I heard and saw things that weren't real. I felt trapped in a bubble, grayness all around. I didn't know what was happening to me.

After about five weeks I started feeling slightly better but was still nowhere near where I needed to be. Henrik wanted to see baby Jake, so I packed up my car and left for the lake. I did the best I could to put myself together, showered, makeup, everything. When we arrived, I set Jake down in his baby carrier and put a few things in one of the side bedrooms. My father was in the kitchen and Mildred walked into the bedroom. Her eyes widened. "Uhhh Fallon, you got fat!"

My mouth fell open in shock. Mildred sucker punched me with her comment. "What did you just say to me? I just had a baby!"

My father ran from the kitchen to quickly intervene. "What's going on here?"

Mildred immediately escaped like a coward.

"I'll tell you what's going on in here," I said, as I watched her leave. "Your wife just called me fat right to my face. I just had a Goddamn baby. She needs to keep her mouth shut." I knew I was so much more than Mildred's cruel words.

"Fallon, you two need to get along."

"I didn't do anything. She needs to get a filter. I don't call her ugly to her face, do I?"

I stormed out, grabbed Jake in the carrier, and sat on the front deck until I cooled down a bit and collected my thoughts. Mildred came outside to water her plants.

"So, Fallon, when do you go back to work?" She showed no signs of remorse.

"I don't know Mildred, five more weeks or so."

"It's too bad that you have to go back to work. In Germany you get six months off for maternity leave and I don't have to work," she said in her gloating tone.

"Well, this isn't Germany. By the way, I like my sales job where I get to work from home when I want. Haven't you said enough today, Mildred?"

"Oh?" Mildred turned quickly, surprised by my rude tongue.

I picked up Jake and made my way through the house.

"I'm leaving. See you later Dad," I yelled out with an edge.

"Why are you leaving so soon?"

"Maybe I'll come back when your wife has a clue, but that might be when hell freezes over."

"Hey, get back here and stop being so rude. You cause so many problems, Fallon."

"Yeah, I'm really the problem here." The door slammed and I was gone. I muttered under my breath, "It's you and your cruel wife who cause the problems around here."

I went to the lake and met Regina by the Brookwood Marina so she could meet baby Jake. On my way home my eyes filled with tears. I called Rachel and shared the latest ridiculous story. Rachel only saw darkness and evil in Mildred's empty soul. She reminded me that only miserable people viciously insulted others to feel better about their own insecurities. "It's about her, Fallon," she said. "Not you. She's jealous of you." I told her that I understood, but that the damage was done.

Five weeks passed, and I started feeling a little better. It was about a week before I went back to work. Rachel, Bob, and Soraya were in Spain, and I was talking with them about their flights coming home. Later that night I had a terrible vision. I was walking back and forth between my bedroom and Jake's nursery and felt myself hyperventilating. I couldn't get the vision out of my mind. I saw a giant fire. I couldn't shake or get away from the thought. I kept repeating the words, "It's a big fire… It's a big fire!" I thought, *Could it be my house, could it be an airplane, could it be one of my customers?*

I felt panic like it was happening to me. I kept walking back and forth between both bedrooms and looking up in the direction of the ceiling fans. After about fifteen minutes the compulsive fear subsided a bit and I calmed myself down. The next morning was September 11, 2001, and I instantly felt jolted out of my peace.

Twenty years later, I watched a documentary on the lost souls in the World Trade Center. I almost fell out of my chair when I heard people talking to their loved ones by phone that there was a big fire in the south and north towers. Lots of people were leaving their loved ones messages on voicemail saying that they heard an enormous explosion but had no idea where the source of the fire or explosion came from.

From my vision, I recall saying the exact words they were expressing to their family. These were family members that they would never see again.

Sam came home from work, and we hunkered down with baby Jake and in disbelief watched the 9/11 footage on the news. The next morning Rachel called me and told me that my sister Soraya was pregnant by her boyfriend. They were still in Spain and the airplanes were grounded. I prayed day and night for my family's safe return and for the news about my nephew-to-be.

A month went by, and just after my thirty-fourth birthday, Soraya got married. Halloween was next, and I dressed Jake up in a giraffe costume. My mother and Soraya came out for the Halloween festivities. Jake was obviously too young to trick-or-treat, but I loved strolling him around the neighborhood that time of year. The colors were beautiful, and the air was cool, but something was missing. I still didn't feel like myself.

Rachel put me in touch with another psychiatrist and a wellness doctor whom she liked, and I dragged myself to their offices. The doctor gave me antidepressants, a different anxiety medication, allergy medication, and something powerful to help me sleep. I was so sick from the depression that I kept having allergy attacks followed by colds every two weeks. I rested at Rachel's house after the appointment. She always made me feel like I was home.

The psychiatrist had agreed with the medications and the wellness doctor made me feel that I would be okay. It is the most difficult thing to work, take care of a baby, and maintain a home when you don't feel like yourself. Soon there was more trouble with my father. I tried to talk to him about my bouts with depression and psychosis, but he couldn't hear me. He simply barked orders at me, telling me that I never called Mildred to check in with her or give her updates on the baby. I told him that I worked, cooked, cleaned, and took care of a newborn, and that I was not feeling like myself. I couldn't even sleep; I was weak and exhausted. He told me that I should have a husband who made enough money so I didn't need to work and that I should make time to cater to Mildred. He called me defiant. I was so exhausted that I couldn't fight back.

I felt like I was on a continuous merry-go-round, and I was fighting to get better. Life was hard enough without having a chronically disturbed parent, yet at that time and for years to come I blamed myself. In the back of my mind, I thought that I must have been a bad child for my father to treat me the way he did. I was always more in fear of the mind-bending retaliation at the hands of my scornful, brooding father and the fallout of what this unstable man could do if I ended contact. I knew that if I cut Henrik out of my life, he would turn every family member against me, make up lies about me, and torture me until I begged for mercy. I remember Rachel begging for mercy when I saw Henrik smash her into the drywall. Henrik did not care how sick I was because he had no concept of empathy. I knew at least he could make my life more of a miserable hell and right now I had to focus on healing.

I continued to confide in Rachel and sought more therapists. I was looking for someone special to help me. I had moments of happiness yet was still so lost and empty. It was not only psychosis that was haunting me but the memories of my childhood. As a child I had absorbed so many moments of trauma that the flashbacks would've been inevitable. Rachel had the courage to walk away from Henrik with style and grace, so why couldn't I do the same? I was a prisoner of my father's abuse. When I met Dr. Michelle Stewart, little did I know that my painful journey was about to get worse before it got better.

"I know you are here for postpartum issues, and I've read your file," said Dr. Stewart. "You've been in and out of therapy since college, right?"

"Yes, the postpartum is only part of the issue."

"I'm glad you transferred all of your records. You have a substantial file on some terrifying events. Looks like your mother went through a lot at the hands of your father. You were a witness to quite a bit."

"My sister Soraya remembers some of it."

"I took the weekend and read your profile. The brutality you witnessed and the physical and mental abuse your mother withstood would be nearly impossible for anyone to bear. Yet here you are."

"I did horrible things too," I said. My throat was tightening, and tears stung my eyes. "You read how I beat my pet rabbit until it died. I was so ashamed of my behavior."

"Fallon, you were a child and witnessed horrendous things. We can get into that later. For now, I want you to stay on the medications prescribed by your other doctor. How are you feeling?"

"Sometimes not so good. Sometimes I feel desensitized, almost like it didn't happen to me. Like I had an out of body experience with it all."

"Many victims of domestic violence have similar feelings. A feeling of detachment is a coping mechanism."

"Domestic violence?"

"Yes, you were part of that abusive situation, even though most of it was happening to your mother, it was also happening to you and I'm sure to your sister."

"I guess I never looked at it that way."

"Any bad dreams, or…"

"Yes, I've had a recurring dream since I was a child. Maybe I can consider it a nightmare."

"Go ahead."

"It's different every time, but I'm always in trouble in the dream. Someone is trying to attack me or get me and out of nowhere, I fly straight up and I'm instantly out of trouble. I end up in the air or the trees or something. Maybe like my angels flew me out of harm's way. I always wake up after that. I catch my breath, and I tell myself it's just a dream."

"This may be difficult but are there any stories that are not in this file? Things we can go over in our sessions. Maybe things from your childhood. We can start there and come into more current time."

"Well."

"Sometimes going into the past can get you where you need to be in the future."

"Some of these stories might sound stupid but some of them hurt me a lot."

"Nothing you can say here will be stupid."

"I was about eleven years old, and I was on a beach in Spain. We were visiting my grandparents, my abuelos. I caught my father videotaping a topless woman and he wouldn't stop. I got that creepy sick feeling in my stomach that what he was doing was wrong. Even though I was a young child, I felt that he was invading her privacy. I felt ill and unsafe. I walked up to my father, and I begged him to stop. He told me to leave him alone. He kept videotaping her. I noticed on the viewfinder that he was zooming in on her breasts. It was disgusting. I was too young to understand what that creepy feeling was, but it was like my father had some sort of perverted engine that kept fueling his desire to film her."

I stopped for a moment and sipped some water to clear my throat before I continued.

"I walked up to my father again and I grabbed his hand to tell him to stop and he turned and shoved me, I went flying into the sand and told me to leave him alone. I had sand all over where I had suntan lotion. I felt odd and humiliated. Looking back, it was as if my father was trying to shame me for what he did. Strange contradiction, I know."

"How did that feel to tell him?"

"I felt violated by the entire incident. I had this urge to tell him off because he always seemed to get away with things. Maybe I viewed this woman as my mom, and I wanted to protect her. I always wanted to protect my mom, but I couldn't. It seems like my father hated women and put most of his vengeance into my mother."

"It's called misogyny, Fallon. A misogynist is a person who despises women. This is good. Let's keep this going."

"I'm trying to think, childhood…something that's not in my file already. There are hundreds and hundreds of incidents with my father. So many hateful nicknames; he used to call me a bull in a china shop, fat ox, stupid. So many fights, I would need an encyclopedia to document them all. I'm telling you…these fights with my father, the windows would shake from his uncontrollable rage."

"I have a feeling, Fallon, that many of these fights came up out of nowhere and you've searched your brain to find out what you did wrong."

"Yes. It's like you read my mind. I know that I'm jumping around a bit, but I have a blurry memory about this. I must have been three or four. I remember opening the fridge and seeing medicine that was not mine. My father was in the kitchen, and he told me the medicine was his. He told me that he had blood in his urine and that was what the medicine was for. I didn't understand what urine was, maybe then he explained that it was pee, I'm not sure. I remember that the story bothered me, so it stuck in my memory. In later years I put it together that he was probably taking penicillin for some of his indiscretions…disgusting. It was almost like he wanted me to find out what he was doing without me even having a remote clue at my age."

"By today's standards that would be considered abuse."

"Well, he definitely had no filter… Oh, I'm remembering this story! We were on the expressway, Soraya, my father, and I. Soraya and I were little, and we were just being kids in the car. I'm not sure if one of us was crying or what was happening, but my father started to scream and took my baby doll that I was holding and, in a rage, threw her out of the window onto the road. We were traveling at high speeds, so the doll was probably mangled instantly by the car in the next lane. When I think back, I still feel unsafe and grieve the loss of something that I loved. I still can't wrap my brain around this one."

Dr. Stewart looked down and shook her head. "Your father seems to fit into a few aggressive and violent categories here. I'll keep a list of subjects to go over later. For now, please go on with any other stories."

"When I was thirteen, Soraya and I were on a canoe trip up at our farm with our father. It was October and just two months before we lost our baby brother."

"I'm so truly sorry about that."

"Thanks, it was a long time ago. I still miss him. Anyways, we were canoeing, and my father was yelling at me. I was in the front of the canoe; he was in the back, he kept telling me to steer a certain way. I did my best and the canoe turned the wrong way. I stood up to try and jostle us free; we were stuck on a fallen tree limb. Out of nowhere my father screamed like a lunatic and called me stupid. He took the canoe paddle and hit me over the head pretty hard. I got dizzy and my knees buckled, I fell back into the canoe. My sister who never yells, turned to him. 'Don't hurt my sister, it wasn't her fault!' she screamed. 'She's trying her best!'

"I couldn't believe she screamed at him and stood up for me. She has witnessed so many fights with my father. She knows that I always stand up for myself."

"His anger seemed to come out of nowhere?"

"That's right. Sometimes he does strange things. I heard that he used to pack his suitcase full of frozen deer meat and fly to Germany with it. That might not sound strange to some people but consider the source. I sure thought it was strange. Another time we were on the farm, and we were all walking the land. Soraya, my dad, and me. Out of nowhere he pulled out a gun."

"On you?"

"Well, no, but he pulled this gun out and pointed it forward, like he was going to shoot something in front of him. I was terrified and confused."

"You were terrified that your dad was going to shoot you?"

"Yes, for a second. I told him to put the gun away and he didn't. It was a strange moment. We didn't know it at that time, but our father was selling our farmland. He was selling it for that skank he married, Mildred. Maybe I'm paranoid but I thought he was taking the gun out to shoot us. He could have buried us on the farmland anywhere and it would have taken bloodhounds to find us. Sometimes I have paranoid thoughts, I believe they stem from my childhood."

Dr. Stewart listened and continued taking notes.

"My father seems to live in his own deep underground unconventional lair. I mean this figuratively speaking. My mother used to tell me stories about my father. There was this little dog that annoyed him. The dog lived kitty-corner from our backyard. My father told my mother that he would give the dog antifreeze and that the dog would be gone. She thought he was kidding. Within a week or so, she never heard the dog again. She believed my father killed it. As a child I felt so unsafe hearing this. If my father could kill a helpless dog, would he hurt us?"

Dr. Stewart breathed in and sighed. She continued taking notes.

"My mother told me another story. Now these can be speculations, but my mother says that she sees things and she sometimes knows exactly when my crazy father is committing these crimes. I see things, too. Sometimes my mother and I see the same vision. She told me that my father, who owned a lot of apartment buildings and homes as rental properties, preyed on older women. One was a widow and my dad wanted to get her home for a really cheap price. He went over to harass her, threatening her that he wanted her house for around $20,000. This was back in the late 1960s and it was under market value. Three days later the woman was dead. My father ended up with her property. In so many words, my mother knew that Henrik killed that woman out of his own insatiable greed."

"Fallon this is a lot."

"Like I said, I can't prove it, but it sounds like my dad got away with murder."

"I know he's made attempts on your mother's life."

"Many! Besides his outrageous…I don't even know what to call it. He goes into these ballistic rages. He explodes for almost no reason. Throwing things, flipping over tables, yanking phones off the wall, breaking things. I've seen him do it almost every week of my life. Like he's a madman out of control. He can't stop himself. He constantly picks fights with me. He would literally look me up and down and fire off new rounds of insults to break my spirit, calling me weak and lost. It's almost like he's programmed for it. He will cut me down and degrade me and put me in the same category as the filth of society. Every time I see him, things are laced with arguments, and chaos. Everything, and I mean everything, is my fault."

"Let me ask you. When you respond argumentatively. Does that fuel him even more?"

"Are you kidding? He goes crazy. I tell him he hurts my feelings, he tells me I'm too delicate or sensitive. If I argue back, it's like putting gas on the fire. He's also a compulsive liar. He is always telling me fabrications about my mother. I know both my parents, and my mother is a wonderful person. This might sound crazy, I love my father too, but at the same time I hate him."

"We're going to address those scars from your childhood so you can grow a new set of beliefs. This might take some time, but it will happen. What kind of lies does he tell about your mother?"

"He likes to make people look bad. He tells me that if it wasn't for him, my mother would be living in a Spanish ghetto. He completely discredits her. I know for a fact that she came from an amazing family. She had star power growing up. My mother lived an incredible life, she's so beautiful and classy, he just puts her down. If anyone came from a ghetto, it was his family and that pig that he married, Mildred. She's the one that came from a ghetto. I've seen her apartment overseas. Also, my father has to have total control over any conversations. He also likes to bring out people's insecurities."

"Can you give me an example?"

"Stupid stuff, like one time I broke up with a boyfriend of mine and in the next sentence he told me I have no one in my life. The stuff he says to me, I feel like I'm going insane. Everything is in my face and intimidating.

He talks to me like I don't matter. Then he would tell me other times that all my boyfriends were cheating on me. Can you imagine playing these high school games with your daughter? With him in my life, I feel like I'm going crazy!"

"I think it's noted here but how many times was your father married?"

"Five times. All catastrophic endings. Except this last crazy bitch is still hanging on. She will leave when Henrik runs out of money." I laughed.

Dr. Stewart smiled. "Does your father idolize any authoritarians, dictators?"

"Uhm?"

"I know, strange question, right?"

"Yes, now I'm remembering. Maybe not so strange. My father has a few books on Hitler and Mussolini. My mother calls my father Hitler. It's a joke between her, Soraya, and me. Maybe a coping mechanism, but we called him a lot of stuff. Hitler, Satan…the Nazi is here! Team Germany, the Nazi Twins, that's what we call Henrik and Mildred. Both of them are just too much for my sister and me. Soraya and I have bonded our entire lives with comedy. It makes our situation tolerable."

"I understand."

"Oh, Dr. Stewart, another thing. This may sound really strange, but my father actually has a list of the Ten Commandments by Henrik Baumann, meaning he wrote them. They're in his kitchen."

"Are you kidding me?"

"Yup, framed and hanging in his kitchen."

"First of all, do you understand what commandments are?"

"Well, they were written by Moses, not Henrik Baumann!"

"They're orders, demands, decrees, they are a divine rule. This is someone, I'm talking about your father, someone who has a 'God complex!' Fallon, whenever you can, please bring me a copy or take a picture of that list of commandments."

"Funny thing doctor, my father is a hypocrite. He has broken all of his own commandments." I cracked a smile.

"Let me read this definition, then we'll take a break until next time we meet: A God complex is a rare medical disorder characterized by inflated sense of self-importance, entitlement, a deep need for admiration, and an alarming lack of empathy."

"Oh my gosh, does it have my father's name under that definition?"

"I think we're going to do some hard work here, but we'll have some fun, too. If you understand your father and what makes him tick, we will be at the root of your depression and anxiety. Also, you're experiencing a flux in post-pregnancy hormones that is putting your life in a tailspin. I think a lot of what you are feeling now is from the past, it's post-traumatic stress disorder from your childhood into adulthood. All the instability and turmoil your brain endured at the hands of your father is now causing you to collapse. I want to study my notes with my colleagues and put together a profile piecing together your father's narcissistic and sociopathic patterns. This may take a while, but it will shed some light on who we're dealing with."

"Wait, my father is a sociopath?"

"I'm sorry but yes, and a lot more. We may never know, but he may have many psychopathic tendencies, as well."

"Don't be sorry, this clears up a lot."

"You have to understand that these are all unofficial diagnoses. Your father is not a patient of mine so we may never know for sure, but we can piece him together. When you can conceive of this, you will understand that none of this was your fault."

I left my doctor's office feeling as if I had been through an enlightening interrogation. The journey inward is always the most difficult. That I knew.

I was pulling up too much from my past, and it was painful. Sometimes it felt like I was cleaning a greasy, grimy pan. At first the grime is so thick, the process seems unbearable and disgusting. With a lot of work and grit, it's possible to make the pan shine again. At that point I didn't know if I could ever feel good and have my life make sense. I had determination, but no reference point to how "good" felt.

I walked out into the freezing February air, and I thought about how much I really appreciated and felt comfortable with Dr. Stewart. I was cautiously optimistic about achieving permanent healing with my past. I sat in my car and the song "Deacon Blues" was on the radio. As I listened, I wondered how Steely Dan could so eloquently put the trials and tribulations of life into a melody, and make it sound like a perfect symphony. I wondered if I could ever compose a masterpiece with my messy life. Making sense out of all that went wrong. After all, I saw my father as a giant mountain of problems, a reoccurring avalanche, and my hand was on a stick of dynamite. At times I thought it was fruitless to try and get better. But I was never a quitter, so I painfully kept moving forward.

22

The Tip of the Iceberg

Two weeks had passed, and I found myself in the waiting room at Dr. Stewart's office. Some days were good, some days not so good. Everything felt messy as though I was shoveling through piles of mental garbage. And there were days that I didn't want to do the work. I felt pity for myself, asking again and again: Why was this happening to me?

I was not only angry at what my father had put my mother through, but what he had put all three of us through. Nothing seemed fair. The tidal wave from my past continually crashed down all around me. I would get up from one wave and another would bear down. From the time I was a young girl, my brain had been wired for trauma and depression. I carried the burden of the scars and dragged them around like a block of cement. I knew with what I experienced, my life would be irreversibly destroyed. My world was like a jigsaw puzzle falling apart into a tailspin. I could hear Henrik in my sleep, barking orders and verbal assaults. I wore the abuse like a tattoo.

When I entered Dr. Stewart's office, I plastered a fake smile across my face. I lied and said I was fine when she asked me how I was doing. We began our usual preliminary back and forth and I tried to fool her about my current mood, not wanting to deal with it at the moment.

"Why don't we pick up where we left off. I also wanted to mention that I talked to my colleagues about putting together a profile on your father's behavioral issues."

"What are they planning?"

"They may ask you to fill out paperwork regarding symptoms or behaviors that you've noted in the past, and the computer can give us some profiles."

"Okay, whatever you think will help."

"Fallon, is everything okay? You seem a little distracted."

"I'm okay, just one of those days." I paused for a moment. "So, I have a few more stories. Nothing really bad. You have most of that in your notes. Just oddball stuff that might help. Oh, here is a copy of the Ten Commandments by Henrik Baumann."

"Thank you. I'll read these later."

"I told you I would get you a copy."

Dr. Stewart shook her head in disbelief. "Fallon, does your father show love toward you, any signs at all?"

"Love…my father is incapable of showing it, feeling it, understanding it. It is a foreign concept to him. He can't even celebrate the good fortune of others. He's extremely jealous if you have something that he doesn't."

"You may be experiencing some trauma bonding with your father. This is normal since from everything I can see, you are an empath."

"Trauma bonding? So many terms I've never heard of. Once when I was away at college, I came home immediately after I heard that my father had an emergency angioplasty?"

"Fallon, you are a good-natured person. You don't want to see anyone hurt."

"Well, Dr. Stewart, some of these stories might sound insignificant but at the time these things really bothered me. This was years ago. The father of one of my friends passed away and my sister and I went to the wake, which started at 4:00 p.m. My father was also friends with this man."

"That's nice of you."

"Not according to my father! I called him up and told him that Soraya and I went to the wake, and he unleashed on me. He threatened that if we didn't go back to the wake around six or seven o'clock when normal people went, we would suffer the consequences. He forced us to go back to the wake a second time. Henrik would be waiting for us at the wake to make sure we listened to his orders."

"What were the consequences?"

"I don't know."

"How old were you when this happened?"

"It had to be late teens. If he would have asked me to do this now, I would have told him to jump off a cliff."

"So, it sounds like your father was manipulating you girls to show you off at the wake."

"But why did I listen to him? Why was I afraid of the consequences? Why didn't I tell him to go fuck off?"

"Because you were a victim of his abuse. It wasn't your fault. Now you can stand up for yourself, but it is still difficult."

"I was also afraid of retaliation. If we didn't listen to him, he would make our lives a living hell. And another thing, I was always expected to give a speech or presentation at my father's birthday celebrations. He would host a big party for himself at a hall and I would have to stoically make a birthday speech. It was ridiculous. After everything he did to my mother, I felt like such a piece of shit for going up there and lying about this man. Looking back, I felt forced to do it."

"The problem is with him, not you."

"My mother says my father is a very sick man and that everything is about him; he needs to be the center of attention. After my speech he would give me a dirty look, start an argument with me, and then snub me. It was weird. So abusive. I always felt that I did something wrong."

"I briefly spoke of gaslighting at our last session. This is what is happening here."

"My father told me once that if I ever went to jail, he would leave me there! I've almost never served detention at school. He's the one that belongs in jail. Dr. Stewart, stuff like this happens all the time, since I was little. He's always in my face. My father says strange things sometimes. He once told me that if I ever ran away from home that I could wash my clothes or underwear in a public toilet. I guess in the tank with the water reserve. What an insane thing to say! I would never run away from my mom and washing my clothes would be the least of my worries! Who would think about washing their clothes in a toilet?"

"Your father certainly sounds disturbed and eccentric along with everything else."

"My sister and I both think he is completely nuts. It's like watching an atomic bomb go off, you stand there in complete shock and there is nothing you can do about it. You just watch the destruction unfold before your eyes! My sister Soraya calls him Henrik, not dad when we talk about him."

"Does your father interrogate, or get excessively angry with your sister?"

"Not really! Mostly me. She's smart, she avoids conflict. I will get in his face and fight back. My father also treated both of us like shit compared to any of his girlfriends' children. They seemed to get preferential treatment. He was always kissing their asses and wanted Soraya and me to do the same. It seems at times that we are peasant children, and we are here to serve the Royal Highnesses. I refuse and it causes more fights with him."

"That's more manipulation on both sides. He was manipulating you girls and his girlfriends."

"I could go on and on. I have a very close male friend who is gay; his name is Mike Daytona, and we planned a ski trip to Colorado before I got married. Mike is like a brother to me, and my father forbade me to go on the trip. He argued with me for weeks about it. I was miserable and my lunatic father called and harassed me nonstop. I put my foot down and I told him to stop ruining my life."

"What happened?"

"I went on the trip. I stood my ground. My father told me that my friendship with Mike was unorthodox, and I should abandon it. I told my father to go blow it out his ass, especially since Sam had no problem with us going."

"Any problems with the old girlfriends, anything criminal?"

"Yes, things always trickle down to my mother and she finds stuff out. A few girlfriends had restraining orders against my father."

"Fallon, what about Mildred? How are things going with her?"

"I really don't know where to start. She only speaks broken English. Her first language is German. She doesn't have a filter. I feel like nothing but saturated filth comes out of her mouth. Soraya and I spend a lot of time making fun of both Henrik and Mildred. That's not to take away any of the painful experiences with him. It's a way we cope."

"Is Mildred manipulative?"

"I think she's a much quieter version of my father, but more sneaky. She gloats a lot and laughs in our faces. In my heart, I know she's a trouble-maker. She constantly is shoving in my face that I have to work for a living, and she doesn't. Mildred will ask me about my vacations, and she will ask me how long I am going on the trip, and she will tell me that my weeklong vacation is pathetic."

"Sounds like your father cloned himself with this Mildred."

"You don't understand, Mildred will call my sister on the day my flight takes off and call other relatives to verify my return! She doesn't care about my trip; she just wants to get in my face and confirm that I'm only going on a week-long trip. I've never seen anything like it. I feel like I'm going crazy!"

"It's all very childish."

"Exactly! She throws it in my face that she goes on six-week vacations and spends my father's money. She goes back to her condo in Germany paid for from the sale of our family farms. She's as ugly as piss, her cooking is horrible. I could talk to you about her for the next three hours and it wouldn't be enough time to tell you all the stupid things she has said. She wonders why we don't like her. How would you like that for a step-monster! Oh, and just a side note, her condo in Germany looks like an old folk's home. It's run-down and dark."

Dr. Stewart shook her head and continued taking notes.

"My father wants Soraya and me to be obedient little puppets while Mildred parades around taking the lion's share of my father's wealth. Then Mildred shoves things in our faces and takes sick pleasure in degrading us. She does this all on my father's cue. My father painted a picture for Mildred of us that is not true. He has told twisted fabrications our entire lives. I should only speak for myself, not for my sister, but I know we both feel the same."

"How do you know he tells fake stories about you?"

"I can just look at his face and I know things, but there are stories that I hear from other family members. My father is a compulsive liar! He spins evil webs. He has done this his entire life."

"Hmm. They both sound like children." Dr. Stewart nodded her head in agreement.

"My father was sitting with us talking about saving money for something and Mildred said, 'Oh Henrik you have so much money.' I made eye contact with her, and my father instantly knew she had put her foot in her mouth."

"She's manipulating you into thinking that you have less than them and are less because of it. I have a feeling that Mildred is a covert narcissist."

"There's more than one kind?"

"Yes, briefly, a covert narcissist craves admiration and needs to be number one. They lack empathy and manipulate their victims. They often aren't aware of the impact of their cruelty. There is research that says there could be a genetic component as I believe there is with your father."

"I know these sound like petty stories, but if you were there, they all are surrounded by a mushroom cloud of contempt. I believe Henrik and Mildred both bully and gang up on me. When that happens, I don't play nice either."

She nodded, encouraging me to continue.

"Stranger still is the kind of food Mildred cooks when we're at their house. Fish heads on a plate, and pink, uncooked grilled turkey with black charcoaled feathers still attached to it. Basically, the turkey was still raw, while some parts were burnt to a crisp. Green mold on the sweet potatoes. Raw herring for breakfast. Cooked fruit surprise. Red cabbage with cloves mixed in, it tasted like potpourri."

"You paint a great picture!"

"I can't tell you how many fast-food drive-throughs we visited on the holidays because of their cooking. Then, my father says emphatically that I'm a horrible cook. I could write an entire comedy skit on meals with Team Germany. On the other hand, my mother and stepfather Bob are both amazing cooks."

"Your father has made you question your own reality in multiple areas of your life with his insults, even with silly things like your cooking."

"This is just the tip of the iceberg. After hundreds and I mean close to a thousand fights throughout my lifetime with my father, you would think that would be the definition of insanity. Actually, with all of his explosive rage, I'm surprised I didn't suffer more physical abuse from the animal. Verbally, I keep getting in his face and fighting with him."

"Can I ask why you think you do that?"

"I know exactly why. I can't let him win. When he yells at me, I have to yell back. After everything he did to my mother, I feel like I fight for her. I don't want my father to have peace after the hell he put us through."

"But your deep-seated anger and hatred for your father is destroying you. It's crushing your peace."

"I know. Why do you think I'm here? When I fight back with my father, I feel that I won, I didn't curl up in a corner and die. But why can't I just walk away? I want to punish him; I want to throw in his face the pain he caused us. If I could get away with it, I would…ugh! I don't know! I sometimes wonder what justice tastes like. My mother, Soraya, and I still have not seen it."

"You will never win against a narcissist. You were…are still an abused child. Don't blame yourself! Remember, revenge is also empty."

"I feel like I made myself more of a victim by fighting back, but I can't stop."

"You were the family rock, and now that rock is temporarily shattered. Your postpartum psychosis is a legitimate concern but this breakdown of yours was inevitable."

Dr. Stewart and I momentarily stopped. I grabbed some tissues and sobbed. I took a deep breath and sipped some water.

"You are going to be okay; you are here! You want to get better. Think of your father as a big bag of noise and the less you give him, that big ugly noise will go away and find another victim. Just know that a narcissist will always need a host to feed on. There's another thing I'm picking up on, and it's quite obvious: you seem to have a lot of animosity toward German people."

"Look Dr. Stewart, even if I don't feel German, I'm still half. I connect much more with my Spanish side. The culture, the people, the warmth. When my abuela from Spain would see me, she would kiss me so hard I thought my ear would fall off. The other side of the family doesn't have that."

"I understand."

"The German culture I grew up with is just colder and alien to Soraya and me. My godparents were German, and I loved them. My Grandpa

Baumann was an adorable man. I don't hate Germans; I don't hate anyone really. I'm just hostile toward some of the Germans in my family because of what I've been through with my father. In my heart, I love all cultures and people who are guided by love and peace. I don't see my father as a peaceful person."

"I can sympathize, I just want you to see the good in the world and that there are bad people not bad cultures."

"Rationally, I know this," I sighed. "But I can't seem to put it all together."

Dr. Stewart and I wrapped up our session. It was a gloomy, chilly day near the end of March, and my eyes and face were swollen with tears. I walked to my car and got in. The stinging tap of icy rain began to sound against my window. I sat for a moment, angry and frustrated with myself. I knew that I was a dumping ground for my father's toxic garbage. Why did I let this happen to my life?

All were symptoms of hopelessness as my mind searched for meaning and purpose. My only freedom was in my isolation inside a hell I couldn't escape. I lived fifty-five miles away from Henrik and he still controlled my every thought and move.

The truth was that I wanted to destroy him, I wanted to annihilate him, punish him. He had no right to be happy. He was manic, miserable, and vicious, and he destroyed many lives in his path. Our father-daughter relationship was built on a foundation already in collapse. Over the years I felt the stress of his unstable behavior. I was filled with rage piggybacking off of his rage. For me this feeling wasn't right, it wasn't who I was in my soul, but I wanted justice for my mother. I wanted to make right all that was wrong. I wanted to bring back parts of our beloved farms, but I couldn't. I wanted revenge; I wanted the childhood that was taken from me. I wanted my peace and instead I sat in a doctor's office trying to figure out the emptiness I felt inside.

Weeks passed. I swallowed my bitterness and tried to hold my composure. I kept up with my appointments with Dr. Stewart and started feeling the medicine kicking in a bit. I was a work in progress but started feeling an occasional smile return. Soraya's baby was born. Adorable baby Tristan came into the world on May 3, 2002. Rachel was overjoyed with her second grandson and we three women felt our family growing.

Soon after Tristan's birth, I started planning Jake's first birthday party. There would be so many families, friends, and neighbors, as well as birthday cake, balloons, Elmo popping in, and a giant bouncy house. Rachel showed up dressed to kill in pleated white pants and a sunshine yellow ruffled halter top. Bob brought in platters full of desserts. I dreaded the arrival of Henrik and Mildred but knew that I would be busy, and their presence would be diluted by the other guests. Avoidance would become another coping mechanism I would latch onto.

The party was running smoothly, there were kids everywhere. I was in the kitchen getting out some of the desserts when I overheard Henrik and Mildred snickering in a whisper by the fridge.

"You see Mildred, this is how she calculates her points on Weight Watchers." Henrik's finger was tracing the printed-out sheet on the fridge. I was standing behind them.

"What are you two doing?" My therapist's powerful voice faded in Henrik's presence.

"Oh, I was just showing Mildred your Weight Watchers points."

"In what world would that be anyone's business but mine? Why would you look at it, let alone explain my private business to Mildred at a party?"

"Oh, Fallon, stop being so self-conscious! This was out in the open for everyone to look at."

"Please mind your own business. Why would you pull a stunt like this at your grandson's first birthday?" I whispered to the clueless couple.

"Everyone always has to walk on eggshells with you!"

I breathed in and the air squeezed out of my lungs, I closed my eyes and shook my head out of sheer exasperation. Henrik painted the walls with my insecurities for everyone to see, this way he looked better facing the mirror. I found Rachel and pulled her outside to tell her the story. The entire scene had undertones of mockery. Who would make fun of someone suffering the past year with postpartum issues? But I had to thank Henrik for the epiphany I had that day. It was now clear as summer rain. Henrik was trying to make me feel less because my successful life was a threat and I had chosen my mother over him.

For the rest of the party Henrik showed anyone who would pay attention a picture of his new boat. I could just hear him scream, "I'M THE CAPTAIN!"

Soraya stayed with me that summer and I was able to book appointments with Dr. Stewart while she watched Jake. Dr. Stewart and her colleagues had finally put together a questionnaire. I never let Dr. Stewart know, but I asked Rachel to come over and help me fill things out. I told her that they were questions about Henrik's personality disorders. I picked up two copies. Rachel jumped at the chance. She was over at my house within a half hour. Her eyes widened as we compared answers. "This man is crazier than I thought!" she said. We both giggled with excitement having stumbled upon enlightening feedback.

Two weeks later, I got a phone call from Dr. Stewart's office to schedule a counseling meeting for the psychological profile. The next day as I sat in Dr. Stewart's waiting room, I could hear the clock tick on the wall. I was nervously fidgeting with some of my notes when Dr. Stewart called me into her office. Rachel and I had taken hours filling out the two-hundred-question form.

"Now, you know this is a very unofficial diagnosis," she said. "So, we understand what we are dealing with."

"Okay."

"I printed out the characteristics, qualities, traits, and, for a lack of a better term, the adjectives that would best describe some of your father's unstable behaviors. These are sub-symptoms of his disorders. Some of this may be repetitive but below is the list of your answers."

I read over the list and felt a bit overwhelmed seeing all of my answers in one clump. It all made sense, but I had to process that this monster, unstable parasite, drama junkie, was my father.

- Lack of empathy/remorse or consequence
- Pathological/compulsive liar
- Explosive rage/anger, disproportionate to the situation
- Unwarranted temper/hostility
- Sexual addiction/predator/deviant
- Power hungry/money hungry
- Manipulator/controlling
- Risky behaviors/impulsivity/reckless driving
- Severe mood swings/agitation
- Unstable relationships
- Abusive/violent/volatile
- Destruction of property
- Deceitful/spiteful/toxic
- Criminal tendencies
- Gaslighting with contempt
- Tyrannical bully/bossy
- Superiority complex
- Callous/calculating/cunning
- Tendency to show off/center of attention
- Plotting malice/depraved
- Neurotic personalities
- Argumentative
- Self-injury (banging head against wall)

- Stalking behaviors/excessive nosiness
- Disregard for others/belittlement
- Outrageous expectations of others
- Tendency for anxiety/depression/manic
- Malicious intent/devious/cruel
- Confrontational
- Incessant talking/monopolizing conversations
- Chronic violent outbursts
- Militant
- Infidelity/cheater/fraudster
- Destabilized victims
- Chronic complainer
- Overly sensitive to criticism
- Overly critical of others
- Meticulous micromanager
- Unprovoked verbal and physical assaults
- Boastful/overbearing
- Erratic behaviors
- Energy vampire
- Psychological projection/blame shifting
- Excessive greed/extreme selfishness
- Coercion
- Eccentric ideology
- Inflated self-worth
- Delusions of grandeur
- God complex

"Fallon, I know this is a scary list. There is actually more, but this is a good overview for now."

"Wow, it's okay, I need to know this, I need to know what I'm dealing with. I've been suffering with this man all my life. What my mother went through, I wouldn't wish it on anyone."

"I had a few colleagues look over your answers. I then put together a profile. It's not a pretty one. Your father seems to fall under what some psychiatrists would call a spectrum or under a large umbrella of combined disorders. I prefer to simply call them cluster disorders." Dr. Stewart handed me a packet with her findings, then she went over them in detail.

"Most of these qualities fall under antisocial personality disorder. The unofficial term would be sociopath. Now, since your father is not a patient of mine and since this is not an official diagnosis, it's difficult to determine if he falls under the sociopath or psychopath label. For our little experiment, I would go out on a limb and say that your father is a sociopath. He checks every box on the sociopathic, narcissistic profile. The narcissist profile that fits your father is connected to his explosive temper."

"Whoa, I know you said this before, but when you put a definition to it, it carries a punch. Why would you say he's more of a sociopath?"

"Psychopaths are born, and studies have shown that on brain scans they lack a neural connection for empathy, whereas a sociopath's empathy is very weak. Sociopaths may have more of an unstable childhood or a history of violence from their upbringing. As a child, a sociopath may have been put on a pedestal or overpraised. Also, sociopaths are more volatile, aggressive, and violent. They can't show emotion in a normal way. Don't get me wrong, psychopaths are dangerous, but I think with your father we are dealing with a sociopath."

"I remember we talked about Grandma Baumann. I can't believe I would be saying this about my grandma, but she was a real bitch. I think she beat the crap out of my father, and she was really strict. The pedestal concept also could have been a factor. I think there was a lot of dysfunction in that family. Grandpa Baumann and Auntie Chloe were the only normal ones."

"Yes, that was a key factor in my thinking. This gives me a snapshot of the instability in your father's life. The problem is we may never know the real story of where things went wrong with him. Sociopaths view the world as an instrument to fulfill their desires. They don't care about others."

"This I know firsthand." I lowered my head and looked toward my lap, shaking my head. I had tears in my eyes once again, feeling overwhelmed with the mounting discoveries.

"The rest of this list is long and disturbing. It looks like we have a cluster of narcissistic behaviors. Your father falls under grandiose narcissist, overt narcissist, malignant narcissist, communal narcissist, and vindictive narcissist. Looks like we have a pathological narcissist on our hands. Fallon, are you doing okay?"

"I'm okay, just a lot to take in." Dr. Stewart handed me a tissue.

"Okay, just checking in with you. Your father's profile is one of the most disturbing I've seen in my practice. Not the most violent, but most disturbing due to the fact of this lengthy list of disorders. These sorts of personalities also tend to spin outrageous fabrications to ruin people's lives. They enjoy creating confusion, contention, and contempt. They twist facts with their compulsive lying. They like fooling people that they can manipulate. They play on the sympathies of good-willed people; they have no empathy for the pain they cause. Their expectations always feel threatening, and they demand control of others."

"Now you know what I've been through, what my poor mother went through!"

Dr. Stewart explained each of the narcissistic behaviors that afflicted my father. "Now, we are branching away from narcissistic disorders. These all feed into each other but let me know if you have any questions."

"Okay, just trying to take it all in."

"Borderline personality disorder, superiority complex disorder, intermittent explosive rage disorder, sexual addiction disorder. I don't think that last one needs any explanation."

"My mom used to tell me some pretty disgusting stuff about my father, but when it spills out and other people start seeing stuff, that's disturbing."

"Your mother was right; your father is a very sick man. A side note on the explosive rage disorder, it's like a terrifying grown-up temper tantrum."

"I know all too well. It's like a nightmare genie that you can't put back in the bottle."

"Exactly! Okay, looks like we are on the last section of this profile. NSSI, non-suicidal self-injury disorder. You told me that your father was caught banging his head against the wall. If you saw it a few times, it's probably happening more than you think."

"He was also caught many times banging the phone against the wall too. Oh, and banging a lot of hookers."

Dr. Stewart and I paused to have a chuckle.

"I have to tell you. You have a great sense of humor going through all of this."

"I have to. Comedy and sarcasm are my only hope!"

And the laughter continued. "What's next on the list, where did I leave off? Ahh…histrionic personality disorder. That's where you have to be the center of attention. Impulse control disorder, we talked about antisocial personality disorder, and it looks like we could have an undiagnosed bipolar disorder, general anxiety disorder, and depression."

"Wow, that's insane!"

"Literally! Are you doing okay?"

"Yes and no, I have a father who's a complete psycho nut job and the worst thing about this is that I can't say one darn thing to him. He refuses to go to therapy. Whenever I bring up his horrendous moods, I would be banished. Even if I uttered a sound or brought attention to his temper tantrums, he would've dismantled me in seconds. He denies that there is a problem. He tells me that I'm the problem. He will not get help for this."

"Your father's insults toward you are nothing more than psychological daggers! In summarizing and putting a definition to your father's mental illness, it looks like...hang on let me look for my notes. Okay, what we have here is a vindictive and malignant narcissist, sociopath with explosive intermittent rage, malicious gaslighting, contempt disorder, with an enormous laundry list of other debilitating psychological and tyrannical disorders."

"That's a lot for an unofficial diagnosis. Almost sounds like during all those years I suffered, I was under a psychological attack. I had no chance."

"He is really hard to put into a definition because he has so many disorders. We're only looking through the peephole of what your father was, but look at what the three of you warriors survived. Meaning you, Soraya, and your mother. This is incredible and brave."

"How come I don't feel so incredible?"

"You all have been through quite a storm, you're still going through it, Fallon."

I grabbed more tissues from Dr. Stewart's desk. I seemed to make her laugh and she made me cry, but I needed to get this all out.

"This may seem obvious, but I believe your father used all of his disorders and narcissistic behaviors to capture and control people's lives. He gives them the illusion that they're trapped and then have no alternatives but to obey him and not leave him. They would be under his control, power, and scrutiny. This way they would not be able to hurt him first. Instead, he would bring the hurt to them. Sound familiar?"

"Yup, like opening up the dictionary and seeing my father's picture."

"These are all aspects of the terrible pain that, according to what you've shared, was inflicted by his mother, and the passivity of his father. How Henrik's mother abused him and mentally tortured him as a child.

How his father stood by and remained silent. Abandonment issues, insecurities."

"So, Dr. Stewart, what you are saying is that my father gets away with this because he's sick?"

"Oh, I don't think he's getting away with anything. I feel sorry for him and Mildred. He seems to live a life of misery under an umbrella of severe mental illness and self-torture. Think about this for a moment. How happy do you think your life would be if you were presented with this many disorders?"

"I never thought about it like that. Wonder what science would find if they cut open his brain."

"I'll tell you Fallon…an entire constellation of darkness and nightmares."

Dr. Stewart and I finished our exhausting yet illuminating session. I told her that I wanted to emancipate from my father. I told her that I had dreamt about it for years. She told me to think long and hard about a decision that could have consequences. I told her that I feared severe retaliation from a man that would make my life a living hell. She told me that emancipation may still not give me the peace that I long for.

I walked to my car, sat for a moment, and turned on the engine. The radio was playing a song by Blind Faith, with Steve Winwood singing, "I can't find my way home." I rested my head against the window, closed my eyes, and let the words sink in. Tears started falling and wouldn't stop. I couldn't…find my way back home. I couldn't find my way anywhere. I didn't feel like I belonged or fit in. I thought for a moment no one on earth could ever understand the devastation and isolation I felt. My past had me in a headlock and the grip was too tight. Even climbing mountains with my struggles, wouldn't set me free.

Are there any answers for me? I wondered. I was envious of my friends who had normal fathers, who hadn't seen their mothers suffer. This feeling had come in waves throughout my lifetime. How could it not? I felt robbed of a basic need, to be cared for by the human being that was supposed to be my pillar. Instead, I felt abandoned in what was supposed to be the happiest time of my life. I had spent so much of my free time in and out of therapy, and none of it was fair.

Dr. Stewart's spotlight on my father's disorders did not cleanse me of the horrendous burdens I carried every day. It took years to come to the realization that a narcissist will never completely leave you alone, until they are six feet under. They will not stop until they ultimately destroy your world. Everything that you make good, they will try and sour. My father succeeded in doing these things relentlessly. He knew no other way; he had a poisonous heart. My life was like a car crash, but sometimes you have to walk away from the twisted metal and mangled pieces to become who you are meant to be. I needed to someday move forward and help others.

I gave myself another moment before I opened my eyes and called Rachel. We talked for over an hour and a half. Rachel always knew there were many layers of distorted syndromes plaguing Henrik but could never put a sentence to it. Now she had an entire definition of who he was.

One advantage that the HOTEL PLAZA has over almost every other hotel in Spain is its rooftop swimming pool. Way up there on the 24th floor PLAZA guests can sun and swim from 11 a.m. to 7 p.m. every day, simply by stopping by the Concierge's desk and picking up an invitation.

In the photo above, the Italian actor, RAF BALDASSARRE, star of the film, JOSE MARIA EL TEMPRANILLO, who has made Spain his second home; at present, he is acting in LOS IMPLACABLES. With him is Miss FALI VAZQUEZ.

At the left, the popular American television and movie star TY HARDIN, also known as BRONCO, who has stayed in our hotel on several occasions.

The Plaza Pool ★ La piscina Plaza

Una ventaja que tiene el HOTEL PLAZA sobre casi todos los otros hoteles de España es la magnífica piscina de su terraza. Los huéspedes del PLAZA pueden subir al piso 24 a tomar el sol y nadar desde las 11 de la mañana hasta las 7 de la tarde, solicitando del conserje su invitación.

En la foto de arriba, el actor italiano, RAF BALDASSARRE; intérprete de la película JOSE MARIA EL TEMPRANILLO, ha hecho de España su segunda patria; actualmente se halla rodando la película LOS IMPLACABLES. En la PISCINA PLAZA junto a la señorita FALI VAZQUEZ; en un día de descanso del rodaje.

A la izquierda, el popular actor de cine y televisión norteamericano, TY HARDIN, más conocido como BRONCO. Ha sido huésped de nuestro hotel en varias ocasiones.

23

Twisted Rhetoric

Henrik and Mildred were in Germany and a snowy Christmas was underway at Rachel and Bob's. Everything glowed around the holidays at their home. The turkey was cooking, and Rachel was making all of her side dishes: rice and sausage stuffing, empanadas, and egg tortilla for an appetizer. The fireplace was roaring, and Soraya was watching Jake and Tristan play with their toys on the floor. Sam was helping Bob get the carving board out of storage.

I was in the upstairs bathroom when I heard the phone ring in the kitchen. Rachel yelled for me to grab it since her hands were in oven mitts. I picked up the phone.

"Fallon?" It was Mildred and her voice sounded panicked.

"Oh, hi, Mildred." I rolled my eyes.

"Something terrible happened to your father. We think he had a stroke. We are not sure."

I sat on the steps near the phone.

Her voice trembling, she told me that my father had complained of double vision, and they took him to the hospital in downtown Hamburg. Hours later, he had jumped out of bed in a panic and couldn't breathe. They put him on a ventilator. She told me that she would call me the next day to let me know what was going on.

Within three days they had a diagnosis of Guillain-Barré syndrome, a rare disorder in which your immune system attacks your nerves. Paralysis can happen quickly after onset, with weakness in the extremities. Henrik was now paralyzed from the waist up, could not open his eyes or speak, and could not breathe on his own. Mildred asked for my help. They were stranded in Germany with my father on a ventilator. Henrik had never bothered to get health insurance and the costs were becoming outrageous.

Soraya and I knew that Mildred couldn't stomach seeing her cash cow getting eaten alive by hospital bills, so she pushed. They were trying to fly my father home to the veterans hospital in Chicago.

The next three weeks I made it my mission to call every airline in the northern hemisphere to see if they could get a portable ventilator and nurse on board in first class. I exhausted all possibilities. Mildred found a Medjet for $35,000 and I hired an ambulance company and timed it to my father's arrival at O'Hare International Airport. The flight took about nineteen hours, landing in Iceland and Nova Scotia to refuel, reaching O'Hare at 7:00 a.m. The waiting ambulance made its way to Hines VA Hospital.

When my father arrived at the hospital, I was in the emergency room. They brought him in on a gurney and a paramedic was using a handheld oxygen pump until they could hook him up to a ventilator. His tongue was protruding out of his mouth, five times its normal size, and grotesquely laying on his neck. At first, I thought he had been poisoned.

Mildred said hello and shortly after, a friend picked her up to take her to Lake Geneva. "I'm exhausted," she said.

I stayed at the hospital with my father for thirteen hours. Within days, his neurologists told us that this was one of the most acute cases of Guillain-Barré the hospital had ever seen. Teams of doctors stopped in to observe him. His ability to walk, speak, and move was gone. He was powerless for the first time in his life. I watched as the silent hammer of justice slammed down. Yet I couldn't bear to see anyone in pain.

Within a few days Mildred moved into our home and spent most of her time at the hospital. Sam and I canceled our trip to Aspen, Colorado so I could help Mildred. Weeks went by and I filled out paperwork to get them financial help and supplemental insurance. I coordinated medicines and strategies with the doctors. Mildred still spoke broken English, so she relied on me to wheel and deal with all the logistics.

The stack of papers was about four inches thick. Two weeks later, they moved my father to a rehabilitation hospital to wean him off of the ventilator and then to Marianjoy, a long-term rehabilitation hospital. Soraya and I took turns visiting. My friend Mike told me that what happened to my father was karma. Mike hoped that if and when Henrik got better, he would somehow dig deep and change his menacing ways.

My company at that time was having financial troubles so I ended up losing my job. Again, I felt the world on my shoulders, and it put a pause on Sam's and my plan to have another baby.

Henrik was progressing slowly, and Rachel came to visit him. After everything he had put Rachel through, she was there out of the kindness of her heart. She brought her friend Carmela who was a healer. Carmela practiced a twenty-minute Reiki healing treatment on my father and within two days his eyes started opening up. My father didn't condone what he called hocus-pocus, but you couldn't argue with the results.

By September, my father was home, still on a feeding tube, needing a walker and months of physical therapy. His speech was different and he was frustrated with everything.

It's funny how all the years I wanted my father to die, yet now I prayed for him to live. My idea of emancipation went out the window. Later that year I felt like I was walking up a mountain pushing a boulder. After losing my job, I took a position in the pharmaceutical industry and was flying across the country, taking care of my son and my home. Henrik was still pulling my attention from everything else in my life. Things were so stressful with the new job that I ended up back on anti depression medication and sleeping pills. I told Sam that I was either going to quit my job or jump out of a window. By 2006, I was back in my old industry; I ended each day exhausted, drained, and on the couch.

By winter of 2007, Henrik was feeling much better, and we had two years where he was quiet and behaving. Many other things in my life, juggling work and my family, were hectic, but for the first time life with my father was shockingly more peaceful. He invited me to go with him and Mildred to Germany, and I agreed under the quieter circumstances. We were scheduled to leave in April 2007, and I let him know that Sam and I were expecting another baby boy. My father never showed much emotion but my mother was overjoyed with the news.

On November 16, 2007, Joshua Michael Colucci was born by another C-section. The doctors said he was perfect. Rachel couldn't wait until she got to the hospital to see him. In Henrik style, he and Mildred showed up right before visiting hours were over. Henrik was back to himself and was yelling at me for planning a C-section. He told me that I always had to be in control of everything, when in fact my doctor had recommended the surgery. Then Mildred teamed up against me and reiterated what my father had just said. Neither of them would leave it alone. I felt that it was an avoidance tactic of theirs because they couldn't show their emotions and were more like robots than human beings. I was back to wondering why my father hated me enough to try and ruin every joyous moment I had. I loved focusing on the people that didn't come with such heartbreak. Sam, of course, was with me all day and his mother brought Jake, who was now six years old. Jake couldn't wait to hold his baby brother.

Days later I left the hospital, my mind stronger than when I had Jake, but I was starting to feel a milder postpartum depression creep in. Within weeks, I was back at my doctor's office, back on anti depression medication. This time, I would be locked into medication for two years. I had to find a new psychiatrist now that Dr. Stewart had moved out of state. I had made such headway with her that news of her move hit me hard. In March 2008, the country was in the middle of a recession and with no work coming in, my company eliminated my position. I was devastated. I had a new baby and was still taking pills for depression. A typhoon whirled inside me and I felt myself tumbling through it.

Before I knew it, I was planning Jake's seventh birthday for early June. I wanted to start taking responsibility for my own life, but Dr. Stewart and other doctors told me that the connections that were formed in my brain as a child had wired anxiety into my system. And that anxiety was fueling everything I did. While friends and family saw Sam's and my beautiful life, I always had the feeling that everything was unraveling.

Jake's party fell on a gorgeous June afternoon. Rachel and Bob had brought a car full of food, desserts, and presents. Rachel cheered up any party where she could wear her latest fashion and indulge in her sparkling personality. I dreaded when my father showed up but knew it was a necessary evil. Now that he was back to his old self, I was not in the mood for an implosion.

In the late afternoon, after the food had been served and we had sung happy birthday to Jake, I walked back into the house to collect paper plates in the dining room, which was bustling with the older partygoers due to the heat outside. Henrik and Mildred were sitting at the dining room table with their coffee when out of nowhere my father blurted, "So, Fallon, when do you collect your food stamps?"

Mildred and Henrik viciously laughed, purposely humiliating me in front of other guests because I was collecting unemployment.

"What?"

"You heard me!"

I whispered. "I'll speak to you later about this."

I walked outside and found Rachel who told me to try and forget it and enjoy the day. The party was now winding down. Henrik and Mildred were at the front door. I could feel my blood pressure boil as I walked up to them.

"Dad before you both leave, I need to talk to you."

"Yup, what's going on?"

"If you ever talk to me like that again at a party or any time, I will ask you to leave on the spot."

"What did I do?"

"You know exactly what you did. You and your wife were laughing at me? You're making fun of me for losing my job? Who do you think you are? That was rude and embarrassing. I'm heartbroken over my job and you embarrass me at my son's birthday party?"

"You're so self-conscious, Fallon. Mildred and I think your husband needs to worry about work. Not you!"

"What is this, the fifties? I'm telling you, don't disrespect me in my own home! I better never hear you speak to me like that again."

"Yeah... Okay, calm down."

I locked eyes with him. When you break the back of a hardworking mom who has worked her entire life for everything that she has, you break the heart of the world. You may or may not notice the pain in her eyes but make no mistake, the bruises are there for a lifetime.

At that moment, I believed I was at a crossroads and was hitting rock bottom. Later that summer, I started writing the first of two novels called *Haunted Nights at Drumheller Castle*. The story was a paranormal tale set in the nearby town of St. Charles. My writing took me away from everything in my life that I had no control over. In my fiction, I could create any outcome I desired. I wrote and wrote, and I wondered where this new obsession was coming from. My recruiter found me a new job and I was back to feeling the burn of being a working mom. I loved and felt pride in my job, but like most young mothers I knew, I was frustrated with the juggle. Still, writing and breaking away from the norm showed what I wanted for my life, even if I didn't yet know how to get there.

Summer was ending and autumn had arrived, a time of inspiration for me as my *Drumheller Castle* tale was set in October of 1967 around Halloween. Witches, black cats, moonlit nights, and the paranormal always fascinated me. Psychic magic ran in my family and my new outlet was flourishing with ideas.

Halloween around my house always seemed like a portal into another world. My kids loved the paranormal mayhem and how our house glowed with the spirit of the season. My blowup pumpkin horse and carriage greeted trick-or-treaters as they passed the spooky cemetery that lit up the night in our front yard. The air was thick as the fog machine worked overtime. Haunting sounds poured out of speakers set up in a nearby window. The sounds frightened the youngest children, who never dared to come to our front door without their parents because first they would have to pass menacing ghouls who hung from tree branches, swinging in the October wind.

Life ebbs and flows with the good and the bad, the happy and the sad twisting together all at the same time. Soraya, Tristan, my boys, and I were at Rachel and Bob's for Christmas, waiting for a phone call from Spain. Our beloved Abuela Esther was not doing well. The day after Christmas my mother got the call. Her best friend and mother passed away at the age of ninety-six. Rachel felt lost without her and the pain burned. She felt guilty that she wasn't with her when she passed and regretted all the years she had lived in the States away from her.

We understand that our grandparents are supposed to leave us on this earth. But it doesn't make it any easier when the people who loved us as much as our mother fade away. Sometimes the end of an era leaves emptiness in our hearts that can never be filled.

24

Non-Negotiable Anchor

By February 2010, Bob, who had become forgetful during the past year, was diagnosed with Alzheimer's. Although he was still able to live at home, Rachel had her hands full picking up after him and retrieving misplaced car keys, paperwork, and his wallet.

At the same time, Henrik called to tell me that he was selling the last twenty acres of farmland still in Soraya's and my names. I reminded him that he had told us he was keeping the land for Soraya and me, but obviously he had different plans. Even though Soraya and I were heartbroken over the sale, it was difficult to argue with him.

"Listen," he said, "I need your signature because the land is in your and your sister's names."

"Why can't we keep the land?" I said. "You've already sold off most of it. It would be wonderful to have a small piece of our childhood to share with our boys."

"Look," he said, "I need the money. I don't have a choice."

I didn't know whether to cry or laugh. I could hear Mildred whispering to him in the background. I was sure that another betrayal was on its way.

"Fallon, you and Soraya will get something," he said. "Once the sale goes through, I'll cut each of you a check for $10,000."

"Okay," I said. "Let me speak to Soraya."

"What are we going to do with the land, anyway?" said Soraya when I called her. "And you know Dad. He'll end up doing whatever he wants."

Still, my father always had an agenda that only served him and Mildred. We went ahead with the signatures, and within a few months the land and the last bit of our legacy was sold. The land that was supposed to go on for generations never made it past the selfish prick that owned it in the first place. We were sure Mildred had a part in Henrik's decision. She had made it clear that she didn't want to see anything going to Soraya and me. That included nine condos Henrik had bought years ago as investment properties with one going to each of his girls. Mildred made sure to foil that possibility from our future.

I told Henrik that in the past twenty years, I had never had a private conversation with him, and I wondered what that was all about. Mildred always had to be there or within earshot on the phone. She would never allow Soraya and me to have a discussion with Henrik without her being present.

And then one night I picked up the phone to hear Soraya's distressed voice. "Fallon! Dad said that now that he sold the last of the farmland, he's keeping the $10,000 he promised us!"

Soraya couldn't believe that another betrayal was on its way.

"But we were the owners," I said. "We signed the paperwork. Over my dead body. He's not going to get away with this!"

I hung up and called Henrik. "You're always breaking promises," I yelled into the phone. "You are crushing Soraya and me. I'm not letting you weasel out of money that's rightfully ours."

Somehow, I got through to him and he agreed to send a check to Soraya and me within ten days.

The hardest part of Henrik's and my relationship was not the money, it was how I allowed myself to be betrayed over and over. I continued with therapy, tried everything really, from divine energy healing to holistic herbs and karmic release. I had even sought out and hugged Amma, the hugging saint, when she visited Chicago.

In some respects, at times I felt I had transformed my anger and had become centered. But everything I tried was only a temporary fix. I was on the same frequency as my father. He was angry constantly and I was consumed with anger at him. It was a vicious cycle that never seemed to end.

Winter turned to spring, then summer. Soraya was in the middle of a turbulent divorce. Sam and I decided to spend a weekend with our boys, Soraya, and Tristan in Lake Geneva.

On Saturday afternoon, they were outside on the front lawn and I was in the lake house kitchen preparing snacks while Mildred rested upstairs. Henrik sat on the couch in the dining room talking to me about the half acre of land he owned adjacent to the house. The land was in Soraya's and my names, but he was concerned that Soraya's soon-to-be ex-husband would try to take it in the divorce.

Suddenly, he started screaming, "Your damn sister is gonna give away the *entire* piece of land next door! Her husband is gonna come here and *just take it*! ALL MY HARD WORK. And for *what*?"

He kept ranting, steaming from his skull. I flew into the dining room. Sparks seemed to fly everywhere, but something was happening within me. The transformation I had so desperately sought for so long came all at once. I suddenly felt a power over him that I'd never felt before.

"You're just a Goddamn bully!" I shouted. "I don't care what you say!"

My voice soared and roared, I found dark octaves I never knew I had, finally drowning out my father's belligerent tone as he shouted at me. Years of abuse and scorn poured out of my soul.

I stood right in front of my father screaming as he stood in his flannel pajamas. "STOP IT! STOP IT! JUST…STOP IT!"

For once, my voice was louder than his. I barked back more viciously.

I could see in his eyes that he saw my mother shining through, something he despised in me. I was tired of getting ridiculed for something that had nothing to do with me, something that my sister's husband might do that was out of my control. Fire raged from my mouth, the lion that had been in me all along was set free.

Henrik fell back against the couch. Mildred raced downstairs and, uncharacteristically polite, ushered me to the front door. Strangely, she seemed to think that Henrik deserved every word.

I walked outside and was still breathing hard; dizzy from a tirade I never knew I had in me. My blood pulsed through my veins as I told Sam and Soraya what happened. We got in our cars and drove with the kids two blocks to the lake. I was trembling and trying to calm down. We tried to enjoy the rest of the day swimming and hanging out on the pier for hours. It was impossible, we couldn't stop talking about the elephant in the room. Mildred came down to the lake to find us. She begged us to come back to the house. Henrik wanted to apologize for his behavior.

"My father is crazy," I said. "And sick."

Soraya, Sam, and I told her we didn't care about an insincere apology. We were all shocked that the word apology even came out of his shameful mouth.

From that moment, my life changed. For the rest of the summer, on my time off, I worked hard finishing up production on my first novel. On September 10, my book was published. By October, I had my fifteen minutes of fame. I was in the newspapers, on Channel 7 news because Rachel knew reporter Terresa Gutierrez, and swamped at my book signing. Henrik made excuses saying he was too sick to attend my book launch.

Two days before Christmas, Soraya, Sam, the kids, and I made our dreaded visit to Henrik and Mildred's house.

Soraya and Tristan walked in the door behind me, Soraya asking, "What's on the menu this year?"

"Another platter of bullshit!" I said, laughing.

Soraya and I kept firing off our comedic banter. It was the only coping mechanism that we had.

"Did you see the movie, *The Devil Wears Prada*?"

"Yeah." I thought Soraya was seriously asking me if I had ever seen the movie.

"Well, this devil wears lederhosen!"

Soraya and I were bent with laughter, secretly making fun of our step-monster, keeping our punchlines to ourselves.

I went into the kitchen and asked Mildred if I could help.

"No thanks," she said. "I've got things covered."

"What are we having?"

She showed me two packages of Stouffer's frozen lasagna.

I asked if I could get out the garlic bread or start chopping veggies for the salad.

"There isn't any," she said.

I found Soraya and whispered, "We're having Stouffer's lasagna for Christmas dinner."

"What?" Soraya snickered.

"Yup, Stouffer's, and no garlic bread or salad."

"She's serving only a frozen dinner?"

"Now you're catching on."

"Wow, she really doesn't have a fucking clue."

Soraya and I were beside ourselves with the giggles over soggy lasagna. We knew that they were going to serve more than frozen food when Mildred's daughter flew in from Germany.

"What's with the Stouffer's?" I said to Henrik.

"We thought you guys like Italian food."

"We do like Italian food, but you could have catered a real lasagna from JoJo's."

"I would have," he said. "But things are tight." I couldn't believe the blatant lie right to my face.

Just then the smoke detector went off and the smell of scorched food infiltrated the house.

Henrik went into the kitchen. We heard him raising his voice. "Who's gonna eat that now? You can't serve dinner like that! You've burnt it to a crisp, you dumb bitch!"

Soraya and I made eye contact and bit our lips.

Trembling, Mildred brought the burnt dish to the table. We dug under the scorched noodle "char-sagna" as we would later call it and ate as much as we could save.

We were all starving by now. Soraya and I sat on the couch and laughed about Christmas the year before. Henrik had approached me and asked if I liked the $150 gift cards he had given to Soraya and me, $350 less than the year before.

That year, I was hosting Christmas dinner and was exhausted from cooking, cleaning, and holiday prep for our extended family. I had been up late and had woken up extra early to tackle all the holiday details.

I had my hands full juggling two pot roasts when Henrik asked what was the matter and why I wasn't joining the party. "I'm fine," I said, and went back to preparing dinner. He stormed out of the kitchen and straight to Mildred.

"What an ungrateful daughter!" Mildred shouted.

"Let's get out of this shithole!" yelled Henrik.

And just like that, they left.

Soraya added a story from the summer before. Henrik had started complaining about seeing us on Facebook living our lives and attending events. He called Soraya and yelled at her for going to a party in the city instead of coming to visit him. He was using Facebook to spy on us and asking other family members to snoop on where we were going. We gleefully blocked him.

As we walked out the door, I was so relieved that we had the Baumann part of our holidays in the rear-view mirror and looked forward to telling Rachel about the yummy char-sagna we didn't eat.

Months passed and over the summer we found out that Henrik had prostate cancer. With treatment the prognosis was good, but I knew without a doubt that Henrik had destroyed his immune system with eighty years of his explosive temper.

On the other side of town our beloved stepfather Bob, who was more like a dad to us, was getting worse with Alzheimer's. The sweet man had set off the alarm system at 3:00 a.m. and the police showed up thinking someone had broken into their home.

By mid-summer I got a phone call from Mildred. She only called me when she needed me, and this was the fourth phone call of its kind. She was in tears, saying that for the past two years, Henrik would go crazy screaming around the house, breaking things and banging his head against the wall. This time when she called the police they arrived, and he suddenly calmed down.

"Call a psychiatrist," I said. "He needs one and they'll help you, too."

"No," she said.

"You're in denial," I said under my breath.

"What can I do?"

"As I said, you need help from a professional."

In between her calls for help, she also let Soraya know that they had sold one of Henrik's condos. I always called it Operation Ramp-Up when Mildred planted the seed for something that was going to happen in the future, as if Soraya and I were naive to her larger goal. Mildred kept trying to lure us to visit Henrik. "He's sick," she said. "He needs you."

They were becoming lonely, miserable, unhappy martyrs, in our view. At times we would visit when our own pity got the best of us. When we got there, we found the same old Henrik whom my sons had nicknamed Grumpa.

October had arrived. Bob had entered a nursing home and was in hospice. Rachel was there every day and I visited often. One morning the nurse came into the hall to tell Rachel that the end was near. Unbelieving, I told her that he looked fine, and he was still talking to us and seemed somewhat normal. But hospice knew what they were talking about. They could see things that we couldn't, or maybe what we didn't want to see.

By the end of October, Bob was mispronouncing my name. By Thanksgiving, he was calling me one of his deceased relatives. By the middle of December, he wasn't saying much of anything. On the Friday before Christmas, I sat with Bob while they spoon fed him lunch. Tears rolled down my face as I talked with him. "Bob…can you hear me?" I tried to have Bob look at my face, but he just stared straight ahead. He was trying to purse his lips to make a sound but couldn't. I left after the nurses were done feeding him.

I called Rachel on my way home in tears. I no sooner pulled into my driveway when Rachel called me back in a panic after speaking with the nursing home. Bob had slipped into a coma and would be on round-the-clock hospice care. We were both in denial that his death was looming.

With not much sleep for any of us, the next morning I took off for the nursing home. Sam and our oldest son Jake were there with me. Tristan, Soraya, Rachel, and all of Bob's children were around him. Bob was such a good man who had never hurt anyone.

My eyes full of tears, I turned to Rachel. "Why would God take Bob from us and leave us this piece of shit father?"

"Querida," she said softly, "it often seems that God takes the good ones first."

Henrik, not to miss an opportunity, called me to complain that no one visited him over the holiday.

At 1:00 a.m. on December 26, Bob passed away with one of his hospice nurses beside him. Bob had secretly slipped through the celestial gateway by the shimmering midnight stars, leaving an emptiness in our hearts.

Rachel and Bob had been married for twenty-nine years. It wasn't always perfect, but Bob had given Rachel safety, and she had someone who treated her with love and respect and whom she could love and respect back. Bob always knew that he was loved not only by her, but also by Soraya and me. He had always been far more of a father to us than our biological nightmare.

The following October my second book in the *Drumheller Castle* series, *Ethereal Quandary,* was published. Another fifteen minutes of fame followed with newspapers and a book launch at the historic Arcada Theater of St. Charles, Illinois. Rachel couldn't get enough of my first book and couldn't wait to read the second.

I showed the book to Henrik and Mildred. Out of nowhere and abruptly, Mildred said, "You know. Your book will be nothing in two years."

25

Fallen Leaves

The year 2016 arrived with its own set of challenges. Mildred saw signs of Henrik's dementia but ignored it, chalking it up as part of the aging process. She made sure, however, to let us know that Henrik had sold more of his condos. Dementia worked in Mildred's favor because she could skew things and fool us in the process. She was also always at her post, keeping a tight rein on the money that would soon come her way. Sam and I had grown apart and were going through a divorce. Rachel, or Yaya as she was called, loved being a grandma and was equally adored.

I met a man named Jim, who changed my life for the better, through the Arcada Theater. I had known Ron Onesti, the owner, for years. He had hosted my book launches, as well as a nonstop flurry of rock concerts and a lot of music from the seventies and eighties which Jim and I loved. Jim and I became part of the culture of the Arcada family and surrounding community. All of the music that I had listened to on our little kitchen radio was there. Now, Jim and I were meeting these music icons who had given us the soundtrack to our lives.

I was yet again researching another holistic remedy to help with my intermittent anxiety and depression, and I found Dr. Kramer out of Naperville, whom I worked with for about four months. In my relationship with Jim, I wanted to be happy and put the past behind me. I never thought that I would discover yet another reason for my messed up brain. The technology was called neurofeedback, and the doctor did a preliminary brain scan on me as a mapping system. When he received the results, he called me into the office. He gave the good news first.

"So, Fallon, in summary of some of these scans, it looks like your brain is healthy and younger than your actual age."

I felt encouraged. Dr. Kramer took his time explaining everything so that I could understand. I told him that I was pretty knowledgeable with medical terminology and that he could speak freely. Then we talked about a few things that I didn't expect.

"On the other part of the testing, I don't see this much, and I don't know how to tell you this…" Dr. Kramer paused. "I don't see brain damage, but I see damage to the four quadrants of the brain. Do you see this scan in bright red?"

I looked at Dr. Kramer, dumbfounded. I felt my heart pounding. "What does that mean?"

"I can't be certain but with damage like this, it can be a high indicator of shaken baby syndrome. Actually, in this office I've only seen damage to three sides of the brain, never four. You are my first."

I sat in silence for a moment. I couldn't even feel my tongue, I had no saliva in my mouth. "May I have a moment?" I asked quietly.

"Yes," he said gently, "Please, take your time."

I tried to calm my breath. I had learned a number of breathing techniques and now I breathed in slowly and out slowly until I felt ready to go on. "Okay," I said. "What else?"

"Do you know if you were ever left alone with a babysitter or if either of your parents ever showed any signs of violent behavior?"

I got up and whispered to Dr. Kramer that I needed to get some air and I would be back in a minute. I walked outside and looked up into the clouds. I knew my angels had protected me when my disturbed father shook me. And while I'd never be able to prove it, I knew for certain my father had indeed done so. I knew in my heart what happened and that my angels had been there. I wiped my tears with my sleeve and walked back into the doctor's office. I looked at him and asked him one question.

"Can you help me?"

"Yes, Fallon, I can help you."

I worked with Doctor Kramer's office for months. It wasn't a forever fix but I started feeling my mind find peace that it never knew before. I understood that the wires of my life could be restored, what was broken could eventually be fixed and that all my crumbled parts could be put back together again.

March of 2018 came in like a lion. I was still living with Sam and trying to stay for my boys. I didn't know what to do. I didn't want to leave them, and I knew Sam needed help raising them, too. Finally, a year and a half after our divorce, I rented a room from a good friend in a historic home in St. Charles. As I moved into my friend's home, my life was taking a momentary detour straight off a cliff. Rachel was beside herself and so sad, she promised to pray for me every day. Even with her prayers, I felt lonely, deserted, trapped, and isolated in my square bubble, missing my children, missing Jim. I felt like I had lost everything in one swoop, my kids, marriage, dog, bed, house, neighbors, my surroundings. Even some old friends deserted me.

I remembered feeling that way when we left our home after Rachel's divorce from Henrik when I was fourteen. I was starting over again with only a few boxes and a carload of clothing. I lived a good life but at this juncture I felt that sometimes inside my brain, I could identify with the people who lived on the fringe of society. I knew what it was like to not belong, to be different, to not fit in, to be awkward, to lose jobs, to be an outcast and an outsider, to have psychosis, depression, anxiety, and ADD, to lose my best friend, to lose my baby brother, to be alone and lonely, to suffer from multiple divorces in my family, to have memories of violence and abuse, to fight for all I had and still lose, and to own only a few boxes with no place to call home. But mostly I knew I had a father who would betray and deceive me, even if I was backed into a dark corner and had nowhere else to turn. That's where I felt most alone, like I was at the bottom of a well looking up at the sky.

I was trying not to feel sorry for myself and I was so grateful to my girlfriend for letting me have a place to stay but knew I didn't belong there. I came from my beautiful house alive and bustling with my boys and our dog Boyd. I felt like a fish out of water. Jim wanted me home with him, but I needed a transitional place so that my boys had time to accept our relationship. I couldn't cry myself to sleep anymore. I moved in with Jim four months later, a six-minute drive to my old home; always keeping close ties with my boys. Sometimes you have to walk away from the person you were in order to transcend into a new form. Sometimes God wants you to hit the reset button.

I went to visit my father at the end of September 2018. He wasn't speaking much the last few weeks, and I was leaving for Italy with my cousin Esther. Those days Henrik was more of an annoying insect than a tyrannical bully. He was homebound, frail, and needed a wheelchair to get between the bedroom and living room, yet he was still ornery. He was diminished to nothing more than crapping all over himself, shitting on the floor and in his bed. I would normally never like to see this happen to anyone but under the circumstances I understood that karma had shown up.

Before I left, I knelt in front of my father's chair. I stared into his dark, empty eyes, not knowing it would be my last time. I told Henrik I was going to Italy, his eyes widened, and he nodded in recognition. My mother was ecstatic that I was going with her niece and told me to bring her something back from the Vatican. Jim drove me to the airport on September 30. I was gone for two weeks. Mildred did not approve.

I flew home the day after my birthday, and I got a concerned call from

Mildred. She told me that her sister had passed away and that Henrik wasn't speaking at all. I told her to stay in touch with me and that I would be out there soon. The next weekend I brought my boys to say goodbye to their grandfather. I sat there for two hours, and my father sat in his chair, eyes closed, not saying a word. I tapped his face; I spoke loud in his ear… nothing.

The next day Soraya was there, and her boyfriend Scott told me Saturday night to come out as soon as I could. In the morning, I was on my way. I left my house at 8:40 for Lake Geneva. I was five minutes from my father's home when an eagle flew over my car. I thought I was going crazy when the eagle doubled back, flew over my car again, and seemed to stare at me with his yellow eyes. In my mind I heard the eagle speak, "Hurry I'm fading fast," and then not another sound. I made it in time. I walked in the door and saw the hospice nurses. I heard my father's death rattle from across the room. Soraya was holding Henrik's hand and asked me if I wanted to take a turn. Mildred was at church. Perfect timing, we thought.

I sat with my father and told him that I was there. Twenty minutes had gone by, and Mildred walked in the door. I told one of the hospice nurses just after they administered medication to keep my father comfortable that it looked like his breathing had changed or stopped all together. They checked his heartbeat and then again after another moment. The man that ruled with an iron fist was gone. Henrik on some level knew that he could not buy back tomorrow, and his money could not save him today. I held his hand in mine, saw him take his last breath and within fifteen seconds of his death Mildred blurted out to the hospice nurses, "I'm so relieved!"

I couldn't believe my ears. My father was still 98.6 and there was Mildred circling like a vulture surrounding her prey.

I don't think I saw the tasteless, tacky, no-class bitch cry. I hugged Soraya then I walked out of the room in tears to call our mother. She told me that it was all over now and I knew what she meant. My next call was to Jim who was at the Bears game, and then I called Mike. After an hour or so the coroner was there for the pickup. Mildred, Soraya, and I waited in the next room. Henrik had a fairytale death he did not deserve. He was in his great room with two hospice nurses, his daughters, and his wife. It was serene and peaceful unlike the life that he left behind. The man who hated women was now surrounded by them in his final moments.

I left my father's home hours later and drove down to the lake just as the drizzle stopped. Jim Croce was on the radio singing "I Got a Name." I loved the lyrics in that song: "And I'm gonna go there free."

All I wanted to be is rolling down the highway…free. Free of the burdens of the last fifty-one years. Before the song ended, I had a lump in my throat. There was emptiness and desolation. I looked at the road ahead, and it seemed to be swallowed up by the October fog. The mist was heavy and sat low in the soggy gloom. The pavement had a finality to it, the streets were silent, and not a soul was around. The air was cool and damp, and the fallen leaves had a mustiness to them. The leaves blew in small gusts, echoing my sadness as I got to the lake. The pier looked momentarily still, lifeless, and empty of boaters. The breeze was numbing. It was all around me, suffocating my breath. I couldn't believe that this monster and the father who robbed me of my childhood was gone.

I sat in the stillness on the bench at the pier overlooking Lake Geneva. I remembered the last words I spoke to my father, telling him that I was going to Italy. The biggest source of anguish in my life had now died, yet I had so many scars that bandages could not hold the wounds. But I knew that my strength and faith would never let me fall apart. It was a superpower given to me by my mother. This was a power that would one day carry me out of the arms of the predator and into my own vindication.

I believe my father's life was one of regret and misery by causing others pain. He was only able to make a connection with another soul when he wanted to manipulate and dismantle them. It was a tragically pathetic existence. During the wake and funeral, I gave the eulogy. Within a few weeks, I read the will. I did a lot of difficult and soul-searching work that others would not touch. In the end, it was the relationship with my father that was not fixable. Our connection was built on decay. It was mechanical, complicated, problematic, and riddled with strife. On one hand I hated my father. On the other hand, I longed for a bond with a dad that was not in existence. I hurt for the dad that was nowhere to be found in my reality. Not even looking for his ghost would fill the void. For a long moment I felt the emptiness…of something I never had.

26

The Knives of Thieves

Two weeks after my father's funeral Soraya and I drove out to speak to Mildred and find a place at the lake for my father's ashes. I read my father's will in its entirety out loud to Mildred and Soraya and couldn't believe my ears. Even though it felt strange to mourn a man I hated at times, I was drained with grief. The duties that were always placed on me weighed down my spirit that wanted to fly away.

It was not a surprise to us, but it looked as if Mildred was getting most of my father's estate. The struggles of the last fifty-one years of my life seemed to capsize me in that moment. Somehow, I thought my father was going to make good on his promises to Soraya and me. Somehow, I thought magic was going to happen, and in the end my father was going to come through for us. It looked as if Soraya and I were left with very little insurance money from children of the veterans, a small life insurance policy, and the empty wooded half acre lot next door. Mildred didn't want the lot because she would have to pay taxes on it. Instead, that was now our responsibility.

Mildred told us sarcastically that she was sorry that all the farmland was gone and reiterated that there was not much left for us girls in the will. Mildred let it be known that within a few years she would sell what was once our summer home and move back to Germany. Soraya and I made joyful eye contact with the news, knowing that someday soon she would be out of our lives forever. Mildred had a hold on the purse strings and the rest of my father's estate. Her new nickname was Houdini because she had made four-hundred acres of farmland, our lake house, boat, bank accounts, and condos all disappear.

The most disheartening part of the will was where it explained in gut-wrenching detail that when Mildred died everything in my father's estate would go to Mildred's daughter Katrina. There was nothing Soraya or I could do about it. Even beyond the grave, Henrik was plotting his evil agenda against us. To punch us more in the stomach, one of the last lines in the will stated, "These are my intentions."

I could hear these final words of betrayal from my father in my sleep! "THESE ARE MY INTENTIONS!" The disparaging pain and unforgiving injustice of these final words collapsed me with the gravest deceit I have ever encountered. Our own father in his final words had turned his back on us, slapping us with the title he had given Soraya and me years before, his "bastard illegitimate children!"

The gravity of this moment was devastating. My body ached everywhere, I felt beaten and crushed. I locked eyes with Soraya and I told Mildred that the will was too much to talk about this soon after our father's death. I was mentally exhausted. An early snowstorm was coming in and we needed to get down to the lake.

"You take the ashes," said Mildred. "It's too much for me!"

I took it upon myself to complete the task that no one else had the stomach to do. I was the last one to leave the pier that day. I watched the murky water as my father's ashes sank to the bottom. I turned to walk back up to my car and there an eagle jumped off a lofty oak tree branch thirty feet above me and flew into the sky.

A few weeks later Mildred flew back to Germany on her broomstick. Before she left, she invited us to an early Christmas at what was now her home. It was six weeks after our father's death. Mildred wanted to give the boys their gifts and made a special mention that she would not be exchanging gifts with Soraya and me. We showed up with our gift, a wooden veteran's flag holder. She had catered dinner and we thanked God that we didn't have to suffer at the hands of her cooking.

After we ate, we watched the boys open their gifts. It didn't take long. Josh got some toys and Tristan and Jake each got one gift. Soraya and I locked eyes and couldn't wrap our brain around what we were seeing. Tristan asked what the gift was. Mildred joyfully answered in her German growl.

"They are jelly jars filled with quarters from your grandfather!"

Jake answered, "What?"

The two jelly jars were wrapped with a red ribbon around the lid and filled with quarters.

Mildred reiterated, "Yes, these are quarters that your grandfather has been saving for years! There should be a couple hundred dollars in each of them."

By no means were Soraya and I ever ungrateful children, but this was Mildred in a very covert form. She was laughing in our faces; we witnessed a new level of systemic greed. Tristan and Jake had a puzzled look of disappointment on their faces. Mildred miscalculated, there was a total of $78.50 between the two jars. She walked into the kitchen, proud of herself.

Soraya pulled me aside. "Fallon," she whispered. "What the fuck? A jar of quarters for Christmas, who does that?" Soraya had a confused and disgusted look on her face.

"I have no idea what this crazy bitch is thinking. Just to let you know, this is my last Christmas at this house. I've played nice long enough. When this fucked-up fraulein gets back from Germany, we're gonna have a talk with her about Dad's will and then I'm done! She's going to fucking hear me!"

"I'm done too, Fallon. She has 95% of our father's estate which was worth four million dollars, she gives us nothing for Christmas, and she gives the boys a jar of quarters. Is this a joke! I'm speechless. What a greedy pig!"

It was almost as if Mildred had morphed into Henrik. The jar of quarters was a slap in our faces. I grew quiet, trying to process everything that was happening. I was alone in my thoughts but knew that Soraya was with me. I was still in mourning and was content to go through it so that I wouldn't have more baggage from the asshole formerly known as my father. I knew that soon I would be grieving the loss of our summer home even though it had been in Mildred's selfish grip so long ago. Soraya and I should have had nothing to do with Mildred after our father's death, but we needed to see all of this through to the finish line. Rachel got the first phone call about the jelly jars the minute the boys and I left Lake Geneva.

You may think this was insignificant, but the quarters were a defining moment in illustrating for Soraya and me how we had been treated, marginalized, and disregarded by the difficult Henrik and Mildred dynamic. Soraya told the bizarre tale to many friends over the next few years. We had a few good laughs about the quarters, but mostly people were dumbfounded in disbelief.

In April 2019, Soraya and I were ready to have our talk with Mildred. The soulless bitch had come back from Germany and then left again. But we waited. She had made it known for years that we were not allowed at the lake house when she was gone. We were not sure if she didn't trust us or our boys, but it was just another way the Cunt of Camelot was telling us to back down and that she was the one who was now ruling with an iron fist. She probably didn't want her trust fund messed with. And I couldn't wait to finally tell her to fuck off!

I often remind myself that the knives of thieves cut deeper because they want what they can't have so they take it. They take all of it like gluttonous pigs shoving every last morsel in their mouths. The thieves will chop at your flesh causing crushing damage. They will take what they want, destroying you in their path, knowing what was yours has now mysteriously emerged in their possession. Henrik and Mildred were two of the most notorious thieves I'd ever known.

Mildred was powerful enough to change wills and trusts just to serve her benefit. There was a debate between Soraya and me about whether Mildred changed what Henrik wrote down in black and white, but Henrik was evil enough to allow this to happen. Mildred had no filter, loved to gloat, and had no class. I had always wanted to slap the stupid grin of that slimy bitch's face with the crooked nose...now I had my chance!

Finally, in November, Soraya and I arrived at Mildred's. I told Rachel I would call her the second we left. I knew I had a job to do. I didn't think today was going to change anything, but I was straight-faced and ready for battle. Soraya and I sat down, and Mildred began to talk.

"Now girls, if you're to ignore me like you have been, then we need to part ways."

"Ignore you? You've been in Germany in a condo paid with the blood of our farmland. You knew we wanted to talk to you about Henrik's will." I did most of the talking that afternoon.

"Both you girls treat me terribly and the way you treated your father!"

I was now ready. "Okay, Mildred, SHUT UP AND SIT DOWN! This is my turn to talk. I've waited thirty years to tell you a few things."

I had a list of things I wanted to cover, and I let Mildred have it. I was fuming, steaming, and I held nothing back. I screamed from my soul, I spoke from the heart, and I wasn't nice. I sounded angry, but really, I was coming from a place of great pain.

Mildred had the nerve to complain that I never came to see my dad and I told her that around my father's death I was there eight different times in a six-week period helping with everything. I told her that if this was any other child, she would have told my father to go fuck off years ago, but I didn't. I gave her a quick summary of what my father did to my mother, Soraya, and me, and how we suffered a lifetime of pain. I expressed the fact that most of the abuse landed on Rachel and me. I also told her that she had been abused by my father too, but she had taken the abuse because she knew she was going to get every last dollar he had.

An hour had passed, and I was still going.

"You've put me down for the last time," I said, my voice a bar of steel. "Boasting about your trips to Germany and how I have no vacation time! You and Henrik treated Soraya and me like garbage. You said you felt sorry for Soraya and me because we have to work. Constantly gloating about your pathetic life. You called me fat right to my face four weeks after I had a baby! What cruel crazy bitch would do something like that? Both you and Henrik *made fun of me* when I lost my job! You laughed in my face when Henrik asked when I was getting my food stamps! *Unbelievable*! You and my father have cut me down for every accomplishment I've ever achieved in my life…leaving me with a lifetime of unbearable pain. You are both sick! But let me tell you, God bless the child that has her own. We are done with your bullshit! DONE!"

Soraya interjected, "Fallon, calm down!"

"No, Soraya! *I'm sorry*, I've had years and years to tolerate their bullshit and now she's gonna hear me!" I looked down at Mildred's trembling hands. It was horrible, but I felt pleasure in her pain, after all the pain inflicted on me and years of mental torture. I was finally getting my point across. I looked at Soraya who was in shock hearing my words, but her eyes encouraged me to go on.

"Mildred, Soraya and I got barely anything from my father's estate. Now, I live a good life in a beautiful home. I travel to many places around the world with my Jim. I have many investments. Soraya has a beautiful lake house and boat with her Scott. I don't need my father's money, but what happened here was *not fair*! You can do the right thing and change that!"

"Change what? I owe you two *nothing*!" Mildred barked.

"Well," I continued, "you filthy, greedy, sewer belching *pig*! You've got your stingy, greasy paws clawing for every last penny, now, don't you? You are not even human…you are a greedy robot with no filter!"

Mildred's face was white as a ghost, and it looked like the slithering bitch wanted to faint, but I wasn't finished with her. I calmed down a bit so that she could hear every word that I was saying.

"Now Mildred I'm gonna tell you about the scum you were married to! I'm gonna tell you about all the whores my dad fucked in your bed while you were in Germany!"

"Oh!"

"*Yup*! When you were in Germany back and forth for years, Henrik was still fucking his old girlfriend, Joanne. He was seeing both of you at the same time. Then I caught my sleazeball father up in your bedroom fucking a twenty-five-year-old crack whore!"

Mildred shrugged her shoulders.

"Oh Mildred, don't pretend that this isn't bothering you! I caught him with his pants down a few times, can you imagine the realistic numbers of his sleazy affairs that I haven't seen?"

"What can I do? That was who he was!"

"THAT'S DISGUSTING! There were more whores than you know! I caught him other times calling me from other women's homes. He would lie about it but I caught him by reading the caller ID! Mildred…I will tell you something, you are nothing more than a *cockroach*! You are just like my father if you accept that kind of behavior in your marriage! You had a miserable marriage *built on lies* with my disgraceful father!"

All the pain and abuse I suffered was pouring out of me. I couldn't stop the verbal attack, even if I wanted to.

"I can't believe you're talking to me this way!"

"I TOLD YOU TO SHUT UP! You had an empty marriage with my despicable father!"

Soraya spoke in a calmer voice. "This is all true Mildred."

"Now Mildred, I want to ask you, when you pass away, everything will go to your daughter Katrina from my father's estate, leaving Soraya and me completely out of the picture! Do you think that's *fair*? On what planet is *that* fair? We were his *daughters*! He made a lot of empty promises to us. This was our father's estate, and you took it for yourself!"

"Well, it's mine now!" Mildred squeaked.

"We know, you selfish *pig*!"

Soraya exclaimed, "Henrik told us that at least one of the condos would go to us!"

Mildred continued trembling and said nothing.

"You and your daughter Katrina are the biggest, greediest fucking pigs I've ever met in my life! I speak for both Soraya and myself. Henrik is no longer our father! By the way, our mother Rachel is beautiful, classy, and kind, and you are an ugly piece of shit! You know it. And we know it!"

I'd been sitting on the edge of the couch. I got up for a second to reposition myself. I continued.

"How pathetic Henrik was! You assholes gave our boys quarters for Christmas and your gluttonous throats were choking on your stupid self-indulgence! How ridiculous, for God's sake, Henrik left *nothing* for his grandsons! WHAT A FILTHY PIECE OF SHIT! Not even his tools, only quarters! Tristan wanted some of his grandfather's tools, and you gave them away! Those boys will never remember their *pathetic*, *cruel* grandfather, or you. I can guarantee this!"

I stood up and looked at Soraya. It was time to leave.

"As for you, Mildred. You sold us out for money! What a disgrace! I hope Jake, Tristan, and Josh spit on you if they ever see you again. This was their summer home, too."

"I'm not kicking you guys out. You can come back to visit," Mildred replied.

"You don't understand. We are *never* coming back! Don't worry, we will still fully enjoy the lake, just not coming back to this shithole!"

I believe Mildred didn't understand all of the curse words I was using, or maybe her brain could not keep up with the mental whiplash, and I didn't care. I hadn't felt that good in years. I looked at Soraya.

"Now we have something better than our birthright, Soraya! We have our fucking freedom! Oh, and we have our own money, we don't have to squat all over someone else's. My job is done here, I've served my time in Baumann's jail!" I glared at Mildred.

I glanced at the mantel. "What is that doing there?" I grabbed my wooden sailboat plaque, and Soraya and I walked to the front door where I picked up my wagon wheel. I turned to the quivering Mildred and spoke one last time.

"By the way, your cooking sucks!"

Soraya and I, still in so much pain, giggled all the way to our cars. It was an unbridled, childlike giddiness I felt inside. I had said outrageous things, but I didn't care. I never had to swallow the slop and anguish that Henrik or Mildred threw my way ever again. We drove to the lake and walked the path, we threw autumn leaves in the air, and I celebrated something that only victims of abuse could understand: a moment of pure exoneration.

What I purged to Mildred on that day in November did not excuse my father or fifty-one years of explosive rage, torture, and abuse that mostly my mother and I suffered at his hands. But it was the only moment of triumph I had in the face of this injustice. I not only did it for myself but for my mother. The past was gone, but I was still living with the burdens and swallowing the agony in the present. When all was said and done, there was no note from our father, there was no letter telling us goodbye, there were no last words with the exception of, "These are my intentions."

Henrik did not even acknowledge his grandsons in his finale. Behind our backs, Henrik made sure that only Mildred was taken care of. In the end, my father said in so many words, "I'LL SHOW YOU!" as he finished his cycle of malicious cruelty.

Now it was a legacy gone…four-hundred acres of sadness, fields of lies, our beautiful lake house, our heritage, promises broken, our birthright in a landslide…*poof*, like they didn't exist. A lifetime of our family culture up in smoke. We were sold out and our spirits left for dead. All of this now was in the hands of the pig that Henrik married. I asked myself: Didn't we have rights as Henrik's children? Why were we made to sacrifice everything that was once given to us? Soraya and I felt tossed away like we didn't belong, our family legacy was thrown away to nothing more than strangers. Our family honor was taken. Soraya and I were two deserving girls robbed of our birthright, bated, switched, and betrayed. It was heartbreak soaked in years of tears and suffering. We were forced to surrender everything to the savages that took their fill.

I knew I had my freedom from the Nazi Twins, but where was my justice? I knew I had to cut off my thirst for vengeance in hopes of seeing fairness Soraya and I so deserved. As far as the world was concerned, Henrik was a shepherd neatly concealed by the flock of society. His evil, sinister ways were only revealed by a small select group of victims. Henrik was not a man…but a coward, a thief of righteousness and truth, disguised behind his sleazy existence.

Ultimately Soraya and I felt an obligation to the farms, our land, and the lake house. They were supposed to be a legacy for our children. We were fighting for our rights; we were fighting for what our nasty father took away from our mother. Henrik had taken Rachel's soul, her happiness, for so many years; I was still aching for him to pay. I wasn't going to just step aside and let Mildred take away what was rightfully promised to us. Soraya and I were going to stand our ground until the end.

It wasn't the money or the land, it was the finality of it all. Legally we didn't have a leg to stand on but where was our document of morality. Who in the end was going to stick up for the two scared little girls who hid inside their closet within earshot from the tirades? Who was going to protect Rachel when she was entombed with more atrocities than one woman should be allowed to suffer as she had at the hands of Henrik? Who was going to fight for Rachel as she tumbled into an unprecedented obstruction of justice? It felt so hopeless, it was like chasing the wind to free yourself of the problem, yet never catching the solution. With the stroke of a pen our father's signature broke our hearts and shoved us out of the circle where we belonged. We were separated out of the final equation in his last performance of absolute betrayal.

Navigating around abuse is never an exact science, but it can take an awakening to understand that it is happening to you. Once you are out, you can ask yourself…what's next? Seeing enough of the dark depths of suffering, I never understood that I kept myself trapped there. I looked back at the echoes of my life…a lost child, a broken spirit, yet I felt a new beginning. I needed to remember that when something is broken and taken from the soul it takes on a new form, turning into something more powerful. It may never be the same, but it now has the potency to build its own formidable resilience. Who you once were, you can now break the mold and mend the wires.

I was grabbing at my roots that were still strong, they anchored my life. I was so desperately trying to remove myself from the darkness that followed me. I knew that my deep-seated rage and arguing with my father had been meaningless, and it had always been a self-destructive path. While I was doing my best to punish him, I was punishing myself in turn. My anger had gotten in the way of my life. Yet how would I forgive someone who had continuously ripped my existence to shreds? I was always in the splash zone inside of a world of abuse, anger, and rage peppered with confusion.

Fighting with my father and finding it unconscionable was the greatest paradox of my life. I never wanted to let the bitterness of my past sour my future or hold others accountable for the burdens I carried. Yet at times it was a difficult shift. My life was a mysterious maze of contradictions.

Truth was, I had become my father in my attempt to overthrow him. I had destroyed my own peace; it was nothing short of ugliness. I knew that I would never put myself in my father's category, I knew I was a giver and not a taker. Yet here I was mimicking Henrik just to defeat him. I hoped that my hatred would die at the hour of my father's death. I ultimately didn't understand that it would take time to bury the consuming bitterness that I tasted at every turn. I hated my father for what he did to my mother, I hated him for how he treated the three of us. He had thrown us away like garbage and had gotten away with it.

I stared at the coppery blue water of Lake Geneva. *Now look at you, Henrik*, I thought. *You live in a shallow grave of muck at the bottom of the lake. The only legacy you leave behind are the daughters who now despise and have disowned you, and grandsons who are only reminded of your pathetic existence by how you hurt them.* Henrik left an endowment of emptiness, only cheating himself by deceiving his own flesh and blood. *In the end, you deserted us and hid behind your cloud of rage to make sure that everyone heard your pain.* It was a fury that only weakened him as he solidified his fate, allowing the transient foreigners to reign as his new heirs. It was the greatest emulation of stupidity I'd ever seen.

Up at the lake the sunlight glistened off the water. The breeze blew sunshine through the leaves on the trees, and the fog lifted. For the first time in my life, I was seeing with clarity and vision like never before. My spirit that was heavy and weighed down was now ready to soar. Difficult roads often lead to destiny. I would learn again to find my voice with peace. Rachel, Soraya, and I were at the beginning of living our souls' purpose that had been derailed for so long.

27

Unsinkable Princess

I continued to research reoccurring symptoms that kept bubbling up. As I was reading, I checked many boxes in the PTSD category. My life was like walking through a minefield. So much violence in my past, yet I still expected to find the explosions that no longer happened. I thought that only soldiers of war and other people suffered that fate. I had the feeling that more psychological therapies would be in my future. I tried not to discuss this with Rachel; I didn't want her to worry. But she always knew when I was sad or burdened. In so many words she told me to take my broken wings and to do something productive with my anger. She let me know that when I let go of my resentment and finally closed the chapter on this deceitful, disgraceful man, good things would happen and doors would be open that were closed before.

After the epic history of fighting with my father, I would be proud of myself, she told me. I was still holding on to those arguments like trophies. I needed to let go. Freeing myself of the bitterness would give me a superpower I never knew that I had. I would be shedding the skin of the past and living in the grace that would magnetize in my direction. Once I could learn the magic and spit out the vengeance, forgiveness and gratitude became the new taste in my mouth.

For myself, I had my own intentions, I had my own framework, I kept my own promises. I would follow through to make sure that my life was a success. I wanted my life to make sense and to do things that mattered. I kept my philanthropy work active, paying it forward and helping those in need. I made lofty strides with my faith. I knew that my greatest gifts were my children Jake and Josh and my nephew Tristan. I knew I had the best sister, Soraya, who was my sounding board for all that we went through.

I lived an amazing life traveling to many parts of the world with the love of my life, my Jim. Music was such a solace in the face of the chaos I had endured growing up. We never realized we would meet because of the music that we both were dedicated to. For Jim and me, music was our antidote, it held answers, and it was an outlet for every challenge life could throw our way. Music has always been there for me in my darkest hours, most magnificent triumphs, and every moment in between.

When I dropped the bitter cup of venom, I had all of this and more. My mother told me that through my courage, my heart was free to follow her.

What I would grow to realize is that my words were my true vindication for my mother, Soraya, and me. With the truth, Henrik no longer lurked in the shadows. We would no longer hide in the shame of what Henrik perpetuated. We would no longer be frightened or held under the thumb of domestic violence.

If you stand your ground long enough, evil will eventually grow tired of the light that surrounds you. Rachel, Soraya, and I chose the light over darkness. We chose prosperity over scarcity. We knew that a higher power was holding us with a shield of protection. We chose to listen to our inner voice and shut out the madman. We needed to raise our vibration, find peace, and always expect a miracle. We fought every step of the way to get there.

Rachel never realized that she defeated Henrik on so many astonishing levels. Rachel ultimately severed the energetic ties to Henrik's debilitating dimensional power and set herself free.

For Soraya and me, Rachel is one in ten billion, a rare and exquisite jewel with a uniqueness seldom seen and the style and flair of old Hollywood. But at her core, she is much more than that. Henrik would only understand his self-centered needs. Henrik actually thought he was leaving a proud legacy behind with his power, money, and influence.

The only proud legacy would be what our mother had taught us, how we lived our lives. Rachel had blazed a trail with her strength, courage, kindness, and perseverance against all odds. Rachel had done some incredible and impossible things in her life that most people could never dream of accomplishing. It's easy to feel on top when you have money and power, when things are going your way. The real winners find strength when they have lost all hope and find courage when things look the bleakest. Rachel's strong spirit stood up to the darkness to protect us, her precious daughters. Rachel fought so that we could live a better life and leave behind the scraps that Henrik threw in our face.

A true hero finds the bravery to grab their children's hands and run across the street to safety at the corner grocery store. It's the valor of packing a bag in minutes, driving to a friend's house to keep your children out of harm's way. It is the strength to face judges, attorneys, and corrupt police officers and not back down as they barrage you with years of injustices. This legacy of resilience was given to us by our mother, not a man with more money that just weaseled us out of our birthright. These were the formidable badges of honor that our mother Rachel gave to us.

Rachel rebuilt her life with pure faith. Out of the ashes she built her world with her character, foundation, and her strong Spanish roots. Rachel knew that what was wronged would one day be made right and what was taken would soon return. Mistakes would transform into miracles, tragedy would turn to triumph, things lost would be found. The truth would now be showcased for the world to see.

The biggest shock Henrik would ever grow to realize about Soraya and me was that the only hero we would have in our life was our mother, Rachel. For the reason of her sacrifices, she was our anchor, our unsung warrior, our champion, our defender, our ambassador of peace; she was the voice in our head. Our mother was our mentor, and the best guardian two daughters could hope for. She was a pioneer and a trailblazer that had no compass on how to navigate out of Henrik's dark forest…but yet she found her way. Because of her, Soraya and I moved forward with our lives as survivors, leaders, overcomers, and thrivers; we are unstoppable and unshakable. We grew fierce and empowered.

Transformation away from tragedy is one of the greatest miracles that you can give yourself; this was something else we learned from our mother. It is because of Rachel that we were saved from the most evil of fates. With the soul of a princess and the heart of a queen, our mother Rachel is our unsinkable princess, our world treasure.

28

Magnificent Cliffs of Galicia

I phoned Rachel every day for support. I still wanted to put my fist through Mildred's throat. I was looking for justice but ran into one wall after another. Still consumed with anger, I knew that forgiveness was a tough pill to swallow. What I needed was a different perspective on things. When you stay suffocated inside your own pain, it makes it impossible to move away from the vile creature that has haunted your past. I no longer wanted to look at what I had lost, but what I had found, what an amazing life that was all around me. History doesn't care about your baggage, but your future does.

My revenge that I carried around because of my father was like choking down gallons of poison. It was a constant intravenous drip of venom running through my veins, tasting the toxic sludge my entire life, just to make my father pay. In the end, I was the only one that paid with the precious gift of time. I wasted it on a man that had no conscience or regard for others. Henrik would never change because his brain was programmed like a robot for only his despicable agenda. What I would learn by putting down the sword was that life was nothing more than a great balance of moving things forward and letting go at the same time. We were not going to allow our past to define us. Rachel, Soraya, and I were finally moving in the right direction.

I let my rant with Mildred sink in. A few days after Thanksgiving, I was in my car listening to the band Yes play "Wonderous Stories." I didn't know if my story was wondrous or not, but I would soon have a tale to tell. I turned down the radio and called Rachel. We talked for about twenty minutes, and I reiterated the entire Mildred story, still needing to vent.

"Fallon, your father is long gone, and we knew that Mildred was going to take everything. Whether she changed the will or not, you may never find out. I want you to forget about Henrik and move on with your life. But before you do, I want you to do something."

"What's that?"

"I want you to slaughter him with your pen."

"You want me to slaughter…who?"

"I want you to write my book. Start at the beginning with the story of my entire life! And yours too! I want you to expose everything your father did. I want you to talk about who I was back in Spain and the amazing life I led. I know you can't put fifty years in a memoir, but you could write some of the highlights!"

"Oh, wow…okay!"

"It's an incredible story! I have all the divorce and settlement papers. I keep them in a small blue suitcase. I can give you all of it to read. Fallon, besides me, you are the only person who knows the truth. You know what happened!"

"Yes," I said. It felt right. And I was ready to tell her story, my story, our story.

We talked for a few more minutes about the details, and I let her know that I would begin soon.

A few weeks later, I picked up the blue suitcase that sat in the corner of my office. It looked heavy, full of painful memories that needed to be freed and liberated. *Yes*, I thought, *the power of the pen is now my equalizer.*

Three months later, I called Rachel with a surprise. "I bought plane tickets for the three of us," I said. "We're going to Spain!"

"What?"

"It's true. You, Soraya, and me. We're taking a flight to Galicia."

I heard her take a deep breath. "When do we leave?" she said, her voice tentative.

"Next month."

"Oh Fallon," she said, her voice filling with joy. "You've answered my prayers."

Our plane landed in Madrid on a warm, sunny morning in June. We went straight to our aunt's house and spent a few perfect days basking in the love of our family.

We were embarking on our own spiritual journey, one that would begin the delicate work of healing and renewal. In the morning, we took the train to Lisbon, Portugal where we made our way up to the Sanctuary of Our Lady of the Rosary of Fátima, patron saint of all mothers and children. In the sacred space of the basilica, sunlight streamed through stained glass windows, bathing us in warmth as we knelt and prayed that our broken hearts would heal.

We were sure that Mary, the blessed mother, already knew we were on a mission to cleanse ourselves of our past. We dipped our fingers in holy water, open and willing to accept her blessing. Our hearts softened, we boarded another train to Santiago de Compostela, stopping in La Coruña and making our way to the Playa de las Catedrales, Cathedral Beach, in Galicia, the Beach of the Holy Waters.

Together, just before sunset, we walked toward the magnificent cliffs overlooking the sea and stopped amidst the wildflowers where the land rose high over the sparkling ocean, its waves pounding the surf below. Radiant mist sprinkled our faces in another sacred blessing. Rachel, Soraya, and I felt as if we finally stood on a formidable pinnacle; we sensed an untouchable power as we were mystically separated from our past.

A smile of contentment spread over Rachel's face as the play of light against the rocks seemed to drench us in magic. Cliffs and arches carved out of giant boulders welcomed the waves that crashed below. The magical air filled us with the warmth of the golden, glowing sunset.

We felt a shift in our souls. A power greater than the three of us. For the first time in the years of trauma, I felt peace settle into my core. Our journey to this place had been long and difficult, but once we reached the cliffs it was so well worth the pilgrimage.

The sound of the surf lulled us into silence. *Here we are*, I thought, *Rachel, Soraya, and me. We've survived a fate so many women have not. We share a sisterhood bound into eternity. There is such a thing as grace. The grace of God lifting us into sunlight.*

Rachel turned to Soraya and me and hummed a Galician melody from our childhood. Soon we were laughing, dancing, and singing songs into the mist of the setting sun.

We paused for a moment to catch our collective breath when Soraya pointed toward the sky. "Look…it's a butterfly!" she said. "I've never seen one so close to the ocean. It's a brave beauty, fighting a lot of downdrafts out here."

"They're tougher than you think," I said, smiling against the wind. "They migrate for thousands of miles." *Kind of like us*, I thought at that moment.

Tears filled Rachel's eyes. "It's my momma," she whispered. "She always comes in the form of a butterfly to check on us, to make sure we're okay, and to let me know how she's doing."

A butterfly, mariposa, delicate as air and strong as crashing waves. I took my mom's hand in the glow of the remaining sunlight. And she took

Soraya's hand. I gazed at the horizon, I tasted victory, I could see it in the clear blue line that divided heaven and earth. I felt the strong breeze on my face, I breathed in the sea air. I felt awake…alive for the very first time. A voice deep within me, my voice, my mother's voice, rose. I felt a calling growing within me, a command, really: "Write your mother's story."

Yes, I thought. *I'll start at the beginning when Rachel's life was filled with promise and beauty. I will share how all of that could be stolen, and what happened to her, to all three of us. The injustices and the pain that wounded our hearts, that threatened to kill us, but didn't.*

I would make sure that the world would finally know the truth and this malignant parasite would finally be exposed. I could see the authenticity of the words imprinted in my mind as the story unfolded before me. This was our moment of second chances, our vision of justice. I heard the ocean speak, felt the roar of its power. The tide crashed toward land, and in that moment, I knew that God and my mother's unwavering love had ultimately removed the storm from our lives.

Photo Album

Family in Spain

Top Left:
Abuelo Alfonso, Tia Carmen
Top Middle: *Tio Manolo*
Top Right: *Abuela Esther*
Right Middle: *Tio Pepe*
Lower Middle: *Alex Levine, Bride Rafaela Faly (Rachel)*
Lower Right: *Tia Esther*
Bottom: *Flower Girl Esther*

Cathedral Beach, Galicia, Spain

The Abuelos
Alfonso and Esther

Clima magazine, circulation in Valencia and different regions of Spain.

Rafaela Faly (Rachel), Cover

Second to Right:
Rafaela Faly (Rachel)

Right: *Famous
Spanish bull fighter
Victor Valencia*

*Victor
Valencia*

Left: *Rafaela Faly (Rachel).*

Right: *Italian movie star Raf Baldassarre.*

One advantage that the HOTEL PLAZA has over almost every other hotel in Spain is its rooftop swimming pool. Way up there on the 24th floor PLAZA guests can sun and swim from 11 a.m. to 7 p.m. every day, simply by stopping by the Concierge's desk and picking up an invitation.

In the photo above, the Italian actor, RAF BALDASSARRE, star of the film, JOSE MARIA EL TEMPRANILLO, who has made Spain his second home; at present, he is acting in LOS IMPLACABLES. With him is Miss FALI VAZQUEZ.

At the left, the popular American television and movie star TY HARDIN, also known as BRONCO, who has stayed in our hotel on several occasions.

The Plaza Pool ★ La piscina Plaza

Una ventaja que tiene el HOTEL PLAZA sobre casi todos los otros hoteles de España es la magnífica piscina de su terraza. Los huéspedes del PLAZA pueden subir al piso 24 a tomar el sol y nadar desde las 11 de la mañana hasta las 7 de la tarde, solicitando del conserje su invitación.

En la foto de arriba, el actor italiano, RAF BALDASSARRE; intérprete de la película JOSE MARIA EL TEMPRANILLO, ha hecho de España su segunda patria; actualmente se halla rodando la película LOS IMPLACABLES. En la PISCINA PLAZA junto a la señorita FALI VAZQUEZ; en un día de descanso del rodaje.

A la izquierda, el popular actor de cine y televisión norteamericano, TY HARDIN, más conocido como BRONCO. Ha sido huésped de nuestro hotel en varias ocasiones.

Bottom Left: *American movie star and star of "Bronco," Ty Hardin.*

Left: *Rafaela Faly (Rachel) Crowning of Miss Galicia shaking the hand of the right hand man of President Franco of Spain, with secret service keeping a watchful eye.*

Rafaela Faly (Rachel) in the Royal Palace of Tetouan, Morocco.

The Royal Palace of Tetouan, Morocco. The Prince of Morocco (middle) and his entourage walking next to Rafaela Faly (in white dress).

Middle: *Prince of Morocco*
Right: *Rafaela Faly (Rachel)*

Left to Right: *Henrik Baumann, Tia Carmen, Rafaela Faly (Rachel), Tio Manolo*

Left: *Mexican movie star Cantinflas… ("Around the World in 80 Days," etc.)*

Right: *Rafaela Faly (Rachel)*

Left to Right:
Rafaela Faly (Rachel),
friend Susie, unkown,
right hand man of
Juan and Eva Peron.

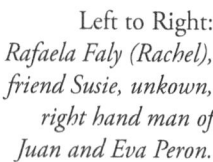

Left: *Rafaela Faly (Rachel)*
Right: *Karin*

Rafaela Faly (Rachel)
photo in New York.

Movie, Modeling and
Television commercial offers
from producers, movie stars
and directors

Top row (from left):
Abuelo Alfonso;
Abuela Esther,
Rafaela (Rachel)

Bottom row (from left):
Faly (Fallon),
Yvonne (Soraya)

Charlie to Rafaela Faly (Rachel),
"With you I want to make time
stand still," were Charlie's words
at this moment

Rafaela Faly (Rachel)
and Bob Hart.

Left to Right: *Author Faly Colaizzi (Fallon) and sister Yvonne (Soraya)*

Left to Right: *Jake, Josh, nephew Tristan*

Acknowledgments

To my incredible editor Joy Stocke, you have given *Unsinkable Princess* the wings that it needs to fly. You have brought clarity to the chaos surrounding every facet of this amazing story. I love that you have pushed me to my limits in fine tuning every last detail, even when you didn't know what dark corners were about to unfold. Your brilliance has brought this book to life.

www.treeoflifetreeofjoy.com

Tim, thank you for the astoundingly beautiful book cover and interior. You have made my mother so proud of this piece of work. I foresee that this book and its cover will be seen in many countries and will go down in our family through the generations as a beautiful piece of art.

www.oglinedesign.com

A special thank you to Ron and Rich Onesti for the tremendous contributions the Arcada Theater makes to the city of St. Charles and surrounding communities. You bring amazing artists, fans, and families together with your passion and dedication to the music we all love. Jim and I have loved every minute being part of the Arcada and St Charles community.

www.oshows.com

About the Author

Faly Colaizzi was born and raised in the Chicagoland area, graduating from Illinois State University with a Bachelor of Science degree. With a 34-year career as a Business Development Manager, she takes pride in being a strong advocate for her clients. Faly is an active member of the Board of Education Committee for BOMA Chicago and also participates in the Western Loss Association. Additionally, she made history as the first female president of the Blue Goose Association in her industry.

In her personal life, Faly is a devoted mother to two thriving boys and is dedicated to philanthropic work through the Saint Charles Women's

Club. Having served on the board for the Saint Charles Women's Club for two consecutive years, she supports various charities that focus on women, children, animal shelters, and local food banks. Faly serves as an ambassador and guest speaker for the Eversight Eye Bank.

Beyond her professional and philanthropic endeavors, Faly is also an accomplished author, having written two novels in the Haunted Nights at Drumheller Castle series. Her achievements in literature were recognized when she was featured on Channel 7 News and became one of the authors in the "Overcoming Mediocrity" series. Faly's association with this series contributed to her becoming an Amazon Best Selling Author.

Her books, especially *Unsinkable Princess*, provide a platform for Faly to address personal struggles, shedding light on issues such as domestic violence, abuse, and tyrannical narcissism. Drawing inspiration from her mother's remarkable life and confronting the challenges posed by a bully, Faly shares, "If I can help even one soul salvage their life and thrive, I have done my job."

For events, photo gallery, and purchases of books, please visit:
www.UnsinkablePrincess.com

If you or someone you love is suffering from domestic abuse, help is available.

NATIONAL DOMESTIC VIOLENCE HOTLINE
available 24/7 in English and Spanish:
800 799-7233

www.ingramcontent.com/pod-product-compliance
Lightning Source LLC
Chambersburg PA
CBHW020430130626
46549CB00001B/66

* 9 7 9 8 9 8 9 7 4 6 4 1 5 *